The Single-Season Home Run Kings

Also by William F. McNeil

*The California Winter League: America's First
Integrated Professional Baseball League* (McFarland, 2002)

*Cool Papas and Double Duties: The All-Time
Greats of the Negro Leagues* (McFarland, 2001)

*Baseball's Other All-Stars: The Greatest Players from the
Negro Leagues, the Japanese Leagues, the Mexican Leagues in
Cuba, Puerto Rico and the Dominican Republic* (McFarland, 2000)

*Ruth, Maris, McGwire and Sosa: Baseball's Single
Season Home Run Champions* (McFarland, 1999)

*The King of Swat: An Analysis of Baseball's Home Run Hitters from
the Major, Minor, Negro and Japanese Leagues* (McFarland, 1997)

The Dodgers Encyclopedia (1997)

The Single-Season Home Run Kings

Ruth, Maris, McGwire, Sosa, and Bonds

SECOND EDITION

William F. McNeil

McFarland & Company, Inc., Publishers

Jefferson, North Carolina, and London

Library of Congress Cataloguing-in-Publication Data

McNeil, William.
    The single-season home run kings: Ruth, Maris, McGwire,
Sosa, and Bonds / by William F. McNeil.—2nd ed.
        p.   cm.
Rev. ed. of: Ruth, Maris, McGwire and Sosa. c1999.
    Includes bibliographical references and index.

    ISBN 0-7864-1441-3 (softcover : 50# alkaline paper) ∞

    1. Home runs (Baseball)—United States—History.   2. Home
runs (Baseball)—United States Statistics.   3. Ruth, Babe, 1895–
1948.   4. Maris, Roger, 1934–1985.   5. McGwire, Mark, 1963–
6. Sosa, Sammy, 1968– 7. Bonds, Barry, 1964– I. McNeil,
William. Ruth, Maris, McGwire and Sosa.   II. Title.
GV868.4 .M38   2003
796.357'26—dc21   2002015189

British Library cataloguing data are available

Cover photograph: Barry Bonds ©S.F. Giants

Manufactured in the United States of America

*McFarland & Company, Inc., Publishers
    Box 611, Jefferson, North Carolina 28640
    www.mcfarlandpub.com*

To my grandchildren

Jessica, Jamie, Jeffrey, Jenna, Morgan, Shannon,
Shane, Katie, Connor, Rachel, Joe and Ari.
It's great to be young.

Acknowledgments

James R. Madden, Jr., has been an immense help in obtaining photographs for several of my books, including the earlier version of the present work *Ruth, Maris, McGwire, and Sosa* and *Baseball's Other All-Stars*, in addition to this book. He has spent literally weeks of his own time scouring the spring training camps of the San Francisco Giants, Chicago Cubs, and Seattle Mariners, among others, to capture candid moments of baseball's legendary players interacting with their fans and cooperating with the media, as well as participating in games. Photographs provided by Jim Madden include Sammy Sosa, Barry Bonds, Ken Griffey, Jr., and Alex Rodriguez.

Jeff Evans, assistant media relations director of Arizona State University, was very helpful in providing photographs of Barry Bonds during his playing career at ASU. The photographs are the property of ASU Sports Information.

Contents

PART TWO : THE STATISTICS

Preface

The home run has been the most romanticized feat in baseball since the 19th century. Big, muscular sluggers who hit baseballs mighty distances have always been the heroes of the game. When Babe Ruth, the New York Yankee "Sultan of Swat," smashed 60 home runs in 1927, it was considered to be one of baseball's untouchable records. And it was, for 34 years, until a smooth-swinging blonde bomber from North Dakota suddenly shocked the world by sending 61 balls flying out of major league parks.

Roger Maris' mark stood the test of time for 37 long years before it fell. Then it was broken twice in the same year. The 1998 baseball season produced the greatest home run race in history, with Mark McGwire, the big red-headed first baseman of the St. Louis Cardinals, and Sammy Sosa, the irrepressible right fielder of the Chicago Cubs, chasing Maris' single-season home run record throughout the spring and summer. McGwire finally caught the Yankee slugger on September 7 when he launched number 61. He passed him the next day.

Sosa was the first man to reach 66 home runs, but the St. Louis slugger finished with a flurry, hitting five home runs in his last eleven at-bats, giving him 70 for the season.

The four home run kings were reviewed side by side in the first edition of this book, titled *Ruth, Maris, McGwire, and Sosa*, and their accomplishments were studied in the context of their times. The conditions under which each of them performed their historic feats were analyzed. The advantages each of them enjoyed during their grueling quests, as well as the disadvantages they had to overcome, were examined in detail.

Only three years passed before the record was challenged again. This time, a muscular left-handed hitter from San Francisco picked up the gauntlet. And once again, as summer turned to fall, the baseball world

1

watched the coronation of a new home run king. Barry Bonds, the Giants' left fielder, assaulted the home run record with a vengeance, blowing by Maris on September 20, leaving Sosa in the dust on the 29th, and finally passing the champion himself, Mark McGwire, with a two-homer outburst on October 5. He added number 73 in the season finale.

This new edition, now titled *The Single-Season Home Run Kings*, adds the Giant slugger to the mix. His early life and his baseball career are examined, and his historic season is chronicled in detail. Then his place in history is studied, alongside his four predecessors.

Once again, the questions are being asked: Whose record-breaking achievement was the most important? Whose accomplishments were the most heroic? Who is the mightiest slugger of them all? This book answers those questions.

PART ONE : THE TEXT

1. The Evolution
of the Home Run

Professional baseball began in 1869 when the city of Cincinnati organized and paid a team to play baseball full time. The club, known as the Cincinnati Red Stockings, toured the United States from coast to coast in 1869 and 1870, taking on all comers. They played some of the top amateur clubs in the country, including Forest City of Cleveland, the Athletic of Philadelphia, and the Mutual of Brooklyn, but for the most part their opposition consisted of local town teams of questionable talent.

In their opening game, they crushed Great Western at Cincinnati, 45–9. Several Reds players hit home runs in the game, including shortstop George Wright. It was a portent of things to come.

The Reds were practically unbeatable, running up an 80-game undefeated streak over two seasons, and outscoring the opposition by an average score of 53–6. The only blemish on their record a 17–17 tie with the Haymakers of Troy, New York. Cincinnnati's first Big Red Machine was finally beaten by The Atlantics of Brooklyn 8–7 on June 14, 1870. The game, played at the Capitoline Grounds in Brooklyn, has been called the greatest game of the nineteenth century. The Atlantics pushed across the winning runs in the bottom of the eleventh inning after the Reds had tallied twice in their half. The Red Stockings disbanded after the 1870 season.

In 1871, a full fledged professional league took the field, when the National Association of Professional Base Ball Players was formed. The first home run hit in a professional baseball league was credited to Ezra Sutton, the 153-pound third basemen of the Forest Citys of Cleveland. Sutton stepped to the plate in the fourth inning against George "The Charmer" Zettlein of the Chicago White Stockings, and sent a drive over the head of center fielder Tom Foley for a home run. Sutton hit another homer three innings later, thus becoming the first player to hit two homers in one game. In spite of Sutton's big day, however, home runs were nothing more than a curiosity in the early days of baseball. The first games were played on open fields, with a ball that was soft and misshapen. Games were high-scoring affairs, but singles, doubles, and triples were the big offensive weapons of the day. In fact, there were only 47 home runs hit in 127 league games in 1871, compared to 434 doubles and 239 triples. The few home runs that were hit were usually inside-the-park jobs, with the batter hitting the ball over the fielder's head or between the fielders, and racing around the bases to score before the relay throw could reach home plate. Both of Sutton's homers were fashioned in that manner.

The first enclosed baseball parks were built for other endeavors, such as horse races or bicycle races. The oval tracks, which were ideal for races, were not well suited for the game of baseball, which was played inside the oval. The fields necessarily had extremely short foul lines of approximately 200 to 250 feet, and obscene center field distances, occasionally exceeding 500 feet.

Charlie Gould, a first baseman for the Boston Red Stockings and a former member of the original Cincinnati Red Stockings, hit one of the league's most exciting home runs on September 5, 1871. The blow, a grand slam home run off former Brooklyn Atlantic ace George Zettlein, whom Gould had faced as a member of Cincinnati's first professional team, actually sailed over the 250-foot left field fence at Boston's South End Grounds, an unusual feat in those days. Newspaper headlines around the league celebrated the historic event.

The National Association, however, was beset by numerous financial, administrative, and disciplinary problems during its turbulent existence. Gambling scandals, thrown games, players jumping from one team to another, and other unsavory practices caused chaos within the league's administrative offices. Unable to control the situation, the owners disbanded the league after five seasons. It was immediately replaced by the National League, which began operations in 1876.

The first National League game was played on April 22, 1876, at Jefferson Street Grounds in Philadelphia, with the Boston Red Caps defeating the Athletics 6–5. Ross Barnes, an outstanding second baseman for the Chicago White Stockings smashed the first National League home run on May 2, 1876. Barnes' drive off "Cherokee" Fisher at Cincinnati's Avenue Grounds carried down the left field line to the spectators' horse-drawn carriages that encircled the playing field. It was Barnes' only home run of the season. George Hall of Philadelphia captured the home run championship with five circuit blows. Charlie Jones of Cincinnati, with four home runs, was the only other National League player to hit more than two.

The first National League baseball parks were nightmares for batters. In most parks, it was impossible to hit a ball over the distant fences. This was especially true for right-handed batters. For instance, the left field fence at the Philadelphia Base Ball Grounds was 500 feet distant while the right field fence was a more comfortable 310 feet away, still a good poke in the old dead ball days. Robison Field in the American Association measured 470 feet down the left field line, 500 feet to dead center, and 290 feet to right field. Exposition Park III in Pittsburgh and National League Park II in Cleveland both had over 400-foot carries to the right and left field foul poles. The average distance to the outfield fences in major league parks in the 1880s and 90s was 358 feet to left field, 473 feet to center, and 322 feet to right. This advantage for lefthanded hitters continued for more than 100 years, benefiting such future home run kings as Babe Ruth and Roger Maris, and penalizing right-handed hitting challengers like Jimmie Foxx, Hank Greenberg, and Harmon Killebrew.

The first bonafide home run hitters emerged during the 1880s to wreak havoc on National League pitchers. For the most part, they were big, strapping left-handed hitters like Dan Brouthers, Roger Connor, and Sam Thompson. In an age when the average player weighed in the neighborhood of 150 pounds, these big sluggers all stood over six feet tall and topped the scales at more than 200 pounds. They averaged between eight and 12 home runs a season each, a hefty total in those days. Sam Thompson once led the league with a monstrous 20 home runs, which by today's standards, could have been in the 50–60 range.

"Big Dan" Brouthers was the most fearsome of the nineteenth century sluggers. Standing 6'2" tall and weighing a muscular 207 pounds, the big first baseman terrorized opposing pitchers. In addition to his nine home runs, he averaged 38 doubles and 17 triples a year, to go along with a .342 batting average. His .519 slugging percentage was the highest of any nineteenth century batter, and is higher than such modern sluggers as Harmon Killebrew, Ernie Banks, and Eddie Mathews.

Another notable slugger of the nineteenth century was Harry Stovey. Unlike the other big boomers of the 1880s, Stovey was a fleet-footed outfielder for the Philadelphia Athletics who had all the qualifications of a superstar. He could hit, hit with power, run, field, and throw. The trim 180-pound gazelle racked up 122 homers during his career, leading the league in that category five times. He averaged 11 homers a year, in addition to 32 doubles, 15 triples, and 90 stolen bases.

As exciting as baseball was to watch, and as difficult as it was to play, the game was not considered to be an honorable profession by most of nineteenth century society. The Victorian Age had become deeply imbedded in the United States by the 1890s, and the moral and social climate in the country decried improprieties of any sort.

Baseball players of the time were looked down upon as ruffians, drunkards, and carousers. The brawling, tobacco chewing, gambling low-lifes that gravitated to the game detracted from the overall clean competition and sportsmanship that actually defined the game. Baseball had such a poor image that law-abiding citizens were embarrassed when a member of their family chose professional baseball as a career. Harry Stovey, whose real name was Stowe, changed it to Stovey when he began playing baseball to protect his mother from public humiliation.

As the twentieth century got underway, the image of the game gradually improved. College athletic programs produced outstanding baseball players like Christy Mathewson, Eddie Collins, and Harry Hooper, who subsequently chose professional baseball as a worthy profession. Over three dozen college men were playing major league baseball by 1916. Eddie Grant from Harvard, Chief Meyers from Dartmouth, Bob Bescher from Notre Dame, Dick Rudolph from Fordham, and Bill Carrigan from Holy Cross, brought a measure of respect and dignity to the game. Gentlemen players like Walter Johnson, Cy Young, and Honus Wagner, whose on- and off-field demeanor was exemplary, further made the game more palatable to the general public. Soon, women and children began attending games in greater numbers, and the sport rapidly grew to become America's national pastime.

The strategy of the game changed during the first decade of the new century. Big, powerful sluggers were no longer in demand in the professional ranks. Baseball owners shunned the burly muscle men, considering them to be brutish oafs, who were defensive liabilities and who clogged up the base paths. Major league players of the 1900s were smaller, faster, and more adept at handling a bat than their predecessors had been. The game evolved into a low-scoring affair, with bunts, stolen bases, and hit and run plays the keys to victory. Home runs declined from an average of 38 per team during the last two decades of the nineteenth century to 22 per team during the first decade of the twentieth century.

Home run champions had modest totals to show for their efforts as the new century got underway. Sam Crawford of Cincinnati led the National League with 16 homers in 1901, the highest total of the decade. Socks Seybold of the Philadelphia Athletics hit 16 homers in 1902 to lead the American League. No other slugger hit as many. In fact, the National

League leader had less than ten home runs five times during the decade, and the junior circuit leader had less than ten home runs four times. Tommy Leach of Pittsburgh led the N.L. with six home runs in 1902.

Things began to change for the sluggers in 1910 when a new cork-centered baseball was introduced. The ball was livelier than the old ball and seemed to jump off the bat when it was hit. It wasn't long before the big boys with the big lumber zeroed in on the friendlier ball. Frank Schulte of the Chicago Cubs, who had hit just 17 home runs in 5½ previous seasons, was the first slugger to exploit it. The solidly built 170-pound left fielder pounded out 69 homers over the next six years, including a league-leading 21 homers in 1911.

The most prolific home run hitter to play major league baseball before the emergence of Babe Ruth was Clifford "Gavvy" Cravath. The 5'10", 180-pound bruiser kicked around the minor leagues for the better part of ten years, with two unsuccessful major league trials along the way. In his early years, from 1902 through 1907, he was a hard-hitting outfielder with the Los Angeles Angels in the Pacific Coast League. His .303 batting average, powerful bat, and 50 stolen bases, brought him to the attention of the Boston Red Sox, who acquired his contract in 1908. After unsuccessful trials with Boston, Chicago, and Washington of the American League, Cravath found himself back in the minor leagues, holding down an outfield spot for the Minneapolis Millers of the American Association. There, at the age of 27, he suddenly blossomed into a dangerous offensive threat. In 1910, the big basher from Escondido, California, led the league in batting (.326), hits (200), and home runs (14). The next year he did even better, showing the way in batting (.363), hits (221), doubles (53), and home runs (29).

That performance brought him to the attention of the Philadelphia Phillies who purchased his contract and inserted him in right field in Baker Bowl, where he remained for eight years. He went on to lead the National League in home runs during six of those years. His league-leading totals included two years with 19 homers and one year with 24 homers.

Over the six-year period from 1912 to 1917, Gavvy Cravath accounted for 7.2 percent of all home runs hit in the National League. By comparison, Harry Stovey, the top nineteenth century slugger hit 5.7 percent of all home runs in the American Association between 1883 and 1889. Babe Ruth, whose career will be reviewed in the following chapters, accounted for 10.8 percent of all American League homers between 1919 and 1924, and 9.5 percent of all homers hit between 1926 and 1931. No other players in major league history have dominated the home run statistics like Babe Ruth and Gavvy Cravath.

Gavvy Cravath's career average of 17 home runs for every 550 at bats was by far the highest average during the dead ball era, and would equate to an average of about 43 home runs in the lively ball era, second only to the great Bambino. In truth, Gavvy Cravath was the Babe Ruth of the dead ball era.

Other changes that were taking place in major league baseball during the first two decades of the twentieth century favored the home run hitters. New steel and concrete stadiums being built in such cities as Philadelphia, Pittsburgh, Brooklyn, Boston, Chicago, Detroit, and St. Louis were more homer friendly. Prior to 1900 most parks had large playing fields surrounded by wooden fences. Center field was usually in the neighborhood of 500 feet distant from home plate, and the left field fence stood a good 350 feet away. Right field was a cozier 322 feet from home plate, but the field opened up quickly to expose cavernous 400-foot power alleys. The new steel stadiums provided more uniform dimensions, but they were still far from perfect. The left field foul line was shortened by 14 feet, but remained a distant 339 feet from home plate. Center field was shortened to 446 feet, a decrease of more than 60 feet. Right field was 329 feet from home plate on average, but six of the 16 major league parks still had right field fences less than 300 feet away. It is not surprising, therefore, that the most prodigious power hitters of the first 100 years of major league baseball were left-handed hitters. Most of the stadiums in use during that period favored southpaw swingers. Only in the 1990s did right handed hitters achieve parity.

The more unusual early twentieth century major league parks included Ebbets Field in Brooklyn, the Polo Grounds in New York, and Fenway Park in Boston. The right field wall in Ebbets Field was only 297 feet from home plate but it rose to a height of 38 feet, with the top half being a 19-foot screen and the bottom half a 19-foot concave concrete wall. It was always an adventure for the right fielder when a batted ball caromed off the concave section of the wall. The Polo Grounds had the typical nineteenth century oblong shape measuring 250 feet, 485 feet, and 249 feet, in left, center, and right. Fenway Park's distinctive feature is "The Green Monster," an inviting 37 foot high green plastic wall hovering over the left fielder, just 320 feet from home plate. The right field power alleys of 380 to 400 feet and the 420-foot center field area give the park respectability.

Off the field, in the everyday world, the economy was strong again thanks to increased industrialization, but several events lurking on the horizon would have a significant effect on the future prospects of major league baseball. World War I, which began in the Balkans in 1914, would soon engulf the United States, drawing hundreds of major league baseball players into the fray. The 1919 World Series between the Cincinnati Reds and the Chicago White Sox would turn out to be a dirty affair endangering the very future of the game. The major league owners would hire a new tough baseball commissioner, former judge Kenesaw Mountain Landis, and endow him with absolute authority over the conduct of the game and its players.

Finally, a hero would emerge to save the game from extinction. A young man by the name of George Herman Ruth would take the popularity of the game to a new level.

2. Babe Ruth— The Early Years

George Ruth was born in Baltimore, Maryland, on February 6, 1895, near the historic inner harbor area of the city. The harbor and the fort that defended it became celebrated events in American history for an incident that had taken place 80 years before Ruth's arrival. During the War of 1812, as British forces bombarded Fort McHenry, Francis Scott Key, a prisoner on board one of the British war ships, on seeing the American flag still flying over the fort at sunrise, penciled a song that would eventually become our national anthem.

The area where Ruth grew up, down by the docks, was a poor, slum-like neighborhood. Visiting sailors wandered the streets, frequenting the dozens of saloons that dotted the waterfront. Derelicts harassed passersby for money. Ladies of the evening decorated the street corners and parks. Fights were an everyday occurrence, with knifings and beatings commonplace.

Although George Ruth, Sr., was Lutheran and his wife Katherine was Catholic, they didn't attend church regularly, and Babe received his moral training on the streets of Baltimore. The dirty, scruffy-faced urchin was on his own, even as a young boy. His father, known as Big George (Babe was known as Little George), worked 14-hour days at the bar. And his sickly mother was kept busy full time trying to care for the family's needs, so young Ruth hung out around the docks with his pals.

According to Mamie, in Dorothy Ruth Pirone's book, *My Dad, the Babe*, "George wasn't a bad boy. He was a mischievous boy." He spent all his time with his buddies, on the streets, looking for excitement. He avoided school like the plague, even defying his parents when they tried to make him attend school.

Babe was only seven years old but, by his own admission, he was a little bum. He didn't know right from wrong. He went where he wanted to go. And whenever he got the urge to do something, he just did it. If he wanted something his parents had, he took it.

One day he tapped the family till. 'I took one dollar,' said Babe, 'and bought ice cream cones for all the kids on the block. When my old man asked me what I'd done I told him. He dragged me down cellar and beat me with a horsewhip. I tapped that till again—just to show him he couldn't break me. Then I landed in the Home, thank God.'"

Babe's parents had him committed to St. Mary's Industrial School, known as "The Home," at Wilkens and Caton Avenue, about four miles south of the city center. The school was not a reform school per se, but more a boarding school, where runaways and incorrigibles were sent to receive the discipline and guidance they failed to get at home. Parents, reportedly, had to pay monthly board to send their child there.

St. Mary's was run by the Xaverian Brothers, a Jesuit order that avows strict discipline. Whippings for infractions were daily occurrences, and young Ruth received more than his share of such rewards for insubordinate behavior. Strangely enough, Babe Ruth came to love the Home. He was once quoted as saying, "I'm as proud of it [St. Mary's] as any Harvard man is proud of his school." He claimed it was the most important time of his life. Brother Matthias, a 6'6", 240-pound human tower, was the Prefect of Discipline at St. Mary's, so he crossed swords with Babe many times over the first few months. Eventually, they became very close, with Babe looking upon Brother Matthias as a father figure.

Babe spent most of the next ten years at St. Mary's, with a few visits home along the way. The youngster learned a semblance of discipline although he never became what could be called a model citizen. He also accepted religion, assuming his mother's Roman Catholic faith at St. Mary's. He even served as an altar boy at the school.

What was most important for Babe's future was that he was forced to attend school, where he finally learned to read and write. He also studied arithmetic, history, geography, and spelling.

Babe's life at the Home was well regimented. His daily routine consisted of 6 A.M. wake-up, breakfast, Mass, about five hours of classwork, another four hours learning a trade, and several hours of free time. The boys at the school had a number of trades they could choose from, including printing, carpentry, farming, and shoe repair. Babe chose to be a tailor. After several years as a student and an apprentice, Babe bragged that he could sew a shirt in 15 minutes.

The priests at St. Mary's tried to provide a well-rounded regimen for the 850 boys at the school, so, in addition to education and trades, they also placed heavy emphasis on athletics. The most popular game at school was baseball, and the school was blessed with several baseball diamonds, which were spacious and well kept. As Babe grew older, the happiest moments in his life were those spent on a baseball field. It became obvious from the first time he held a bat that the former juvenile delinquent had a natural affinity for baseball. Brother Matthias noticed this and took Babe under his wing. He spent countless hours working with him, perfecting his pitching and fielding. The big, gentle priest caught Babe's pitches day after day, so Babe could improve his control and his movement on the ball. Brother Matthias also hit Babe hundreds of fungoes, and watched as the youngster happily ran them down. According to Marshall Smelser, Babe noted, "I could hit the first time I picked up a bat, but Brother Matthias made me a fielder." Ruth called the Xaverian brother the greatest man he ever knew.

In 1913, the Red Sox won the school championship, led by Babe Ruth who went undefeated as a pitcher, striking out 22 batters in one game, and who hit a lusty .537 to boot. Babe was big for his age, and by this time, at the age of 18, he stood 6'2" tall and weighed in at a trim 150 pounds. He was a southpaw pitcher with a blazing fast ball, a sharp-breaking curve, and a decent change of pace. At bat he was already noted for his long distance clouting.

The St. Mary's baseball teams played other schools around the Baltimore area, in addition to playing intramural games. Jack Dunn, a former major league pitcher who once won 20 games for the Brooklyn Bridegrooms and was now the owner and manager of the Baltimore Orioles of the International League, heard about Ruth from friends in the city, including Bill Byers, a former player for Dunn at Baltimore. Byers coached an all-star team that was defeated by Ruth's St. Mary's team in 1913, with Ruth fanning 20 batters along the way. Byers, who was not only impressed by the Babe's pitching savvy, but also by his big bat, told Dunn he thought Ruth should be an every day player.

The following February, Dunn visited St. Mary's Industrial School and signed Ruth to a Baltimore Orioles contract for $600 a year.

The world that Babe Ruth entered in 1914 was a far different world from the one he left when he entered St. Mary's in 1904. The world was changing at breakneck speed, with technological advances bringing automation into American manufacturing and farming. Spectacular new inventions were increasing the quality of life.

The gasoline-driven automobile, introduced in 1893, was an important means of transportation by 1911. Over 100,000 Ford Model T's, selling for $600, were already on the road.

Motion pictures, invented in 1893 by Thomas Alva Edison, were being shown for five cents in 10,000 nickelodeons by 1908.

The first subway train sped beneath the streets of New York in 1904, traveling eight miles from the Brooklyn Bridge to 145th Street at Broadway.

The Wright brothers flew an airplane 120 feet in 1903. The first cross-country flight took place only eight years later.

Cities were being lighted by electric lights. Telephones were becoming consumer items. Railroads criss-crossed the country, making long distance travel practical.

And the *San Francisco Chronicle* began publishing comic strips in 1907.

Babe Ruth began his professional career on March 7, 1914, when he took the field for his first intra-squad game for the Orioles in Fayetteville, North Carolina. Playing for the Buzzards against the Sparrows, the powerful southpaw swinger wasted no time in impressing his teammates, as well as the coaches and the fans. In the seventh inning, he sent a monstrous 400-foot drive over the right fielder's head and raced around the bases for a two-run home run. The Buzzards won the game 15–9, and Babe sparkled both at shortstop and on the mound.

It was about this time, that young Ruth received his nickname. Many of the Baltimore players started calling Ruth, "one of Dunn's babies." The newspapers quickly picked up the statement and began referring to the 19 year old southpaw as "Dunn's Baby," in the spring training reports. Over a period of weeks, it was modified to Babe. The name stuck.

The International League season opened on April 21, with the Orioles hosting the Buffalo Bisons. Ruth pitched the second game of the season, and whitewashed the Bisons by a score of 6–0. He also began his professional baseball career by scorching a single to right field in his first at bat.

After dropping his second start, a 2–1 pitchers duel to Rochester, the southpaw sensation tossed a 1–0, ten-inning shutout at the Montreal Royals, doubling home the winning run himself. For two months, the young rookie pitched regularly, winning some, losing a few, and gaining valuable experience. His 14–6 record through the end of June helped keep the Orioles in first place, but the hand writing was on the wall. Unfortunately, the Orioles were not drawing many people to their games, being outdone by the outlaw Federal League's Terrapins. Jack Dunn did everything he could to keep the team solvent, but to no avail. By the first of July, he was forced to conduct a full-scale fire sale.

On July 9, 1914, Babe Ruth, along with pitcher Ernie Shore and catcher Ben Egan, was sold to the Boston Red Sox for $20,000. The teen-ager made his major league debut in Boston's Fenway Park on July 11, against the cellar-dwelling Cleveland Indians. The rookie pitched a cred-itable game, going seven innings and yielding three runs on eight hits. Tris Speaker's RBI single in the bottom of the seventh brought in the run that made Ruth the winning pitcher.

A feeling of impending doom permeated the United States of Amer-ica in 1914 as a World War raged in Europe and the clouds of war were coming closer and closer to the homeland. The feeling of desperation would reach its lowest point in 1918 when more than 4,000,000 men would march off to war.

The mood in the country was even affecting major league baseball. Attendance, which had reached an all-time high of 7,200,000 in 1909, declined the following year, and by 1914 it had fallen off almost 40 per-cent, to 4,400,000.

World events, even those affecting his own country, didn't interest the Babe however. He was only interested in playing the game of base-ball. His major league career lasted five weeks, during which he pitched in four games, winning two and losing one. Manager Bill Carrigan, whose Red Sox were not quite ready to make a run at the powerful Philadelphia Athletics, decided that further seasoning with the Providence Grays would benefit Ruth more than sitting on a bench in Boston.

Carrigan was right. Babe Ruth's eight wins helped the Grays capture the International League pennant by four games over his old team, the Baltimore Orioles. His hitting improved also. After a tepid .200 batting average in Baltimore, the Babe hit a more respectable .247 for Provi-dence, with ten triples (in just 121 at bats) and one home run. The homer on September 5 in Toronto came in support of his own one-hitter. It was a three run shot in the sixth inning of a 9–0 whitewashing.

Nineteen fourteen was a significant year in the life of Babe Ruth in another respect. He got married. The young, virile major leaguer, who was now earning $2500 a season after another raise, was always on the prowl for good-looking women. While in Boston, Ruth regularly had breakfast at Landers Coffee Shop on Huntington Avenue. He became infatuated with a waitress named Helen Woodford, a 17-year-old immi-grant from Nova Scotia. Supposedly, after visiting the shop a couple of dozen times over a period of three months, Ruth proposed to her during one of his morning visits. She accepted, and on October 17 of that year, they were married in St. Pauls Church in Ellicott City, Maryland.

The next year, Babe Ruth came of age as a major league pitcher. When the season got underway, the St. Mary's graduate was not being counted on to be a major contributor to the Red Sox drive to the top of the American League. Bill Carrigan had rightys Ernie Shore, Rube Foster, "Smokey Joe" Wood, and Carl Mays, and southpaws Dutch Leonard and Ray Collins in the rotation. Ruth was odd man out.

On May 6, when Ruth got one of his infrequent starts, against the New York Yankees, his record stood at 1–1. In the third inning of a scoreless game, Yankee pitcher Jack Warhop tried to throw a fastball past the youngster, and Ruth promptly hit a mighty wallop into the upper right field stands at the Polo Grounds. It was his first major league homer, and a tape-measure shot at that. Although Ruth lost the game 4–3 in 13 innings, he impressed manager Carrigan with his pitching skills.

The new Boston slugger had a return match with Jack Warhop less than one month after their first encounter. This time Babe hit another towering home run to practically the same spot as the first one, only longer.

The 20-year-old rookie hit another tape-measure job on July 21. He slammed a towering drive over the right field pavilion in Sportsmans Park in St. Louis. As reported by William J. Jenkinson in the SABR *Home Run Encyclopedia*, the ball "cleared the wide breadth of Grand Boulevard and landed on the sidewalk approximately 470 feet from home plate."

In spite of the fact that the 6'2", 198-pound phenom could pound the ball with authority, his teammates resented the fact that he insisted on taking batting practice with the team. In those days, pitchers were not allowed to take batting practice. Some players decided to teach the young upstart a lesson. They sawed his bats in half when he was not in the club house.

Ruth also drew criticism from the players because he was so relaxed with everyone. He never held anyone in awe, which some people took as a sign of disrespect, particularly with regard to the veteran players on the club. But Babe was just being Babe. He treated presidents the same way he treated kids—as equals. One time, several years later, on meeting President Coolidge, he remarked, "Hot as hell, ain't it Prez."

Some players resented him because he was generally uncouth. He had horrible table manners, his language was disgusting, and his hygiene was deplorable. All these things were true. Over time, he improved in some areas like hygiene, but he was never able to clean up his language. One player claimed Ruth wasn't recruited. He was trapped. Other players called him "The Big Baboon."

The talented southpaw eventually moved up in the pitching rotation and pitched some outstanding games down the stretch. One memorable game took place in Fenway Park on August 14, when he faced the great Walter Johnson. Ruth prevailed 4–3. The pitching duels between Ruth

Babe Ruth began his career as a left-handed pitcher for the Boston Red Sox in 1914. He won 65 games for the Sox between 1915 and 1917.

and Johnson became legendary over the years. The two fireballers met on the field of battle ten times Between 1915 and 1918. The Red Sox southpaw came away the winner on six occasions, while Johnson was the .victor twice. Three times, the two hooked up in brilliant 1–0 pitching duels, with Babe Ruth winning all three. One of the games went 13 innings.

In another key game against the second-place Detroit Tigers, Ruth outpitched 24-game winner, Hooks Dauss, 3–2.

By season's end Babe Ruth was tied with Ernie Shore for the second best record (18–8), just one game behind Foster's 19–8, and was third in innings pitched. In addition to his fine pitching, Babe's batting statistics were an omen of things to come. He batted a healthy .315, and accumulated 15 extra base hits in only 92 at bats—ten doubles, one triple, and four home runs. Braggo Roth of Cleveland led the American League in home runs with seven in 384 at bats.

Babe Ruth's total of four home runs in 92 at bats is even more impressive when you realize that the entire Red Sox team hit a total of only 14 home runs. No one on the team hit more than two homers, and only seven position players in the league hit more than four.

Bill Carrigan's Red Sox won the 1915 American League pennant by 2½ games over the Detroit Tigers. In the World Series, the Sox faced the National League champion Philadelphia Phillies. It was strictly no contest. Carrigan, going with his veteran pitchers Shore, Foster, and Leonard, took the title in five games. Ruth watched from the bench, except for one pinch hitting chore in game one.

In 1916 Babe Ruth became Bill Carrigan's ace. He began the season in grand style, knocking off Walter Johnson by a score of 5–1 on April 17. "The Big Train" lasted only six innings, being raked for 11 hits by the Sox batters. On June 1, Ruth took the measure of Johnson again, this time by a slim 1–0 score. The Senators managed to hit just one ball out of the infield against the Boston southpaw. On August 15, the two great pitchers met a third time. This one was a sizzling pitching duel, with both pitchers at the top of their game. After 12 innings, the score stood at 0–0. Then in the bottom of the 13th, the Red Sox bunched three hits together to win the game 1–0. Ruth won a fourth encounter, 2–1, with Johnson finally taking a 4–3 decision on September 12.

The pennant race was a nail biter, with Boston, Detroit, and Chicago bunched together on September 14, as the Red Sox began a grueling ten-game road trip. They immediately dropped the opener of a three-game set to the White Sox, then righted themselves to take the next two. They went on to sweep the Tigers in three, and win two more at Cleveland, opening up a three-game lead over Chicago. They clinched the pennant six days later.

Ruth and Johnson dominated the league's pitching statistics for the season. In spite of going 1–4 against the Bambino, "The Big Train" led the league with 25 victories, 228 strikeouts, 371 innings pitched, and 36 complete games. The 21-year-old Ruth, with a 23–12 record, showed the way with a sparkling 1.75 earned run average and nine shutouts, still an American League record.

Boston's opponent in the World Series was the Brooklyn Dodgers, who had captured the National League pennant by 2½ games over the Philadelphia Phillies. The Dodgers, who had a better all-around team on paper, and were favored in the Series, were beaten by Boston, four games to one.

Babe Ruth pitched the best game of the Series, defeating hard luck pitcher, Sherry Smith of Brooklyn, 2–1 in 14 innings. Ruth's 13⅓ consecutive scoreless innings plus Larry Gardner's game-winning single in the bottom of the 14th were the highlights of the Series. Ruth's 14-inning complete game is still the longest complete game in World Series history.

Babe Ruth was on the verge of becoming the best left-handed pitcher in major league baseball. On the heels of his sensational year in 1916, the Boston ace won 24 games against 13 losses in 1917 and led the league in complete games with 35. He split two decisions with Walter Johnson, winning 1–0 and losing 6–0.

Even though Babe Ruth was a world class pitcher, 1917 was his last full year on the mound. The following year, he split his time between the mound and left field. He still pitched enough to be the number four man on manager Ed Barrow's staff, winning 13 games against seven losses, with an ERA of 2.22 in 166 innings, but his main value was as a world class hitter.

In a war-shortened season of 126 games, the Boston Red Sox took the American League pennant by 3½ games over the Cleveland Indians. In Boston's pennant clincher, Babe Ruth tossed a 6–1 three-hitter over Philadelphia, and contributed a single and a double to the cause. For the season, the Bambino, playing 110 games in left field, stroked the ball at an even .300 clip, and tied for the league lead in home runs with Tilly Walker, with 11. Many of his home runs were tape-measure jobs that excited the fans and brought flowering comments from the sports writers.

In the World Series against the Chicago Cubs, the big southpaw went 2–0 on the mound, establishing a Series record of 29⅔ consecutive scoreless innings, including 13⅓ from 1916. The record stood until 1961 when it was broken by Yankee ace Whitey Ford.

Ruth took the opener of the World Series, 1–0, over Hippo Vaughn. The only run of the game came across the plate in the fourth inning on a walk and consecutive singles by Whiteman and McInnis. Ruth also took game four, 3–2, with ninth-inning help from Joe Bush. Boston took the sixth game and the Series, 2–1 behind Carl Mays.

The big baseball news of the winter concerned the prodigious slugging feats of George Herman Ruth. The Babe was already being called the greatest home run hitter in baseball history, at the tender age of 23. His legendary exploits with the bat had the entire country mesmerized. It soon became obvious to Boston Red Sox management that his future was as an outfielder, not as a pitcher.

Babe Ruth appeared in 130 of the team's 140 games in 1919, but only 17 of them were as a pitcher.

Over the winter, the Boston strongman worked out diligently at his Sudbury, Massachusetts, country home. His regimen included clearing the trees behind his home, chopping wood, and running. Helen saw to it that he maintained a healthy diet.

As a result, he arrived at spring training camp in Tampa, Florida, in top physical condition. And he arrived with the mentality of a hitter. In his book *The Tumult and the Shouting*, when Grantland Rice called Ruth a good hitting pitcher, Babe replied, "I may be a pitcher, but first off I'm a hitter. I copied my swing after Joe Jackson's. His is the perfectest."

Joe Jackson was considered by many experts, including Ruth and

Ted Williams, to be the greatest natural hitter of all time. Both sluggers copied their swings after "Shoeless Joe." At the time he was barred from baseball for life, Jackson had a career batting average of .356, #3 all-time.

Baseball owners shortened the baseball season to 140 games in 1919 but went back to the 154-game schedule the following year. From a team standpoint, 1919 was a disaster. Shortly before the season began, Red Sox owner Harry Frazee sold three of his star players to the New York Yankees, outfielder Duffy Lewis and pitchers Carl Mays and Ernie Shore. Mays had won 21 games for the Sox in 1918 while Lewis and Shore were both in the army.

The Red Sox started slowly in 1919, hovering around the .500 mark for two months, then collapsing completely, finishing in sixth place, 20½ games behind the pennant-winning Chicago White Sox. Babe Ruth, catcher Wally Schang, and pitchers Allan Russell and Herb Pennock were the only bright spots in an otherwise dismal year.

Ruth got off the mark quickly when the season began, smacking a home run against the Yankees, in support of Carl Mays' 10–0 shutout of the New York team. For the first couple of months, Babe Ruth alternated between the mound and left field, but the wear and tear of the dual role finally brought the experiment to an end. Babe became a full-time outfielder.

As summer wore on, Babe's spectacular hitting exploits had the baseball writers rushing to their record books to verify the existing home run record. At first it was thought that Buck Freeman's 25 home runs in 1899 were the record. Then someone discovered that Ned Williamson had dropped 27 balls over the short fence in Chicago's Lake Front Park in 1884.

No matter, Babe would not be stopped. His first challenge, Sock Seybold's American League record of 16 home runs, set in 1902, fell before a fussilade of home runs, on August 14. Within weeks Ruth passed Gavvy Cravath's modern major league record of 24 set in 1915, then beat Freeman's mark of 25. On September 20, the mighty Bambino tied Williamson's mark with an unusual Fenway Park home run. Ruth, a notorious pull hitter, hit an outside pitch from Lefty Williams of the White Sox over the left field wall in the bottom of the ninth, to win the game. Finally, on September 24, Ruth hit #28, to pass Williamson. The record-breaking home run came in the ninth inning of the second game of a doubleheader against the New York Yankees, in the Polo Grounds. It was hit against New York's 20-game winner, Bob Shawkey, and was called the longest home run in Polo Grounds history, clearing the right field stands and landing in Manhattan Field which adjoins the stadium. He

Babe Ruth, in his first full season as an outfielder in 1919, set a new home run record when he socked 29 round trippers.

hit one more home run before the season ended, finishing with 29, an unbelievable total in those days of the dead ball and trick pitches. And— he outhomered four American League teams.

The 1919 World Series pitted the powerful Chicago White Sox against the National League champion, Cincinnati Reds. Although the White Sox were heavy favorites, betting was light because there were already rumors that the Series was fixed. Ed Cicotte, the White Sox ace, who went 29–7 during the season, was clobbered in the opening game of the Series, then lost game four, 2–0, when his two errors in the fifth inning led to both Cincinnati runs. Lefty Williams, a 23-game winner during the season, went down to defeat three times, compiling a suspicious 6.61 earned run average. The only bright spot in the Chicago lineup was the pitching of little Dickie Kerr, who did everything in his power to win the Series. He shut out the Reds 3–0 in game three, then won game six 5–4 with a gutty ten-inning performance. But it wasn't enough. Cincinnati took the best five of nine Series in eight games.

On October 28, 1919, the United States Congress passed the 18th amendment to the Constitution, making the manufacture and sale of alcoholic beverages illegal in the country.

Prohibition would have a profound effect on American society during the decade of the 20s, but not in the way its adherents expected.

On the baseball front, the big news of the off season was the sale of Babe Ruth to the New York Yankees. Harry Frazee, the owner of the Boston Red Sox, experienced serious financial difficulties in 1919. He had lost a considerable sum of money producing Broadway plays he had loans due to Joseph Lannin, the former Red Sox owner, and Ruth was squeezing him for more money. In desperation, Frazee sold his "franchise" player to New York for $120,000 and a $350,000 loan. The deal was finalized on January 5, 1920.

Ruth's sale was followed in subsequent years, by the sale of Waite Hoyt, Herb Pennock, Joe Bush, Sam Jones, Everett Scott, and Wally Schang, to those same Yankees. Frazee's disgraceful acts destroyed the greatest team of the decade, a team that had captured four World Championships between 1912 and 1918.

The wholesale shipment of Boston's star players to New York led to the creation of the great Yankee dynasties that dominated the major leagues from 1921 until 1964.

Boston has never recovered from the Babe Ruth fiasco. They have won only four American League pennants in the ensuing 80 years. They have never won another World Championship.

3. Babe Ruth—
A Hero Emerges

Nineteen hundred and twenty was a historic year in major league baseball. Prohibition went into effect. "The Roaring Twenties" got underway. The major leagues began using a new juiced-up baseball, establishing the lively ball era in professional baseball. Babe Ruth joined the New York Yankees, and broke all single season home run records. Trick pitches like the spit ball were banned forever. And the Black Sox scandal captured the public's attention.

The beginning of the lively ball era was not a figment of someone's imagination. The ball shot off players' bats like it was shot from a cannon. Major league home runs increased by 41 percent from 1919 to 1920. They continued to increase over the next decade as more and more batters began to swing for the fences instead of just trying to make contact with the ball.

Major league hitters pounded out a total of 447 home runs in 1919. They hit 631 homers in 1920, and a mind-boggling 1565 homers in 1930. There were two major culprits, the new ball and Babe Ruth. The A.G. Spalding Company, manufacturer of major league baseballs, reportedly began using Australian yarn in 1920. The new yarn, which was stronger and tougher than American yarn, could be wound tighter, giving harder, livelier balls than those manufactured prior to 1920.

Babe Ruth himself contributed significantly to the home run craze. His mighty blasts created such excitement around the country that other players soon began to copy his swing. Until Ruth revolutionized the game, players were more concerned with making contact with the ball than they were with hitting it out of the park. The baseball mentality was such that it was a disgrace to strike out, so most players just protected the plate when they had two strikes on them, making sure they put the ball in play.

The tremendous increase in home runs however, is not the reason that so many modern-day hitters strike out 100 to 150 times a year. In 1930, when major league hitters pounded out 1,565 home runs, which was an increase of 250 percent over 1920, strikeouts only increased by 9 percent, from 7,282 to 7,936.

Today's hitters arc guess hitters, who commit to swinging at a pitch before they know what kind of a pitch it is. Yesterday's hitters were controlled hitters, who waited on a pitch until the last moment before swinging at it. As a result, they knew what kind of pitch they were swinging at and were able to put it in play more often.

The other factor that impacted significantly on the home run production in the major leagues was the banishment of trick pitches from the game. Pitchers were no longer permitted to throw the spitball, emery ball, shine ball, and other trick pitches, but major league pitchers who threw the spitball were grandfathered. They were allowed to continue throwing it until they retired. Burleigh Grimes was the last of the spitball pitchers, finally retiring in 1934.

As the 1920 season got underway, Miller Huggin's New York Yankees were poised to make a run for the top. The previous year, they won 80 games against only 59 losses, finishing in third place, 7½ games behind the Chicago White Sox. Now, with Ruth in tow, Huggins was confident he could take it all.

Babe Ruth was already referred to as the Sultan of Swat by the baseball community after his long distance bludgeoning of opposing pitchers during the preceding two years. His record-breaking clouts brought the fans out by the thousands. Even opposing players held Ruth in awe. Players and fans alike stopped whatever they were doing to watch the Bambino take batting practice before a game.

The big slugger was an imposing sight at the plate. He was one of the bigger players in the league at 6'2", and 210 pounds, and his chiseled body seemed to be designed for destruction. His broad shoulders and huge chest, tapering down to a svelte waist and powerful legs, exuded power. His swing was vicious but graceful. It was copied from "Shoeless Joe" Jackson's swing, except that Babe Ruth kept his feet closer together than Jackson did, so he could stride into the ball, utilizing all his power at the moment of contact. As Ruth said, his swing was an all-or-nothing swing. He either hit the ball with tremendous power or he looked good striking out.

Ruth was the most glamorous and exciting player in baseball history. Unlike his contemporaries who swung the bat level to the ground in order to hit line drives back through the infield, the Yankee slugger used his powerful wrists to uppercut the ball, sending the little white pellets into orbit whenever he connected.

Ruth got off the mark slowly when the 1920 season opened however, going homerless in New York's first 11 games. Then, on May 1, Babe Ruth hit his first Yankee home run, a towering drive over the right field roof at the Polo Grounds, also known as Brush Stadium, sparking the team to a 6–0 whitewashing of the Red Sox. The Yankees were tenants in the New York Giants home park for ten years, until they moved into their own stadium, in 1923. Ruth played in the Polo Grounds for three years and enjoyed tremendous home run success in the homer-friendly park. He averaged an astounding 63 home runs for every 550 at bats in the Polo Grounds.

The Yankee slugger hit 11 home runs in May and 13 in June as he took baseball to a level it could never imagine. On July 15, in just his 93rd game of the season, Babe Ruth tied his own major league mark with home run number 29. Five days later, he broke the record, smashing #30 against the Chicago White Sox in the Polo Grounds.

The excitement of Babe Ruth's home run rampage was brought back to earth on August 16, when tragedy visited the Yankees' home park. In a game against the Cleveland Indians, New York submarine pitcher Carl Mays hit Cleveland shortstop Ray Chapman in the temple with a fastball after Chapman inadvertantly ducked into the pitch. The 29-year-old infielder died within 24 hours, becoming the only fatality in major league baseball history.

Cleveland, under manager Tris Speaker, wore black arm bands the rest of the season, in tribute to their fallen comrade. The Indians went on to capture the American League pennant after eight Chicago White Sox players were suspended for complicity in fixing the 1919 World Series. They also won the World Championship, beating the Brooklyn Dodgers five games to two.

Ruth continued his cannonading through the months of August and September. He hit a milestone on September 24 when he launched #50 off the right field facade at the Polo Grounds in the first game of a doubleheader. He hit number 51 in game two. The Sultan of Swat climaxed his explosive season by hitting home run #54 on September 29, breaking his own record by 25 home runs.

Babe Ruth's inaugural season in New York was a smashing success. He not only set a new major league home run record, but he also showed the baseball world he was not a one-dimensional player. The big outfielder ripped the ball at a sizzling .376 clip, with 36 doubles and nine triples to go along with his 54 home runs. His .847 season slugging average lasted more than 80 years until Barry Bonds broke it in 2001.

Babe Ruth totally dominated the major leagues in 1920. He led the majors in runs scored (158), home runs (54), runs batted in (137), bases on balls (148), on base percentage (.530), and slugging average (.847). And he outhomered every team in the American League!

Nineteen twenty was the beginning of the decade that has been called the Golden Age of Sports. It has also been called the most hedonistic decade of the twentieth century—the Jazz Age, the Roaring Twenties. The two—sports and the Roaring Twenties—went hand in hand. Everything seemed surrealistic during the 20s. The athletes were larger than life. The nightlife was one wild, never-ending roller coaster ride. On the athletic front, until the 20s, baseball and boxing were essentially the only sports that most Americans were familiar with. Then beginning in 1919, when increased leisure time made spectator sports more popular, the entire field of athletics exploded with legendary figures. Babe Ruth stood baseball on its ear with his electrifying home run feats, personally carrying the game to a new level of popularity. In the ring, a young fighting machine out of Colorado, named Jack Dempsey, captivated the sporting public. The Manassa Mauler, a veritable tiger at only 182 pounds, manhandled heavyweight champion, Jess Willard, to win the title on July 4, 1919. Dempsey, in as ferocious an attack as had ever been seen in the squared circle, knocked the 6'6" 250-pound "Pottawatomie Giant" to the canvas six times in the first two minutes of the fight, en route to a third round TKO. He would rule the division for seven years until dethroned by Gene Tunney in 1926.

Other sporting figures who captivated the American public over the next decade included football legend Red Grange of Illinois University, Notre Dame's famed Four Horsemen, golfer Bobby Jones, Tennis champions Helen Wills and Bill Tilden, swimmer Gertrude Ederle, and aviator Charles Lindbergh.

American society changed dramatically in the years following World War I. Call it a fatalistic attitude brought on by the horrors of war, just another step in evolution, or the result of a booming economy. Whatever it was, it turned the country upside down.

The automobile had made long-distance traveling practical. By 1929, there were 23 million autos on the country's highways. Stock market investments made thousands of millionaires overnight. Even the small investor was living comfortably as a result of the huge profits being generated by American business. And movies were influencing the morals of the country. Movie stars like Rudolph Valentino and Claire Bow, the "It" girl, exuded sexuality on screen. The public flocked to movie theaters in record numbers. When Valentino died in 1925, after an appendectomy,

30,000 people stormed Campbell's Funeral Church in New York City to view the body. By the time Al Jolson, another graduate of St. Mary's, made the first talking picture, *The Jazz Singer*, in 1927, over 100,000,000 people were attending movies every week.

Prohibition, which banned the manufacture and sale of alcoholic beverages, instead of curing the country of the ills of alcohol, drove it to new heights, and in the process, led to the rise of gangsterism in the United States.

Before the ink was dry on Amendment #18, crafty racketeers, ready to take advantage of every opportunity, were making arrangements to obtain illegal alcohol from other countries, and from illegal manufacturing operations (known as moonshiners), inside the country. Other mobsters were opening secret nightclubs, called "speakeasies." It was the beginning of "The Roaring Twenties."

The atmosphere in the country was fueled by the passage of Amendment #19 to the United States Constitution, the law that gave women the right to vote. The female sex was becoming more independent and was beginning to establish its own identity in the country.

Speakeasies contributed to the lawlessness in the country in another way. In illegal night clubs, there was no "legal" drinking age. If you were big enough to reach the bar, you were big enough to drink. And the booze flowed freely, much of it coming into the country on fast motor boats from the West Indies. Other sources of supply included Mexico and Canada. People also brewed their own liquor at home. It was called Home Brew or Bathtub Gin.

A significant amount of the illegal alcohol came from industrial alcohol that was diverted to making synthetic liquor. In 1926 alone, it was estimated that 60 million gallons of industrial alcohol were diverted for illegal uses.

The Roaring Twenties were a time of fun and games. The new jazz music filled the speakeasies with a sensual, rhythmic beat. Combined with the effects of alcohol, it produced wild orgies in thousands of clubs across the country. Unconventional young women in short dresses, known as flappers, danced away the nights, drinking and behaving wildly. The men followed suit. Rich, old men, known as "Sugar Daddies," took advantage of the situation to latch on to young, willing companions. The attitude seemed to be "eat, drink, and be merry, for tomorrow we die."

Throughout the twenties the nation partied, and Babe Ruth was right in the middle of it. The Babe could drink and party with the best of them, even before 1920. In fact, manager Bill Carrigan of the Boston Red Sox, tipped off by a hotel employee that Ruth didn't get back to the team hotel until 6 A.M. one morning, broke into the Babe's room and found him under the covers fully clothed. After several arguments and a suspension, Babe agreed to leave a note on Carrigan's door telling him when he got back to the hotel every night. Carrigan, for his part, said he would never check on Babe again, as long as Ruth did not lie to him. Sure enough, the Red Sox manager would find a note on his door every morning that would say something like, "Bill. Got back at 3 A.M. Babe." Babe never lied, and Carrigan never checked on him again. He was satisfied as long as Babe's night life didn't affect his performance on the field.

Prohibition proved to be a monumental disaster for American society. Instead of eliminating the consumption of alcohol, it actually resulted in an increase in consumption, because of the inability to monitor the drinking age. Other results of prohibition were an increase in prostitution, an increase in arrests for drunkenness, a rise in alcoholism, an increase in deaths from poisoned alcohol, and the growth of organized crime. Crime figures like Al Capone and Lucky Luciano got their starts bootlegging during "The Roaring Twenties," eventually expanding into racketeering and protection.

Prohibition was finally repealed by the passage of the 21st Amendment to the Constitution, on November 7, 1933. Laws against drinking however, remained in effect in some localities across the country. Throughout the remainder of the twentieth century, drinking was regulated on a state by state basis, or by a town or a county within a state.

Once back in the states, Ruth retreated to his home in Sudbury, Massachusetts, to relax and to enjoy the life of a gentleman farmer. He also worked out on a regular basis to stay in shape.

When the 1921 season rolled around, Babe Ruth was ready. Baseball fans across the country held their collective breaths, wondering what the Sultan of Swat would do for an encore. The first thing he did was fascinate the people who visited the Yankees' spring training camp. The Babe was an extrovert, and he loved to entertain the fans, both on the field and off, and he spent hours signing autographs whenever he had the time. Over the years, Babe Ruth probably signed more autographs than any other sports figure. And he loved the kids most of all. His close relationship with kids went back to his years in St. Mary's where, as a teenager, he defended the little kids from the school bullies, remembering how tough life was for him when he was little.

The New York Yankees of 1921, unknown to them at the time, were about to embark on a memorable, record-setting journey. Their pennant victory would be the first of 35 such trophies over a period of 78 years, an extraordinary achievement unmatched in the annals of professional sports. Two years later, the Bronx Bombers would win the first of their 24 World Championships. Babe Ruth anchored the attack for the first seven American League pennants and the first four World Championships.

The Yankee team, who by this time had obtained pitcher Waite Hoyt and catcher Wally Schang from their supply house in Boston, started the season in fine fashion, blasting the last-place Philadelphia Athletics, 11–1. Babe Ruth led the attack with five hits, including two doubles. Three days later, on April 16, the Sultan of Swat banged out his first homer, as Miller Huggins' boys took the A's in tow once more, this time by a score of 3–1.

New York struggled during the first month of the season, but by mid–May they were cranking on all cylinders, and moved into second place behind the defending World Champion Cleveland Indians. Through the summer and into September, not more than two games separated the two combatants.

Ruth's home run count reached 14 by the end of May, 26 by the end of June, and 36 by the end of July, leaving him about even with his 1920 pace. The Yankees trailed the Indians by a mere one game.

On August 11, New York beat the Chicago White Sox to move into first place by one percentage point. The dogfight was on. The lead changed hands several times over the next five weeks, as the two teams jockeyed for position. Ruth's cannonading continued unabated through August and into September. On September 9, in Shibe Park, the Bambino tied his own home run record when he unleashed a mighty wallop against the A's. One week later, in the cozy confines of the Polo Grounds, he hit #55 against the St. Louis Browns.

The pennant race finally reached its climax on September 26, when Tris Speaker's Cleveland Indians, trailing the Yankees by ½ game, invaded New York for a crucial four-game series. With the two teams tied at one game apiece, the Yankee bombers unloaded on the hapless Cleveland pitchers. In game three, they completely destroyed the visitors to the tune of 21–7. In the finale, the Sultan of Swat, with two home runs and a double drove in five runs as the Yanks prevailed 8–7. They clinched the pennant on October 1.

The Bambino hit his record setting 59th home run on October 2, in the last game of the season. He hit it in the Polo Grounds with two men on base, as the Yanks edged the Boston Red Sox, 7–6. It was a record-setting season all around the major leagues. Home run totals increased from 630 in 1920 to 937 in 1921, a jump of 49 percent. Still, Babe Ruth was in a class by himself. His nearest competitor in the American League was teammate Bob Meusel with 24 homers. The National League champion, George Kelly of the Giants, hit 23.

Once again, the kid from Baltimore showed himself to be a superstar of immense proportions. His season was arguably the greatest of his career, even better than his fabulous 1920 season. In addition to his 59 home runs, Ruth led the league with 177 runs scored (still the all-time major league record) and 171 runs batted in. His 204 base hits included 44 doubles and 16 triples, good for a .378 batting average. His 16 triples, along with 17 stolen bases, were indicative of his exceptional speed on the bases.

Two "firsts" were set when Miller Huggins' Yankees met John McGraw's Giants in the World Series. It was the first time two teams that shared the same home ballpark met in the Series. It was also the first World Series broadcast on radio. Station WJZ in Newark, New Jersey, covered the game, with legendary sports commentator Graham McNamee doing the play by play. Unfortunately, the Yankees dropped the best of nine series, five games to three. The Yanks got off fast, taking the opener 3–0 behind Carl Mays' five-hitter, and capturing game two, 3–0 on a brilliant two-hitter by Waite Hoyt. Then it was downhill, with the Giants taking five of the last six. Injuries kept Ruth out of the lineup for the last three games, all of which the Giants won.

Babe Ruth's years in New York were hectic and turbulent ones. He always resisted authority, and had continual run-ins with manager Miller Huggins, owner Jacob Ruppert, and Baseball Commissioner Kenesaw Mountain Landis. He even punched an umpire in the jaw one time, resulting in one of his dozen or more suspensions. Those incidents never hurt his popularity however. He was an idol to the fans, young and old alike, and he also had an excellent rapport with the newsmen.

New York went on to take the American League pennant again in 1922, this time beating a strong St. Louis Browns team by a single game. But Ruth personally had a difficult year. He allowed himself to get out of shape over the winter and performed poorly all year. The boos of the crowd made him testy, resulted in frequent altercations with the umpires, and brought about four more suspensions. The frustrated slugger was also removed as the Yankee captain after he chased a jeering fan through the stands. And he lost a one-sided fight to teammate Wally Pipp to boot.

Babe Ruth's season statistics were not something he was proud of. He played in only 110 games, hit 35 home runs, batted in only 99 runs, and hit a sub par .315—a career season for some players, but an embarrassment for an icon like Ruth.

The New York Yankees met the Giants in the World Series once again. This time they were swept in four games, much to the chagrin of Miller Huggins and Jacob Ruppert. The Yankees were a lesson in futility, scoring only 11 runs in five games (one game ended in a tie) and never scoring more than three runs in any game. Babe Ruth hit a paltry .118, with just one RBI in the Series. Bob Meusel at .300 and Wally Pipp at .286 were the only Yankee batters to hit over .250.

Ruth worked hard to get in shape for the 1923 season, determined to redeem himself in the eyes of the New York fans. Meanwhile Ruppert dipped into the Boston well one last time and came up with southpaw pitcher, Herb Pennock. The slender six footer went on to win 164 games for the Yankees over a period of 12 years.

The year 1923 was a memorable period in New York Yankee history. Yankee Stadium, known as "The House That Ruth Built," opened on April 18. Fittingly, the "Sultan of Swat" responded in typically heroic fashion. He slammed the first stadium home run, a three-run shot into the right field stands in the third inning, as the New Yorkers won, 4–1, behind Bob Shawkey. The Yanks went on to capture their third successive American League pennant, this time leaving the rest of the league in their dust and finishing a comfortable 16 games ahead of the Detroit Tigers. They capped off their spectacular run with a six-game victory over their arch rivals, the New York Giants, in the World Series.

Babe Ruth had a great season all around. He led the league in home runs again, this time with 41. He also led in runs scored (151) and runs batted in (131), and he hit a career high .394. In the Series, he ripped Giant pitching for three home runs and a .368 batting average.

Babe Ruth continued his sensational slugging through the 1924 season. Even though the Yankees fell to the Washington Senators in the pennant race, the Bambino won his only batting championship, with a sizzling .378 average. He led the league in runs scored with 143 and home runs with 46. And he also drove in 121 runs.

The big outfielder went on another typical eating binge in the off season, and arrived at spring training overweight and out of shape. His 256 pound bulk finally caught up with him as the team headed north. He collapsed on the train platform in Asheville, North Carolina, and was rushed back to New York for medical treatment. He was operated on for an intestinal abscess, putting him out of action for seven weeks. Newspapers popularly reported the incident as "The Bellyache Heard Round the World."

Ruth returned to the Yankee lineup on June 1, but he never did regain his batting form. He hit below .250 most of the summer but continued to enjoy the night life all around the American League. Finally, in desperation, manager Miller Huggins fined his star $5000.00 and suspended him indefinitely. After the usual threats to quit the team, Ruth recanted, apologized to Huggins, and was eventually reinstated.

His return couldn't help the Yankees however. They struggled through a disastrous season, finishing in seventh place. Their 69–85 record left them a distant 28 games behind the Washington Senators. Ruth played in only 98 games, batting .290 with 25 homers and 66 RBIs. Bob Meusel was the only bright spot on the team, leading the league in home runs with 33 and runs batted in with 138. Rookie Lou Gehrig hit a respectable .290 with 20 homers and 68 RBIs.

The embarrassed Sultan of Swat punished himself over the winter, determined to get back into playing condition. He worked out religiously at Artie McGovern's gym on 42nd Street and Madison Avenue. The regimen paid off. He dropped 42 pounds in five months and arrived at spring training camp in St. Petersburg weighing a svelte 212 pounds. The camp was upbeat as the proud New Yorkers were determined to atone for their dismal showing the previous year.

Miller Huggins' boys got off the mark quickly in 1926, anchored by a new double play combination of Tony Lazzeri at second and Mark Koenig at short. Lou Gehrig at first, with one full year under his belt was about ready for stardom. The Yankees opened the season on April 13, with a 12–11 triumph over the Red Sox in Boston. A 16-game winning streak in May left them with a 30–9 record and a healthy 14-game lead over the Philadelphia Athletics.

A late-season slump by the Yankees and a surge by the Cleveland Indians closed the gap by the end of the season, but New York still took the pennant by three games. Unfortunately they lost the World Series in seven games, to the St. Louis Cardinals, when grizzled veteran Grover Cleveland Alexander came out of the bullpen in the seventh inning with the bases loaded, two out, and the Cards clinging to a slim 3–2 lead. "Old Alex" fanned "Poosh 'em Up Tony" Lazzeri to end the threat, then protected the lead over the final two innings to give the Cards the World Championship. Babe Ruth, who walked with two out in the bottom of the ninth, was thrown out attempting to steal, ending the Series.

Overall, the Bambino had performed brilliantly, both during the season and in the Series. Playing in 152 games, he once again led the league in runs scored (139), home runs (47), and runs batted in (145), while rapping the ball at a .372 clip. In the World Series he smashed four home runs in seven games, while walking 11 times.

In 1927 George Herman "Babe" Ruth achieved the pinnacle of his career. At 32 years of age, he was beginning to settle down, take his conditioning seriously, and limit his evening escapades. After a winter of vigorous training, he arrived in Florida ready for action. It was reported that he took young Gehrig under his wing, and told Lou he could hit 40 to 50 home runs a year if he held his bat down at the end and swung with bad intentions. He also suggested that Gehrig try to pull the ball more to take advantage of the short right field porches in most American League parks. Coincidentally or not, Lou Gehrig suddenly blossomed into a feared slugger, increasing his home run production from 16 in 1926 to 47 in 1927. His output in Yankee Stadium jumped up from four homers in 1926 to 24 homers in 27, indicating he did in fact learn to pull the ball. Gehrig went on to average 37 home runs a year over the next 11 years.

The 1927 New York Yankees, who would forever be known as "Murderers Row," and may have been the greatest team of all time, opened their season in Yankee Stadium against the Athletics, before 72,000 fans. Their 8–3 victory gave them a share of first place. They never lost it. By the end of April, they held a one-game lead, and Ruth had just four home runs.

Both Ruth and the Yanks picked up the pace in mid–May. The Yankee slugger began the month by hitting two homers at home, against the A's, on May 1. Then he had a dry spell of eight days before slamming #7 against Milt Gaston of the St. Louis Browns. Gaston became a favorite target of Ruth's during the season, yielding four of Babe's 60 home runs. Southpaw Rube Walberg of the A's also gave up four homers to the Yankee bomber. After a 10–3 streak mid month, the Yanks 23–10 record gave them a 4½ game lead over the Chicago White Sox. On May 22 in Cleveland's League Park, the Sultan of Swat hit his tenth homer, a tape-measure job, off journeyman right-hander Benn Karr.

Babe had nine home runs in June, including two two-homer days. He pounded out two home runs against lefty Garland Buckeye of Cleveland, in Yankee Stadium, on June 11, then duplicated the feat in Boston, against Hal Wiltse, on the 22nd.

On June 13, Babe hit #21 in Cleveland. Following a habit he established at the start of the season, as reported by Bill Koenig, he put a notch around the trademark of his favorite bat, a model R43, 40-ounce, 35" Louisville Slugger. Notch #21 was the last notch he put on the bat. He broke the bat before hitting #22.

The New York team continued to terrorize opposing pitchers with their long ball attack. In addition to Ruth and Gehrig, Bob Meusel and Earl Combs were stroking the ball at a better than .330 pace, and Tony Lazzeri was over .300 for the New York wrecking crew that was averaging more than six runs a game.

During the heat of the summer, according to Samuel Fuller in *Cult Baseball Players*, Babe Ruth swaggered into the City Room of the New York Journal one day, announcing to the reporters, "Gentlemen, that bathtub gin is poison," pointing to the half dozen water coolers around the room that, in fact, were filled to the brim with homemade prohibition gin. Ruth was followed into the room by six uniformed cops, carrying six cases of genuine whiskey. Typewriters were left silent and telephones were left ringing as Ruth, the reporters, and the cops drank to each other's health from paper cups.

The Babe hit nine more homers in July, as the Yankees widened their lead in the American League pennant race. After sweeping Bucky Harris' Washington Senators by scores of 12–1 and 18–1 on the fourth of July, their lead mounted to a hefty 11½ games. Lou Gehrig had two homers in the sweep giving him the home run lead over Babe Ruth, 27–26. Babe kept the pressure on however, hitting a homer off Don Hankins in Detroit on the 8th of the month, then following that with two homers off the Tigers' Ken Holloway the next day. He also hit two more off his "cousin" Milt Gaston of the Browns, on July 26. He finished the month with 34 home runs, still in a neck and neck race with his teammate Lou Gehrig.

The Senators stayed hot through July, but when they slumped in August, the Tigers and A's jockeyed for second place, a good 16 games behind the league-leading Yankees. Lou Gehrig, or Larrapin' Lou as he was called, kept pace with Ruth through the dog days of August. On August 10, Lou was in the lead 38 homers to 35. The Sultan of Swat connected for #37 in Chicago on the 16th, becoming the first player to hit a ball out of the remodeled double deck Comiskey Park. He got even with Gehrig on August 22 when he victimized "Lefty" Joe Shaute in Cleveland, smashing his 40th home run of the season. Babe hit nine home runs in August, finishing the month with a total of 43 homers.

Gehrig jumped out in front of the "Sultan of Swat" again, 45 to 44, on September 5. The Yankee lead at that time was a comfortable 15 games. On September 6, Miller Huggins' crew visited Boston to play the last-place Red Sox. Facing Tony Welzer, the Bambino launched two home runs, giving him 46 for the season. He hit #47 later in the game against Jack Russell, moving in front of Gehrig by two. The following day, the big slugger punished Boston pitching for two more homers, increasing his season total to 49. When he homered off Gaston of St. Louis, in New York on the 11th of the month, it gave him an even 50 home runs with just 17 games left in the season.

The New York Yankees clinched the pennant on September 13 when they swept the Cleveland Indians by identical scores of 5–3. Ruth

Babe Ruth dominated the American League for 16 years with his spectacular home run feats. (Brace photo)

homered in each game, giving him 52 for the season. The New York triumph was the earliest pennant clinching in American League history. Now the only race of interest for the fans was the home run race, and the race was over as far as Gehrig was concerned. He hit just two more home runs after September 6, finishing the season with 47. Now it was just Babe against Babe.

Babe Ruth was in an enviable position as he chased the record. He was chasing himself, so there was no pressure on him to break someone else's record. There were no radio or television interviews to contend with and no combative newspaper reporters prying for sensational personal exposes.

In Ruth's time, the major leagues were confined to a relatively small geographical area that stretched from Boston in the north to Washington, D.C. in the south, and St. Louis in the west. Travel was less hectic than it is today. Trains carried the New York team to Boston or Washington in three hours. The longest trip of 976 miles to St. Louis was a comfortable overnight ride in a sleeper car.

The New York newspaper reporters traveled with the team when they were on the road. They shared sleeping and eating accommodations with the players, on the train, and they spent their free time playing poker and shooting the breeze with them. They also hung out with the players in the hotel, the restaurants, and the local nightspots. For all intents and purposes, the reporters were just one of the boys. Their reporting was restricted to events on the baseball field. They did not pry into a player's private life or report on any negative off-field incidents.

Future home run challengers were not so lucky. They would come under intense media scrutiny, both before a game and after a game. Their private lives were fair game, their indiscretions laid bare for all to see. Future home run challengers lived life in a goldfish bowl.

Babe still trailed his 1921 record pace of 59 home runs as the month approached its final two weeks. When he put #55 in orbit against Sam Gibson of Detroit in Yankee Stadium on September 21, he was still five games behind '21. He was still three homers behind with just four games to play.

According to Robert W. Creamer, when Babe hit his 56th homer he carried the bat around the bases with him. A kid rushed onto the field and grabbed the bat as Babe rounded third, but Babe continued on, crossing the plate, dragging the bat and the kid behind him.

He smashed his 57th home run, a grand slam, off future Hall-of-Famer Lefty Grove at the stadium, in game #151. Two days later, on September 29, playing against the Washington Senators at home, the Sultan of Swat propelled more two balls into the stands, tying his own record of 59 home runs. His first homer came with the bases empty in the first inning. His second homer was a grand slam in the fifth as the Yankees romped 15–4.

Babe Ruth had two more games in which to break his own record. He needed only one. On Friday, September 30, the Washington Senators were in town to close out the season. Tom Zachary, a 6'1", 187-pound curve ball artist was chasing his ninth win of the season, opposed by 18-game winner, Herb Pennock. The two southpaws locked up in a pitchers duel, with the score knotted at 2–2 after seven innings. Ruth had singled and scored both Yankee runs, one in the fourth and one in the sixth, to offset a two-run fourth by Washington. In the eighth inning, Mark Koenig tripled with one out, bringing Ruth to the plate again. The Babe had a perfect day at that point, with two singles and a walk. With a count of 1–1, Zachary uncorked a low, inside fast ball, and Babe jumped all over it. He sent a sizzling line drive down the right field line, barely fair. The ball came to rest about half way up the stands, with the umpire signaling a home run. Tom Zachary argued that the ball was foul, but to no avail. Babe rounded the bases to the cheers of the screaming New York fans. Hats and torn scraps of paper floated down on the field as the wild celebration continued for another ten minutes.

Babe's 60th also turned out to be the game winner as Pennock shut down the Senators in the ninth to win 4–2. During the clubhouse celebration following the game, the Babe exulted, "Sixty. Count 'em, sixty. Let's see some other sonofabitch match that."

Curiously, only 10,000 fans turned out to witness history in the making. Apparently it was no big deal to the blase New Yorkers, who had already seen Babe Ruth set two home run records. They thought he would continue setting records for years to come. So #60 was nothing special to them. That mentality would change drastically as the years passed.

Babe Ruth's glorious season, in addition to his 60 home runs, included a league-leading 158 runs scored, 164 runs batted in, and a .356 batting average. Once again he outhomered every team in the league.

Ruth, Lou Gehrig, and the rest of "Murderers Row," continued their cannonading through the World Series. They swept the timid Pittsburgh Pirates in four straight but, truth be told, they probably won the Series even before the first pitch was thrown. The day before game one, during batting practice, manager Miller Huggins told his charges to see how many balls they could put out of Forbes Field. The bombardment that followed completely demoralized the Pirate players who were outscored 23–10 in the Series.

Nineteen twenty-seven was by no means Babe Ruth's swan song. He hit 54 home runs in 1928, followed by 46, 49, 46, and 41 the next four years.

4. The 1930s, '40s, and '50s—An Historical Perspective

On October 29, 1929, a day that would go down in history as "Black Friday," the stock market crashed, wiping out the financial assets of millions of investors and starting a depression that would last for ten years. The 1920s had been a glorious decade for investors and speculators as the business economy boomed. Much of the prosperity, according to "News of the Nation," was built on credit. Stocks were bought with low down payments and with speculators borrowing to get on the bandwagon.

When the stock market lost 50 percent of its value from September 3 to late October, small investors lost their life savings, even their homes. The resulting depression continued through much of the 1930s. By 1933, 12 million people, or 25 percent of the workforce, were unemployed. The new president elect, Franklin Delano Roosevelt, promised to wage war on the depression by instituting government programs to get the people back to work. One such program, the WPA, employed thousands of men to build roads, bridges, and national parks.

Naturally, baseball attendance dropped precipitously during the depression, falling from 10.1 million fans in 1930 to a low of 6.1 million fans in 1933. The game survived, however, and got even stronger with the introduction of the All-Star Game in 1933 and with a bumper crop of bonafide new sluggers filling the rosters of the big league teams. When Babe Ruth retired in 1935, he left a legacy of awesome power unmatched in the annals of professional baseball. His long ball-hitting exploits have since been passed down from one generation to the next. Rawboned sluggers, arriving on the scene periodically, have taken dead aim on his slugging records. Some records have been broken over the years, but others will probably never be broken. The legend of Babe Ruth lives on.

Ruth's impact on major league baseball was not immediate. Many of his contemporaries, who had played major league baseball during the dead ball era, were too set in their ways to change. They continued to choke up on the bat and slap at the ball rather than taking a full cut. It was the mentality of the day when it was considered a disgrace to strike out. A few players like Rogers Hornsby, Tilly Walker, and Ken Williams changed their batting grips to go more for distance, and their home runs increased dramatically. But, for the most part, the change to a Babe Ruth–type long-distance mentality took a generation or more to complete.

One of the first major leaguers to emulate Ruth and go for the fences was a young Maryland farm boy. His name was James Emory Foxx. He was born in the tiny farming community of Sudlersville, on October 22, 1907. A life of hard physical labor on the farm gave young Foxx the rugged physique of a body builder, with bulging biceps and a powerful chest. He was discovered playing for a local team by former Philadelphia Athletics third baseman, Frank "Home Run" Baker, who quickly signed him to a professional baseball contract.

Sixteen-year-old Jimmie Foxx, who was influenced by the awesome slugging feats of Babe Ruth, began his career as a catcher for Easton, Maryland, in the Class D Eastern Shore League. He was already a formidable presence on the diamond, standing 6' tall, and weighing a brawny 195 pounds. Like Ruth, he held his bat at the end and swung from his heels. He punished opposing pitchers in his rookie season, driving out 31 extra base hits, including ten home runs, in just 260 at bats. Defensively, he led league catchers in assists with 73.

The following year, after playing 41 games for Providence in the International League, Foxx was called up to the A's. He appeared in ten games, and batted a sensational .667, with six hits in nine at bats. The 17-year-old strongman was a major leaguer.

The handsome, genial slugger impressed everyone who saw him. Bill Dickey, the great Yankee catcher, once said he could tell when Jimmie Foxx was at bat, even blindfolded. "He hit the ball harder than anyone else."

Old "Double X" was not just a power hitter. He could hit for average, had decent speed (125 lifetime triples and 87 stolen bases), and was a good fielding first baseman.

Foxx led the American League in home runs four times, in runs batted in three times, and in batting twice. He was voted the Most Valuable Player in the American League three times, tying the major league record.

He batted over .300 in 13 of his first 15 seasons in the majors, including four years over .350. In 1933 "The Beast" won the triple crown, batting .356 with 48 homers and 163 RBIs. The previous year, he just missed the triple crown. He led the league in homers with 58 (a major league record for right handed batters until McGwire and Sosa broke it in 1998), and in RBIs with 169. His .364 batting average was only three points below the league leader.

Foxx's 58 home runs in 1932 came within two of tying Babe Ruth. In fact, if Foxx had played under the same conditions that Ruth enjoyed in 1927, he might have hit as many as 66 home runs. "The Beast" hit five balls off the right field screen in St. Louis and three balls off the left field screen in Cleveland. Neither screen was in place when Babe hit his 60.

Another big right-handed slugger surfaced in the early 1930s. Hank Greenberg, a powerfully built 6'4", 215-pound first baseman from New York City, starred in the majors for 13 years. He missed an opportunity to go down as one of the greatest sluggers of all time when he missed one full season because of an injury and four other seasons in the U.S. Army during World War II. He returned from the war in 1946, played two more years, then retired at the relatively young age of 36.

"Hammerin' Hank" arrived in the American League as a fuzzy cheeked 22 year old in 1933. Two years later with the Detroit Tigers, he led the league in homers with 36, in runs batted in with 170, and batted a solid .328. In 1938, Greenberg came within a whisker of catching Babe Ruth in the home run race. He had 58 home runs with five games to go but went homerless the rest of the way. In two home games against the St. Louis Browns, Greenberg was held to one single in nine trips to the plate. Then, in three road games in Cleveland, the best he was able to do was hit a double off Bob Feller.

Hank Greenberg was a fearsome major league hitter for 13 seasons. In addition to home runs, he also hit more than his share of doubles and triples. He led the league in doubles with 63 in 1934 (fourth highest all time), and 50 doubles in 1940. His extra base hit percentage of .150 trails only Babe Ruth. Greenberg was one of the most efficient run producers ever to play the game. His 183 runs batted in, in 1937, is the third highest RBI total ever, trailing only Hack Wilson's major league record of 190 and Lou Gehrig's American League mark of 184. His career average of .915 RBIs per game (1,276 RBIs in 1,394 games) is #2 all time, just .005 points behind Lou Gehrig's .920.

While Greenberg was playing out his career with the Pittsburgh Pirates in 1947, he tutored a young slugger named Ralph Kiner. Kiner, who was born in Santa Rita, New Mexico, on October 27, 1922, was a

Jimmie Foxx slugged 534 home runs during a brilliant 20-year career. (Brace photo)

6'2", 195-pound right hander who had led the National League in home runs in his rookie season with a modest 23.

Pittsburgh management, in an attempt to increase Kiner's home run output, constructed a chicken wire fence from left field to left center field, reducing the home run distance in left from 365 feet to 335 feet and in left center from 406 feet to 355 feet. The 24-year-old slugger responded with 51 home runs in 1947. He went on to lead the National League in homers his first seven years in the league, including a 54 home run season in 1949. Kiner, like Greenberg, retired early, putting his spikes away

Hank Greenberg was the most prolific slugger in the major leagues during the late 1930s. (Courtesy Transcendental Graphics)

when he was just 32 years old. His average of 39 home runs for every 550 at bats is third all time, trailing only Babe Ruth's 50 and Mark McGwire's 52.

Ralph Kiner's career had a profound impact on future baseball players. His statement that "Home run hitters drive Cadillacs. Singles hitters drive Chevys," influenced a whole generation of hitters. Young boys who dreamed about playing major league baseball began gripping the bat down at the end and swinging for the fences.

During the 1920s, after the introduction of the lively ball, and while Babe Ruth was demonstrating his home run prowess to his contemporaries, the average number of home runs per team per season was 72.

During the 1930s, as more and more boys came into the major leagues with a Babe Ruth–type swing, the average number of home runs rose from 72 to 84. The 1940s were not representative of major league baseball because the able-bodied men were away fighting a war from 1941 through 1945, and the players who filled the major league rosters were not up to big-league standards. The average number of home runs per team per year plummeted to 62 during that time.

The decade of the 1950s was influenced by two factors. First, there was the "Kiner syndrome," which attracted hundreds of free swinging sluggers to professional baseball, players intent on "driving Cadillacs."

Second, integration had a major effect on the batting philosophy of professional baseball players. Integration was the single most significant social change in America in the twentieth century, and it began with major league baseball. Baseball Commissioner Happy Chandler, after seeing black soldiers fight and die side by side with white soldiers during World War II, believed they deserved the right to share equally in the American dream, which included playing organized baseball. When Brooklyn Dodger President, Branch Rickey, approached him in 1945 with his intention of signing a black player to a Brooklyn contract, Chandler gave Rickey his full support. Jackie Robinson subsequently broke the color barrier that had existed for more than 45 years, opening the door for other black players to walk through.

From 1947 until 1959, over 100 former Negro league players made the transition from the Negro leagues to the major leagues. Some of the greatest sluggers in baseball history made their major league debuts during this period, established Negro league sluggers like Roy Campanella, Luke Easter, Larry Doby, and Monte Irvin, as well as young budding Negro league superstars like Hank Aaron, Willie Mays and Ernie Banks.

The 1950s are often called the "Golden Age" of major league baseball, and that is probably true. Certainly, with integration the quality of play in the major leagues was far superior to the quality of play prior to integration. Negro league legends like Josh Gibson, a slugger of the ilk of Babe Ruth, Satchel Paige, one of the greatest baseball pitchers ever, pitchers "Smokey Joe" Williams, Martin Dihigo, and "Bullet Joe" Rogan, shortstops John Henry Lloyd and Willie Wells, third baseman Ray Dandridge, and outfielders "Cool Papa" Bell, Turkey Stearnes, and Oscar Charleston, were prevented from playing major league baseball during the 1920s, 30s, and 40s because of their color.

Over the last 40 years, the quality of major league baseball has once again deteriorated, probably due to several factors, such as the dilution of talent caused by athletes participating in other professional sports like basketball and football, major league expansion, and an improved economy which attracts more and more young men to a business career, rather than a career in professional sports.

The mentality of hitting has also undergone a drastic change from the hitting philosophy of the first half of the twentieth century. Until the

1950s, most hitters were taught to wait on a pitch until the last moment, then when they could identify what kind of pitch it was and where it would cross the plate, they would commit their swing. Beginning in the 1950s, batters began guess hitting—guessing what kind of a pitch would be thrown, and where it would be thrown—and they would start their swing as soon as the pitcher released the ball, hoping they had guessed correctly. Batters became guess hitters in the mistaken belief they would hit more home runs that way. Statistics show that guess hitting does not result in more home runs. It only increases strikeouts and lowers batting averages.

From 1950 to 1960, home runs increased by just 2 percent, while strikeouts shot up 34 percent. From 1950 to 1988, home runs actually decreased by 12 percent, while strikeouts were up 33 percent. Big swingers like Reggie Jackson (35 homers, 145 strikeouts, and a .262 batting average), Mike Schmidt (36 homers, 124 strikeouts, and a .267 batting average), and Dave Kingman (36 homers, 150 strikeouts, and a .236 batting average) glorified the new mentality.

The old-time sluggers, like Babe Ruth (50 homers, 87 strikeouts, and a .342 batting average) and Jimmie Foxx (36 homers, 89 strikeouts, and a .325 batting average), belie the modern hitting philosophy however. And Ted Williams, who wore out opposing pitchers from 1939 until 1960, remains the epitome of batting excellence. He combined a sharp batting eye with world class power. The "Splendid Splinter" averaged 37 homers a year during his career while batting a torrid .344, the sixth highest career batting average in baseball history. He accomplished these outstanding feats while striking out only 51 times a year, proving that truly great sluggers can hit for both average and distance without piling up a lot of embarrassing strikeouts.

Roger Maris, who arrived on the major league baseball scene in 1957, although not the possessor of a high batting average, showed the world it was possible to hit for distance without whiffing every third or fourth time at bat. Maris averaged 30 homers a year during his career while striking out only 79 times.

5. Roger Maris—
The Early Years

Babe Ruth's single season home run record of 60 home runs stood for 35 years. He was actually the single season home run champion for 43 years, going back to 1919 when his 29 home runs broke the all-time record set by Ned Williamson of the Chicago White Stockings in 1884. He subsequently broke his own record three times, with 54 homers in 1920, 59 homers in 1921, and 60 homers in 1927.

The man who would break the Bambino's record was born Roger Eugene Maras on September 10, 1934, in Hibbing, Minnesota, a town of about 15,000 people located in the northeastern part of the state, about 100 miles south of the Canadian border. The family name was subsequently changed to Maris when Roger was a teenager.

When Roger was ten years old, the Maris family moved to North Dakota, eventually settling in Fargo, on the Minnesota border. North Dakota is essentially a treeless, wind-swept plain, with an average temperature of 39 degrees. Summers (and baseball seasons) are short, and winters are long and bitter. Farming is the primary industry with over 85 percent of the land used for agriculture. Wheat, barley, and rye constitute the bulk of the farm production.

Rudy Maris, Roger's father, worked for the Great Northern Railroad, providing his sons with a good, middle-class work ethic. He also gave his sons a love of sports, having been a good athlete himself, in his younger days.

Roger Maris was an all-around athlete in high school, playing basketball and track, in addition to football. He also starred for the Fargo American Legion baseball team for three years, winning the Most Valuable Player award in 1950, and helping the team capture the American Legion state championship in 1951.

That summer after Roger graduated from high school, General Manager Hank Greenberg of the Cleveland Indians signed the young outfielder to a $5000 bonus contract to play professional baseball. He was assigned to play in his hometown, for Fargo-Moorehead of the Northern League. That same year, 1953, he married his high school sweetheart, Patricia Ann Carvel, beginning a 32 year married love affair that was blessed with six children.

The smooth-swinging, left-handed hitter thrived in the Class C Northern League, under the tutelage of manager Zeke Bonura, a former major leaguer with a career batting average of .307. Maris finished the year with a .325 batting average, nine home runs, and 80 RBIs in 114 games. He also proved to be an aggressive baserunner, and an outstanding defensive player. Fargo-Moorehead won the pennant by 13 games over Duluth, and went on to win the playoff as well. And 18-year-old Roger Maris was voted Rookie of the Year.

Maris moved up a notch in his second year in professional baseball, playing with Keokuk, Iowa, in the Class B III League. While there, he was taught to pull the ball by his manager Jo Jo White, a former major league outfielder. Maris learned his lessons well. He deposited 32 baseballs over the fence, on his way to a .315 season with 111 runs batted in.

In 1956, at the tender age of 21, Roger Maris fine tuned his talents at Indianapolis in the American Association, just one step away from the major leagues. He had an outstanding season, batting .293, with 17 homers and 75 RBIs. The Indianapolis Indians won the American Association pennant by five games over Denver, captured the league playoffs, and went on to win the Little World Series, beating the International League champion Rochester Red Wings in a four-game sweep.

The young slugger became a major leaguer in 1957, settling in right field for Cleveland. He got off to a fast start for the Indians, going three for five against the Chicago White Sox on opening day, April 16, then hitting a game-winning grand slam home run in the 11th inning the next day. Maris played in a total of 116 games for Cleveland, batting .235 in 358 at bats, with 14 home runs and 51 runs batted in.

The next year, he was traded to the Kansas City Athletics with two other players for Vic Power and Woodie Held, just before the June 15 trading deadline. His batting average for the season was still on the low side (.240), but he showed improved power with 28 homers and 80 RBIs. He came back to hit .273 in 1959, with 16 homers and 73 RBIs, in 150 fewer at bats than in '58. After the season ended, he was sent off to the New York Yankees in a seven-player swap, with Kansas City getting Don "No-Hit" Larsen and Hank Bauer as part of the deal.

Roger Maris was born to be a Yankee. As Robert Wuhl noted in *Cult Baseball Players*, "Roger Maris had THE perfect Yankee Stadium swing. Short. Quick. Powerful. Left handed." And he was the ultimate team player, ready to sacrifice himself, if necessary, for the good of the team. He was a long ball hitter, and a clutch hitter, but he also knew how to handle a bat. Unlike most sluggers, Maris could bunt or hit-and-run as the situation warranted. He was an outstanding baserunner and slider, and one of the best at breaking up a double play. Many baseball experts consider him the best defensive right fielder ever to play for the Yankees, and according to Mark Gallagher in *The Yankee Encyclopedia*, "He often dove into Yankee Stadium's right field seats to rob opponents of HRs."

Roger Maris played for Cleveland and Kansas City for three years before being traded to the New York Yankees in 1960. (Brace photo)

Usually batting just ahead of Mickey Mantle in the power-laden New York Yankee lineup, the kid from Fargo came into his own in the big city. As spring training wound down, Yankee fans wondered if their team could come back from the 1959 debacle. When they lost the final game of the spring, 2–0 to the Boston Red Sox, it left them in last place in the Grapefruit League standings, with a disheartening 11–21 record.

Al Lopez's Go-Go Chicago White Sox were favored to repeat in 1960. They had one of baseball's all-time great double play combinations in future Hall-of-Famers Nellie Fox at second and Luis Aparicio at short. They had explosive speed on the bases, led by Aparicio who topped the American League with 56 stolen bases, and Jim Landis who had 20. As a team, the Go-Go Sox led the American League in stolen bases with 113. They also had outstanding pitching led by Early Wynn (22–10 in 1959), Bob Shaw (18–6), Billy Pierce (14–15), Gerry Staley (14 saves), and Turk Lown (15 saves).

The Cleveland Indians, with Rocky Colavito (42 homers, 111 RBIs), Minnie Minoso (.302, 21, 92), Billy Martin, and pitchers Cal McLish (19–8), Gary Bell (16–11), and Mudcat Grant (10–7), were also expected to be in the hunt.

The season opener, in Yankee Stadium, on a seasonably warm 62-degree day, was a success all around. The Bronx Bombers pounded Boston Red Sox pitching for 17 hits, en route to an 8–4 thumping of manager Billy Jurges' troops. Roger Maris, batting in the leadoff position, led the New York attack with a single, a double, and two home runs into the right field bleachers.

Big 6'4" right hander Jim Coates, on his way to a fine 13–3 season, was the recipient of the early season barrage. The Yankees raked Boston starter, Tom Brewer for six runs in 4⅓ innings, before 35,162 enthusiastic fans. Ted Williams provided the only excitement for the Boston contingent when he blasted his 494th career homer into the right field seats.

Two weeks later, Coates upped his record to 3–0, in Baltimore, as Casey Stengel's boys bombed the Orioles 16–0, scoring five runs in the first and never looking back. Maris cracked two doubles and a home run (his third), driving in four runs. His cohort, Mickey Mantle just missed a home run by a couple of feet, his long drive off the wall going for a triple. The win snapped a three-game New York losing streak, and sent 33,000 Baltimoreans home sad. As the month ended, the Yanks' 8–4 record gave them a 1½ game lead over the Chicago White Sox and Detroit Tigers, with Baltimore another ½ game behind.

The Yankees treaded water most of May, struggling to an 11–13 record for the month. Maris was one of the bright spots, batting .322 and leading the league in both home runs (11) and runs batted it (30). Big Jim Lemon of Washington was second in home runs with ten, while shortstop Ron Hansen of Baltimore had 29 RBIs. Jim Coates was still cruising along with a spotless 5–0 record, but Mickey Mantle was mired in a horrible slump, hitting only .244.

As the weather warmed up in June, so did the Yanks. The M & M boys, Maris and Mantle both went on a tear, and the Bronx Bombers won 20 of their last 25 games, giving them a 21–10 record for the month, and a 1½ game lead over the O's. The pennant race, which was a five-team affair for two months, was now a four-team race as the Detroit Tigers fell by the wayside.

On a hot 87-degree New York day, the Yankees completed a sweep of the Kansas City Athletics, for their 21st victory of the month. Only 8513 fans witnessed the 10–3 victory, or saw the five New York home runs leave the Stadium. First baseman Bill Skowron banged two homers, his ninth and tenth of the year, while Tony Kubek, Roger Maris, and Mickey Mantle hit one apiece. For Maris, the long drive into the upper deck in right field was his league-leading 25th of the season, and 14th for the month of June. Mantle's round tripper gave him 12 for the month and 18 for the year.

July 4 is the generally accepted halfway point of the season, and the league leaders at that point are considered to be the favorites to win the pennant. In 1960, the New York Yankees held a 3½ game lead over their nearest American League rival, Joe Gordon's Cleveland Indians, while the Pittsburgh Pirates held a similar lead over the Milwaukee Braves in the Senior Circuit. Maris was the home run leader with 25. He trailed Babe Ruth by one.

The Washington Senators ruined New York's holiday by knocking them off, 9–8. Roger Maris was nursing a cold and did not play. Mantle hit a three-run shot in the first, giving Jim Coates (9–0) a quick lead, but Coates couldn't hold it. He was still leading 8–6 when he left the game, after giving up six runs and ten hits in less than six innings, but three New York relievers blew the game. The last Yankee pitcher, Ryne Duren, walked in the winning run with two out in the bottom of the ninth, before 16,913 happy home fans.

Cleveland swept a doubleheader from the Chicago White Sox, by scores of 4–0 and 7–4, reducing the Yankee lead to a mere 1½ games. But that turned out to be the high point of the season for the Indians. They immediately self destructed, losing 18 of their next 25 games and dropping out of the race. Jimmy Dykes was brought in as manager in August, but he couldn't right the ship, winning 26 games against 32 losses the rest of the way.

The pennant race was reduced to three teams with the demise of Cleveland. New York, Chicago, and Baltimore were left to battle it out. The Yankees went into another slump in July, leaving the door open for Al Lopez's White Sox. And the White Sox capitalized on it, winning 20 of 29 games, to move into the top spot, by 1½ games over Stengel's boys, who could manage only 13 wins in 27 games. Baltimore was even worse, going 12–15 for the month.

As July wound down, the Yankees were in Kansas City for a doubleheader with the A's, while Chicago played two with Washington. The White Sox swept the Senators by scores of 5–2 and 9–5, while New York and K.C. split a pair. New York scratched and clawed for single runs in both eighth and nineth to tie game one, but two wild throws by third baseman Hector Lopez gave the A's three runs and the victory. Maris drew the collar in five trips to the plate, while Mantle hit #27. Johnny Kucks pitched a strong eight innings, yielding only two runs.

In game two, the Bronx Bombers righted themselves, winning 9–0 behind Art Ditmar's seven-hit shutout. Mantle (1–3) and Maris (1–4) were not factors in the game.

Roger Maris held on to his top spot in both the home run race and the RBI race. The Yankee right fielder had six homers and 17 runs batted in, in 27 games, while Mantle hit nine homers for the month, giving him 27 for the year, four behind Maris. Bill "Moose" Skowron, with 71 RBIs, trailed Maris by ten.

On August 5, in Kansas City, Art Ditmar edged the A's 4–3, to the disappointment of 28,111 loyal A's fans. Maris hit a two-run homer off Johnny Kucks in the third, giving New York a lead it never relinquished. It was Roger's 33rd of the season, putting him six homers ahead of Mantle.

The next day, the Stengel men routed K.C. 16–4 under stifling 97-degree skies. The 24,039 sun worshippers in the stands saw Roger Maris crack his 34th and 35th round trippers of the year, putting him seven games ahead of the mighty Bambino.

On Friday the 12th, the Bronx Bombers returned home to do battle with the Washington Senators. They should have stayed in Chicago. The game was an embarrassment. New York pitchers issued 11 free passes, and the defense played like high schoolers. Washington won easily, 12–7. Roger Maris was one of the few bright spots in the Yankee lineup. He went 2–4 at the plate, with two RBIs and, in the field, he went over the right field fence into the bullpen in a futile attempt to catch Harmon Killebrew's 18th home run. Berra and Skowron homered for the Yankees.

Whitey Ford got the Yanks back on track the next day, tossing a three-hit 1–0 shutout at Cookie Lavagetto's club. The only run of the game came in the seventh inning, when Maris laced a triple to right center field, and Mantle brought him in with a sacrifice fly to deep right.

The joy was only temporary however, because the Stengelmen took multiple big hits on the 14th. Not only did they drop a doubleheader to the Senators, but they lost their star right fielder for 18 games, in the process. In game one, Maris and Mantle were held to a combined 2–9 (one single each), as Washington routed Bullet Bob Turley with a big five spot in the fifth, to win 5–4. Winning pitcher Camilo "Hot Potato" Pascual took Turley down town with the bases loaded, sparking the big rally.

Washington completed the sweep with a 6–3, 15-inning win in game two. Ralph Terry, who entered the game in the 15th, was touched up for three runs, dropping his record to 5–7. A bigger loss occurred in the sixth inning. With Roger Maris on first base, Mantle hit an infield grounder. Maris slid hard into Billy Gardner at second base in an attempt to break up the double play. He took Gardner's knee to the ribs in the process, sending him to the Lenox Hill Hospital for observation. Fortunately nothing was broken, but his badly bruised ribs would keep him out of the lineup for almost three weeks. Mickey Mantle's failure to run out the double play ball brought Stengel's wrath down upon him. He was immediately yanked from the game and given an early shower.

New York held a slim one-game lead over the Baltimore Orioles on the morning of September 1. They compiled a record of 22–11 during August, compared to Baltimore's 22–14 mark. The White Sox were four behind while the Indians slipped out of the race, 12 games behind.

It was a bad month for Roger Maris. The Yankees' hard nosed outfielder, knocked out of action on the 14th of the month, missed 18 games. He still held his lead in homers (35 compared to Mantle's 31) and RBIs (96), but when he returned to the lineup, he couldn't swing with his old aggressiveness, and his home run total suffered as a result.

In the National League, Danny Murtaugh's Pittsburgh Pirates had opened up a 6½ game lead over the Milwaukee Braves, with the St. Louis Cardinals another ½ game behind.

Casey Stengel's Bronx Bombers turned on the afterburners down the stretch, after a slow start. Through the first two weeks of September, the New Yorkers, the Orioles, and the White Sox, continued to jockey for position. New York, coming off a double loss to the last-place A's, that left them at 7–7 for the month, hosted Baltimore for a critical four-game series. The Yanks and the Orioles were tied for first, with Chicago lurking only two games behind, ready to take advantage of the New York-Baltimore skirmishes. Prior to game one, Casey Stengel was quoted in the *New York Times* as saying, "The main trouble is that our guys aren't mad at anyone. They like everyone, don't argue with anyone…. We've got to play the best, the hardest baseball we know how, and we've got to do it right now…. I'll wrap it up for you. My ballclub is too erratic."

The Yanks got hot just in time. In game one, with 49,217 screaming Yankee fans trying to jump-start their boys, Whitey Ford, "The Chairman of the Board," pumped up by the crowd, threw nothing but zeroes at the O's for eight innings, while New York ran up a 4–0 lead. When Paul Richard's team loaded the bases against the Yankee southpaw with two gone in the ninth, Stengel brought in Bobby Schantz to quell the rally. The Yankee closer was touched up for a two-run single, but settled down to fan Marv Breeding for the last out, with the tying runs on base. The New York crew had scored a single run in the fourth, two in the fifth, and another singleton in the sixth, off Baltimore's 21-year-old rookie, Steve Barber. New York's first run was a wind-blown, opposite field home run by Hector Lopez. The ball actually hit the pocket of right fielder Jackie Brandt's glove, before bouncing into the stands. Roger Maris deposited #39 deep into the right field seats in the fifth, with Bobby Richardson on base after a single. It would be Maris' last home run of the season. He would not homer over the last 14 games. The homer itself was a surprise, since Maris was hitting only .180 against southpaws.

On Saturday the 17th, a Ladies Day crowd of 49,055 whooped it up all afternoon. The Yanks jumped out in front 2–0 in the first, thanks to a two-run homer into the top deck in right field by Mickey Mantle, following a Lopez single. Baltimore pushed across one run in the fifth, then tied the game in the sixth, on Gus Triandos' long home run into the left field seats. Berra immediately untied it in the bottom of the same inning with a homer. Gene Woodling tried to give Baltimore another tie in the seventh, but Maris robbed him of a homer with a great running catch in front of the New York bullpen in deep right center field. Unfortunately Jim Gentile followed with a titanic shot that Maris couldn't catch. It landed in the upper deck in right field to knot the game once again, at 3–3. In the bottom of the eighth, Yogi Berra reached on a bad bounce single. After Skowron was intentionally walked, Blanchard drew an unintentional walk to load the bases. Bobby Richardson then lined a two-run single back through the middle, and New York was home free, 5–3.

The series closed out the next day with a doubleheader. Stengel got outstanding pitching in both games as New York swept the O's, by scores of 7–3 and 2–0. In game one, the Yanks pummeled 21-year-old Jack Fisher for four runs in the third, on a Kubek homer to right field, singles by Lopez and Maris, a walk to Mantle, and a two-run double by Yogi Berra off reliever Hoyt Wilhelm. Art Ditmar won his 15th game against nine losses. In game two, Bill Terry (9–8) outpitched another of the Baltimore baby brigade, 21-year-old Milt Pappas (13–11).

From there to the end of the season, the Yankees just kept winning. On September 28, Mickey Mantle hit his 40th home run, to take a one-homer lead over Roger Maris, who was still bothered by bruised ribs.

The final standings showed New York with a substantial eight-game lead over Baltimore, and a ten-game bulge over Chicago. Mickey Mantle captured the home run crown with 40, and led the league in runs scored with 119, and total bases with 294. His sidekick Roger Maris won the RBI title with 112, and led the league in slugging percentage with .581. First baseman Moose Skowron hit .309 with 26 homers and 91 RBIs. The pitching staff was led by Art Ditmar (15–9), Jim Coates (13–3), Whitey

Ford (12–9), and Ralph Terry (10–8). Little Bobby Schantz saved 11 games to lead the bullpen corps. As a team, New York led the league in runs scored with 746, slugging average (.426), shutouts (16), saves (42), and earned run average (3.52).

New York's opponents in the World Series were the Pittsburgh Pirates, whose 95–59 record gave them a seven-game bulge over the Milwaukee Braves. Pittsburgh, like New York, was a high-scoring team whose 734 runs scored led the league. They also led in doubles (236), batting average (.276), and double plays (163). Their 3.49 ERA was comparable to New York's.

The two teams were rated even coming into the fall classic. Danny Murtaugh's club was led by the immortal Roberto Clemente, a true superstar, Bill Mazeroski, one of the greatest fielding second basemen in history, and all-star shortstop Dick Groat, who could beat you with either his glove or his bat. The outstanding pitching staff included Vernon Law (20–9), Bob Friend (18–12), "Vinegar Bend" Mizell (13–5), and Elroy Face (10–8 with 24 saves).

The 1960 World Series turned out to be one of the strangest World Series ever played. The Yankees set new Series records for runs scored (55), RBIs (54), total bases (142), base hits (91), extra base hits (27), and team batting average (.318). They routed the Pirates in three games by scores of 16–3, 10–0, and 12–0. They outscored Pittsburgh by more than a 2–1 ratio in the Series, 55 runs to 24.

New York was awesome. But Pittsburgh won the Series.

The World Series opened in Pittsburgh on October 5, with Art Ditmar facing 20-game winner, Vernon Law. The Yankees got on the scoreboard first when Roger Maris put a Law pitch into the upper deck in right field. But the Pirates bounced back to rout Ditmar in the bottom of the inning, scoring three runs on a double, two singles, a walk, and an error by Kubek.

Vernon Law was in control throughout the game. He left after seven innings with a comfortable 6–2 lead. Elston Howard's pinch hit two-run homer in the ninth made it close, but Pittsburgh prevailed, 6–4. Roger Maris and Tony Kubek, with three hits each, led the Yankee attack, but three Pirate double plays did them in.

The Bronx Bombers erupted in games two and three, outscoring their opponents by a combined score of 26–3. In game two, "Bullet Bob" Turley and Schantz were the recipients of a 19-hit Yankee attack, with Turley being credited with the 16–3 win. Kubek and Richardson had three hits each, while McDougald, Mantle, Howard, and Skowron chipped in with two apiece. Mantle's two hits were both homers, the last one being a tremendous 475-foot drive over the center field wall.

The next day, in Yankee Stadium, Whitey Ford handcuffed the Pirates 10–0, with a four-hitter. Mickey Mantle once again led the attack, ripping four hits, including a double and a long home run into the left field bullpen. Bobby Richardson's grand slam homer into the left field stands in the bottom of the first, capped a six-run outburst against Pittsburgh starter "Vinegar Bend" Mizell, and Ford coasted from there.

Most other baseball teams would pack it in after being routed by such lopsided scores, but Danny Murtaugh's boys were made of sterner stuff. Game four belonged to Vernon Law again, as he won for the second time. A Moose Skowron home run in the fourth went by the boards in the fifth, when the Buccaneers put a big three-spot on the board. Law was in the middle of the rally, doubling in one run and scoring another. Pittsburgh won 3–2 to even the Series.

Another excellent pitching performance the next day by Harvey Haddix with relief help from Elroy Face brought Pittsburgh home a winner again, 4–2, putting them in the driver's seat, up three games to two, with the final two games to be played in Pittsburgh. Maris thrilled the New York crowd when he hit a towering home run into the third deck of the right field stands in the third inning, but it was not enough.

The vaunted Yankee bats came alive again in game six. Seventeen base hits, including four doubles and three triples, rattled around Forbes Field, much to the chagrin of the 38,580 Pittsburgh fans who came to see their beloved Pirates wrap up the title. Maris, Berra, and Blanchard pounded out three hits apiece, and Skowron and Richardson each had two, as Whitey Ford tossed his second straight shutout, this time a 12–0 laugher.

Game seven turned out to be one of the most exciting and dramatic World Series games ever played. Bob Turley started against Vernon Law. Pittsburgh KO'd Turley early, scoring two runs in the bottom of the first, on a Rocky Nelson homer, and two more in the second on three singles. New York got one back in the fifth on a Skowron homer, then drove Law to cover in the next inning when they pushed across four more runs. A three-run homer by Yogi Berra was the telling blow.

The Stengelmen upped their margin to 7–4 with another deuce in the eighth, but Pittsburgh roared back again. In the bottom of the inning, they put up a five-spot on four singles and a three-run home run over the left field wall by catcher Hal Smith.

Pirate ace Bob Friend came on in the ninth to close it out, but he couldn't get it done. After yielding consecutive singles to Richardson and Long, he was replaced by 35-year-old Harvey Haddix. "The Kitten," as he was called, finally retired the side, but not before New York scored two runs to tie the game.

In the bottom of the ninth, with Ralph Terry pitching, defensive genius Bill Mazeroski hit the second pitch over the left field wall to win the game and the Series. It remains the most dramatic home run ever hit in World Series history.

November 10 was a big day in the life of Roger Maris. He was voted the Most Valuable Player in the American League for 1960, edging out his teammate Mickey Mantle by three votes, 225–222. Roger Maris deserved the award. He batted a consistent .283, with 39 homers and a league-leading 119 runs batted in. In addition to his slugging, he was a dangerous baserunner, and a brilliant right fielder with a shotgun for an arm. He was also the ultimate team player, one time, in the middle of the home run chase, squeezing in the winning run, much to the surprise of his teammates.

Roger Maris also captured a Gold Glove for his work in the outfield. Teammate John Blanchard was quoted in *Season of Glory*, as saying "Roger Maris in 1960 was the greatest baseball player I've ever seen,"

6. Roger Maris— Home Run Champion

After the 1960 season ended, many players hit the banquet circuit, to earn a little more money, and to bask in the adulation of the fans around the country. Roger Maris, on the other hand, went home to Raytown, Missouri, where he and Pat were raising their family. Pat was pregnant with their third child, and the little ranch house was bursting at the seams. Over the winter, Roger rolled up his sleeves and went to work remodeling the house. He added another bedroom, and built a laundry room and a play room.

The winter sojourn also included contract negotiations with the Yankee brass. Mickey Mantle had signed for 1961, for $75,000, making him the highest paid player in the major leagues. Whitey Ford came in at $35,000, and Yogi Berra got $52,000. Maris, who was paid $20,000 for his MVP year wanted a raise to $40,000. After some haggling back and forth, he settled for $38,000, a veritable bargain for GM Roy Hamey.

When spring training began in St. Petersburg, Florida, a serious problem that had been festering for years, finally surfaced. Florida was still a segregated state, with segregated schools, housing and restaurants, as well as separate public drinking fountains and rest rooms, for blacks and whites. Black players were not permitted to stay in the same hotel as the white players. Elston Howard, who joined the Yankees in 1955 as their first black player, had always stayed in a private home during spring training. Now New York had three black players, Howard, Hector Lopez, and Al Downing, and it was difficult to find decent accommodations for them.

Yankee management tried to make arrangements with the Soreno Hotel to allow the black players to stay there with the rest of the team, but the Soreno wouldn't allow it. Accommodations for the black players were finally located in private homes. The next year, the Yankees moved to Ft. Lauderdale, and the entire team was housed at the Yankee Clipper.

Another interesting topic of conversation during the spring was whether or not someone would break Babe Ruth's home run record. It was the beginning of a new era in major league baseball—the expansion era—and baseball experts feared that the expected dilution of talent would cause many of the cherished baseball records to tumble. The expansion era actually began back in 1953 when the Braves pulled up their teepees in Boston and set them down in Milwaukee, the first team to relocate in 50 years. They were quickly followed by the St. Louis Browns who moved to Baltimore in 1954, and were renamed the Orioles, and the A's who moved from Philadelphia to Kansas City in 1955 (and later to Oakland). The game finally became a truly national sport in 1958, when the Brooklyn Dodgers moved to Los Angeles and the New York Giants moved to San Francisco.

The next step in the evolution of baseball was increasing the two major leagues from eight teams each to ten teams. The American League expanded first, adding the Los Angeles Angels and the Washington Senators in 1961. The new Washington team replaced the old Washington Senator team that moved to Minnesota that year and became the Twins. The National League followed suit the next year by adding the New York Mets and the Houston Colt .45s.

With two new teams in place in the American League, baseball experts began discussing the possibility that someone would break Ruth's record. After all, ten times since Ruth set the record of 60 home runs in 1927, players had hit more than 50 home runs in a season, with Jimmie Foxx and Hank Greenberg topping out at 58. The addition of two teams meant that 20 percent of the pitchers in the American League in 1961 would have been minor league pitchers if expansion hadn't taken place.

The two most likely candidates to break the record were Harmon Killebrew of the Minnesota Twins and Mickey Mantle of the Yankees. The 24-year-old Killebrew was just coming into his own as a big league slugger. He had hit 42 homers in 1959, and followed that up with 31 more in 1960. He was a big, powerful right-handed batter who was capable of hitting tremendous home runs in bunches. Mickey Mantle, the 29-year-old New York slugger, already had a 52 home run season under his belt, and was the favorite to surpass the Babe. Mantle's teammate Roger Maris, who had 39 homers in 1960, was considered a longshot since he had never hit more than 28 home runs in any year prior to '60. Another longshot was Rocky Colavito of the Detroit Tigers, a 27-year-old bomber who had two 40+ home run seasons with the Cleveland Indians in '58 and '59.

New York Yankee manager Ralph Houk had other things on his mind than home run records, however. His team got off to a rocky start in the early exhibition games. As the losses mounted, New York reporters pressed Houk for reasons. The hassled manager, as reported in *Season of Glory*, spouted the typical excuses. "There are things you've got to find out about your players, and spring training is the time to find them out." Houk didn't believe his own explanation—he was as puzzled by the team's poor showing as everyone else—but he couldn't put his finger on the problem. He just hoped it would work itself out by the time the season opened.

Spring training did shake out some of the question marks for Ralph Houk. He decided that Elston Howard would be the catcher, with Johnny Blanchard as his backup. Yogi Berra would be the left fielder. Clete Boyer beat out Deron Johnson at third. And Luis Arroyo, Bill Stafford, and rookie Rollie Sheldon won spots on the pitching staff, Stafford and Sheldon as starters, and Arroyo as the closer.

The Grapefruit League season came to a merciful end in St. Louis, where the Bronx Bombers dropped two games to the Cardinals by scores of 7–6 and 16–12. New York finished the spring with an embarrassing 9–19 record.

Two days later, on Tuesday April 11, a windy and cold day in Yankee Stadium, only 14,607 fans braved the elements to root for their heroes. Pre-game ceremonies included the raising of the 1960 American League pennant, and the presentation of the Most Valuable Player plaque to Roger Maris. The game, unfortunately, followed the same script that was used during spring training. The Minnesota Twins, behind the three-hit pitching of 25-year-old Pedro Ramos, blanked Houk's boys, 6–0. The New York offense consisted of singles by Berra and Skowron, and an infield hit by Whitey Ford. Ford, the Yankee starter, stayed with Ramos for six innings, but couldn't make it through the seventh. With the game still scoreless in the top of the seventh, Bob Allison hoisted a home run into the lower left field grandstand. After Earl Battey doubled down the left field line, Rene Bertoia walked, and Billy Gardner sacrificed both runners along. Ramos then helped his own cause by slashing a single over third for two runs. Bertoia added a two-run homer to left in the eighth.

Six days later, before a chilled group of 1947 Yankee Stadium fans, the Oklahoma Comet unloaded a two-run homer in the first inning, as Whitey Ford pitched a 3–0 complete game. The weather during the month of April was horrible; cold and damp. At one point New York played only three games in nine days.

On the 20th, another chilly day, but at least without rain, New York swept a doubleheader from the Los Angeles Angels. Mantle homered twice in game one, a first-inning shot that landed about ten rows up in the right field grandstand, and a fifth-inning dinger, his second and third homers of the year. Mantle hit another one the next day in Baltimore, giving him four homers in four games. The newspaper reporters were all around him after the game, asking him how it felt to be eight games ahead of Babe Ruth's record pace. It should be noted that, over the years, literally dozens of players have been ahead of Ruth's pace during the season, primarily because Ruth hit only 43 home runs through the month of August. He finished up the year with a flurry, banging out 17 homers in September.

On April 26, a frigid day in Detroit, Roger Maris finally hit his first home run of the year. It came in the Yankees' 11th game, against right hander Paul Foytack. Whitey Ford was staked to a 6–0 lead in the game, but couldn't hold it, being raked for ten runs and 11 hits in 6⅓ innings. He was still clinging to an 8–6 lead in the seventh, when Bob Scheffing's club exploded for five runs. Mickey Mantle hit his sixth home run of the year off Jim Donohue, with a man on, in the eighth inning to tie the game at 11–11, then crushed his seventh homer off Hank Aguirre, into the upper left field deck, with Hector Lopez on base, in the tenth, to win it. The loss ended an eight game Detroit winning streak and increased New York's record to 6–5. It was the eighth time in Mantle's career that he homered from both sides of the plate in the same game. Little Luis Arroyo, the pride of Puerto Rico, hurled two scoreless innings for the victory.

Mickey Mantle was off to a sizzling start, batting well over .300, with seven home runs in 11 games. He was determined to have a big year for his new manager, Ralph Houk, whose strategy was to praise the Yankee star at every turn. It was a different approach than was used by Stengel, who looked upon Mantle as a son, and who constantly nagged the youngster to mature and become a team leader. But growing up in the big city was difficult for the kid from Commerce, Oklahoma. As a member of the unholy triumvirate, along with Whitey Ford and Billy Martin, he saw the inside of every nightspot from Kansas City to Manhattan. Now, at the age of 29, having sown his wild oats for a decade, he was beginning to settle down and become the leader Stengel had hoped for. Unfortunately, from a career standpoint, it was too little, too late. His years of living in the fast lane, and his serious leg problems, sapped his tremendous skills, cutting short a potentially legendary career. The powerful switch hitter had more home runs by the age of 30 (404) than any player in baseball history. Hank Aaron had 366 homers, while Willie Mays had 319, and Babe Ruth just 309. After 1961, Mantle would add just 162 home runs to his total of 374, with just two more years of 30 or more homers.

New York had a 9–5 record in April, leaving them one game behind Detroit. Mickey Mantle, hammered seven homers, drove in 17 runs, and batted .327 for the month. He was three home runs ahead of Babe Ruth, and was already being cornered by the reporters asking him if he thought he could break the record. Mantle, who was now a seasoned veteran, fielded all the queries gracefully and politely, giving thoughtful answers, and always smiling.

Roger Maris, on the other hand, was suffering through a deep slump, with one home run and a .204 batting average. Yankee management called him in at one point and asked him if he was having eye problems. They also inquired as to whether he was having personal problems, to which Maris replied, "That's none of your business."

On May 3, in Metropolitan Stadium, Minnesota, Maris hit #2, but Mantle whacked #9, a 405-foot blast to center field, in the top of the tenth inning, to break a two all tie. The Mick was now 11 games ahead of Ruth, who had six in the same number of games.

Roger Maris hit #3 off Eli Grba in Los Angeles on May 6, then went another ten days before hitting #4. Beginning on May 17, he picked up the pace and got in the race. He cracked nine home runs over the last 14 days of May, bringing his total up to 12. On the last day of the month, the Yankees piled up 11 hits against Boston Red Sox pitching, quieting Fenway's 17,318 paying customers, and edging their beloved BoSox 7–6. Rookie Rollie Sheldon won his first major league game, with 6⅔ innings of four-run ball. Reliever Luis Arroyo was ineffective, but Danny McDevitt came in to shut down the Sox in the bottom of the ninth. After New York tallied one run in the first, Maris hit his 12th homer of the season in the third inning, a thunderous 425-foot blast into the right field bleachers. Four more New York runs crossed the plate in the fifth, on two singles, an error by Don "Bootsie" Buddin, and a 400-foot homer into the right field bullpen by Mantle.

New York's 19–12 record was an improvement over April, but left them in third place, 3½ games behind the red hot Detroit Tigers, who had a 29–16 record. Cleveland was in second place with 26 wins against 17 losses. Mickey Mantle was hitting .318, and leading the league in home runs with 14. Mick's sidekick, Roger Maris, had his average up to .245, and his home run total up to 12.

New York began June by winning 15 out of 19 games, but Detroit kept pace, sparked by first baseman Norm Cash, who was having a career season. Cash, a lifetime .271 hitter, was on to his way to winning the batting championship (.361), with 41 homers and 132 RBIs. Whitey Ford paced Ralph Houk's Bombers in June, racking up a perfect 8–0 mark, a new American League record. It matched the National League record of Rube Marquard, who compiled an 8–0 record in June 1912, on his way to a major league mark of 19 consecutive victories. Closing out the month, "The Chairman of the Board" whipped the Washington Senators, in D.C., by a score of 5–1, with a complete game five-hitter. Maris and Mantle did most of the damage. Dick Donovan (3–8) was up 1–0 after five innings, but the roof caved in on him in the sixth. Richardson singled through the middle to lead things off. He stole second and went to third on a fly ball to right by Tony Kubek. Maris then smashed a ground rule double into the right field seats, to score Richardson. Mantle followed with a tremendous drive to dead center field. The ball struck the wall just to the right of the 461-foot sign. When it bounced back over center fielder Willie Tasby's head, Mantle turned it up a notch, and circled the bases in record time, for an inside-the-park homer. It was Mantle's 25th of the season, leaving him two behind his teammate, Roger Maris, who had a big month, with 15 homers. New York closed out their scoring in the eighth. Richardson singled and Kubek doubled. Then with the infield drawn in, Maris ripped a ball through the right side for two runs.

As June ended, Roger Maris had his batting average up to .260, was leading the league in home runs with 27, and was third in RBIs with 62. Mantle was hitting .312, and was second in homers.

During June, Maris completed the most extraordinary home run hitting feat in the annals of baseball. Beginning on May 17, when Roger hit his fourth home run of the season, and continuing through June 22, the sweet-swinging lefty pounded out 24 homers in 38 games, an achievement unmatched by any baseball player who ever lived. Babe finished his record season in 1927 with a similar run, hitting 24 homers in his last 41 games.

When the sun came up on July 4th, the standings were:

Detroit 49–27
New York 47–27—1
Cleveland 45–34—5½
Baltimore 42–36—8

Roger Maris was at 30 home runs, putting him eight games ahead of Babe Ruth, while Mickey Mantle was four games ahead of the mighty Bambino. The press was beginning to pay more attention to the home run chase now, referring to the two Yankee sluggers as the M& M boys, but most of the coverage was still on Mantle. He was the favorite of the press, the fans, and even some of the Yankee players and Yankee brass. After all, Babe Ruth had been a Yankee and Mickey Mantle was a Yankee.

Roger Maris, on the other hand, was an interloper, a late arrival, and not a real Yankee. From this point until the end of the season, the intense media pressure continued to mount. It was on Mantle initially, but would swing over to Maris in a big way in late August, after he became the first player in history to hit 50 home runs before September 1st.

Roger Maris, after reaching 27 home runs by the end of June, kept up his pyrotechnics through July. He hit #35 on the 15th, putting him a full 20 games ahead of Ruth. Mantle was nine games ahead. Four days later, both sluggers hit home runs in the second game of a doubleheader against the Baltimore Orioles, but the homers were lost when rain washed out the game before the required 5½ innings were played. That same day, baseball Commissioner Ford Frick announced that, in order to break Babe Ruth's record, a batter would have to do it in the same number of games Ruth played, 154. If the record was broken after the 154th game, it would have a "distinguishing mark" after it, to differentiate it from Ruth's record. Poor Frick. He never lived down that ruling. He was known as Mr. Asterisk until the day he died.

The Yankees took over the top spot in the pennant race, as the dog days of summer wound down. Their 67–36 record on July 31, gave them a 2½ game bulge over the Detroit Tigers and a 9½ game bulge over the Baltimore Orioles. Cleveland self destructed during the month, losing 16 of 27 games after July 3, to fall out of the race. Twenty-six-year-old Norm Cash, in his first full year as a Detroit regular, was belting the ball at a torrid .365 pace, 14 points higher than Yankee catcher Elston Howard. Roger Maris led the home run race with 40 dingers, and the RBI race with 98 RBIs. Mickey Mantle had 39 homers and 95 RBIs.

Frank Crosetti was acting manager as the Bronx Bombers hosted the Kansas City A's in a twin bill on August 2. In the opener, Whitey Ford, looking for his thirteenth consecutive win, brought a dazzling 19–2 record into the game, but he didn't have his usual stuff on this day. It was not an artistic outing for the stylish lefty, and he left after eight innings, with the score tied at 5–5. He almost pulled off his twentieth win, but it wasn't to be. In the bottom of the eighth, with the bases loaded, Ford punched a single over third for two runs, giving himself a 5–3 lead. But in the top of the ninth, he threw a home run ball to Haywood Sullivan with a man on, to tie the score. After the next batter singled, Luis Arroyo relieved him and retired the side. In the bottom of the ninth, the Yanks loaded the bases with none out, on a single by Maris, a double by Mantle, and a walk to Howard. After Berra popped up for the first out, Cerv hit a bouncer to third, as Maris raced for the plate. Third baseman Wayne Causey pounced on the ball and gunned it home, but Maris, being an old line backer himself, plowed into catcher Joe Pignatano, causing him to drop the ball, and ending the game. The home plate collision was a typical Maris maneuver. He was a hard-nosed player, who put his body on the line on every play. He did whatever it took to win.

The second game was a laugher. Ralph Terry (7–1) saw his team go up 12–0 after five, and they hung on to win, 12–5. New York scored three in the first, two in the third, and seven in the fifth. Mickey Mantle clubbed his 40th home run of the year, and 360th of his career, in the first, a two-run shot into the third deck in right field. His outfield partner, Roger Maris, got hit by a pitch in the third, bruising his leg. He left the game to put ice packs on it, but was back in action the next day.

During August, the home run race heated up as both Maris and Mantle kept the pressure on. Maris had a dry spell after July 25, hitting only one homer over the next 17 games. Then, on August 11 he found his stroke again. He banged out his 42nd home run, and went on to hit ten homers in the next 16 games. Mickey Mantle, who took the lead away from Maris when he hit numbers 41 and 42 on August 5, went into a slump of his own, hitting only one homer between August 13 and August 29.

On the twentieth day of the month, the Yanks swept a twin bill from the struggling Cleveland Indians in Cleveland Stadium, before 56,307 hopeful fans. Ralph Terry won his tenth game against a single loss, throwing a complete game, four-hit shutout, winning 6–0. Mickey Mantle hit his first home run in a week, a three-run shot in the first to give the New York contingent a jump start. Mick also chipped in with two singles and a base on balls. Roger Maris broke out of an 0–13 slump with his first homer in four days, a singleton in the third. It was his 49th of the season, putting him 11 games ahead of Ruth.

In game two, Mantle went 1–2 with two walks, and Maris took the collar in two trips. Rollie Sheldon (9–3) went the distance with an eight-hitter, and the Yanks won 5–2, taking three out of four in the series, and moving on to Los Angeles.

Baseball fans around the country were anticipating Maris' 50th home run as the New York club took the field in Los Angeles, to face the Angels. Wrigley Field's inviting 345-foot power alleys in right and left center field were custom-made for the M & M boys. In fact, more home runs were hit in Wrigley Field in 1961 (248) than any park in major league history.

The media circus began to heat up about this time, and the press started to focus its attention on Roger Maris. Where before, most of the attention was paid to Mickey Mantle, now Maris was in the spotlight. And Maris hated the spotlight. He was a quiet, reserved individual, who cherished his privacy. Under questioning, he gave short answers in a monotonous monotone. He was colorless and emotionless. And he told it like it was, no PR platitudes, no political evasiveness. What you saw was what you got.

Roger Maris loved his time on the playing field. He enjoyed all aspects of the game, the home runs, the squeeze bunts, the stolen bases, the exciting outfield catches. But he detested the claustrophobic interview sessions that would become part of his life for the next five weeks. The media pressure before and after the game would eventually take its toll on his mental and physical health. He would begin to lose his hair by mid–September.

He didn't lessen the media circus with his performance on August 22. Bill Stafford, the Yanks' 21-year-old rookie, faced off against L.A's crack right hander Ken McBride, before a packed house of 19,930. McBride tossed a complete game six-hitter, but he was saddled with the loss when Yogi Berra cracked his 17th homer in the ninth inning, for a 4–3 Yankee win. The Angels had scored three runs in the first inning, then were shut down the rest of the game by Stafford and a bevy of relievers. Roger Maris, making history, whacked his 50th home run of the season, with a man on, in the sixth inning to deadlock the game and set the stage for Berra's dramatics. With his home run, Maris became the first major league player to hit 50 home runs before September 3rd. Babe Ruth in 1921, and Jimmie Foxx in 1932, both hit their 50th home run on the 3rd of September.

The next night, the Yanks won again, this time 8–6 in ten innings. In the process they routed former teammate Ryne Duren.

The Angels also routed New York ace Whitey Ford, in the fourth. The game went to the tenth inning, tied at 6–6. Then Roger Maris walloped a 400-foot triple to center field to drive in the go-ahead run. He scored minutes later on a wild pitch.

On the 31st, in Metropolitan Stadium, Minnesota, Jack Kralick, a lanky southpaw, toughed out a complete game, 11-hit struggle, to win 5–4. A Ladies Day crowd of 33,709 screamed with delight as Minnesota roughed up Sheldon for all their runs in the third inning. The last two runs crossed the plate on a home run by Jim Lemon, off Jim Coates. Mickey Mantle slugged home run #48 in the fourth inning, after hitting #47 the previous day. Trying to add a little humor to the home run race, Mantle, referring to Lou Gehrig, who hit 47 home runs in 1927, told Maris, "I got my man. Now you have to get yours." Maris was five games ahead of Ruth.

The crucial series of the season took place in Yankee Stadium from

September 1 to September 3, as the Detroit Tigers invaded the Yankee lair to do battle with Houk's sluggers. The New York lead, as the series began, was a slim 1½ games. On Friday the 1st, with 65,566 Yankee rooters packing the Stadium, Whitey Ford, Bud Daley, and Luis Arroyo, combined on a shutout, and New York edged the Tigers 1–0 with a run in the ninth. Don Mossi, a slick southpaw, on his way to a 15–7 season, matched the Yankee arms pitch for pitch until the ninth. Then, after retiring Maris and fanning Mantle, he hit the wall. Elston Howard cracked a two-out single, Berra moved him along with another single, and the "Moose," Bill Skowron, drove him in with yet another single. It was a stunning defeat for the Detroit crew, who came into the series with a record of 86 wins against only 47 losses.

In game two, 50,261 fans sat transfixed under an intense sun as Yankee killer Frank Lary (19–8) dueled Ralph Terry (12–2). The Tigers jumped on Terry for two runs in the top of the first. Roger Maris, after doubling in the fourth, ripped his 52nd home run of the year in the sixth, to give New York a 3–2 lead. Then, in the eighth, he smashed his 53rd with a man on, as the Bronx Bombers KO'd Lary with a big four spot. Luis Arroyo, in his 55th appearance of the year, pitched 1⅓ shutout innings. He also started New York's eighth-inning rally with a single.

Manager Ralph Houk sent big Bill Stafford to the mound to face eventual 17-game winner Jim Bunning, in the Sunday finale. This was do or die time for Detroit, who now trailed New York by 3½ games. They couldn't afford to fall any further behind with just 26 games left in the season. Neither pitcher was around at the end, although Stafford pitched a creditable game, giving up only two runs in seven innings. He left the game with the lead, but the Yankee bullpen blew it. Mantle and Berra both homered in the New York first to give their team a 3–1 lead. By the time the ninth inning rolled around, New York was on the short end of a 5–4 score. Mickey Mantle, who was playing despite a strained muscle in his forearm, injured the previous day, slugged his second home run of the game, and 50th of the season, to knot the score at five all. After a single by Berra and a walk to Skowron, Elston Howard stepped to the plate with two men out, and sent the fans home happy by slugging a game-winning, three run-homer.

The New York Yankees were now in a comfortable position, holding a healthy 4½ game lead over Detroit, heading down the stretch. On Labor Day, the Yankees swept a doubleheader from Washington while Detroit took the pipe for the fourth straight time. The following day the Yankees beat the Senators again, and the Tigers dropped two. Ralph Houk's boys were suddenly up by 7½ with just 25 games to go.

The Yankee win streak reached 13 before they lost, while the Tiger losing streak bottomed out at 9. When the dust settled, New York had a commanding 11½ game lead, with just 18 games remaining.

The media attention now shifted back to the chase of Babe Ruth. After every game, anywhere from 15 to 50 newspapermen would pin Roger Maris against the wall and barrage him with questions, while photographers' flash bulbs popped incessantly. Some of the questions were enough to make a grown man retch. One reporter asked him if a right hander's curve ball broke in on him. Maris, not trying to hide his sarcasm, said, "It probably does, since I bat left handed." Another reporter asked him if the ball was livelier this year, to which Maris replied, "No, the players are."

Unlike in Babe Ruth's day, when clubhouse banter was protected, every comment uttered by Roger Maris, every minor complaint and off-the-cuff remark made in the friendly atmosphere of the locker room was boldly reported in the next edition of the New York newspapers. Negative comments made by Maris about an umpire or about the New York fans were the next day's headlines. At one point, a distraught Roger Maris said to Mantle, "I can't take it anymore," to which Mick replied, "You have to."

Once or twice, in self-defense, Maris closeted himself in the safety of the trainer's room, which was off limits to the press.

The media pressure on Maris increased with each passing day. The Yankee slugger banged out homer #55 in game 141, keeping him seven games ahead of Ruth. The post-game questions were the same after each game. "Are you hitting so many home runs because it's an expansion year and the pitching isn't as good?" "How many home runs do you think Babe Ruth would hit this year?" "Do you really want to break Babe Ruth's record? He was a great player."

On road trips, fans mobbed the hotels where the New York Yankees stayed, trying to track down Maris and Mantle for autographs. Some people just wanted to touch the two heroes. Several times, the M&M boys had to sneak down the back stairs to avoid the crowds. It was unpleasant.

Even worse was the public recognition Maris now received as a celebrity. He couldn't go anywhere without being accosted by inconsiderate people looking for autographs. He couldn't frequent his favorite New York restaurant or even attend Mass in peace.

Maris became almost paranoid during the final weeks of the season. He complained about the reporters, the fans in the right field stands, even the Yankee management. He was sure his teammates as well as the

Yankee management wanted Mantle, not him, to break Babe Ruth's record.

The press reported all Maris' negative comments about players, officials, and fans. The comments alienated him from the New York fans, and his complaints about being misquoted, and his refusal to talk to reporters after some games, alienated him from the media. As Robert W. Creamer noted in *Season of Glory*, "If you feel, as William Congreve did, that hell has no fury like a woman scorned, you've never seen a sportswriter scorned." Louis Effrat, a writer for the *New York Times*, wrote "While (Mantle) answered all questions and volunteered information, Maris ... remained in the trainer's room and sulked."

The sweet-swinging lefty, trying to find peace on the playing field, banged out homer #56 against Mudcat Grant of Cleveland on September 9, then went a week before hitting another. After going homerless in three games in Chicago (he had four singles), Maris had just one single to show for nine trips to the plate in a doubleheader win in Detroit. Whitey Ford captured his 24th victory against only three losses, in the opener, and the Yankees won their 100th game of the season in the nightcap. Yogi Berra hit a home run to tie the major league team record of 221 home runs in a season, then Moose Skowron hit one out to set a new record. When the season finally ended 16 days later, the New York Yankees' victory total had risen to 109, and their home run total stood at 240.

Mickey Mantle, by this time, had dropped out of the race. Bogged down by a cold and by an injured forearm muscle, the Commerce Comet hit only four home runs after September 3. On the team's last road trip to Chicago, Detroit, and Baltimore, covering a total of ten games, he was unable to connect even once.

Roger Maris slammed #57 against Frank Lary in Detroit on the 16th of the month, and #58 against the Tigers' Terry Fox the next day. Then it was off to Baltimore, the birthplace of Babe Ruth, where Maris would play games 153, 154, and 155.

In a Tuesday doubleheader, Maris went a combined 0 for 8. Steve Barber, Baltimore's 22-year-old southpaw sensation, bested Whitey Ford in a pitchers' duel, 1–0, in the opener. Mantle sat out both games.

Wednesday, game #154, drew only 21,032 paying customers to Baltimore's Memorial Stadium (capacity 49,375), to witness Roger Maris' attempt to catch the mighty Babe. Memorial Stadium had a short 309-foot foul line in right, but quickly opened up to a distant 380-foot power alley. Center field was a healthy 410 feet from home plate. The Yankees' Ralph Terry (15–3) was opposed by young Milt Pappas (13–9). In the first inning, Maris hit a routine fly to right field. Two innings later, he caught

Roger Maris set a new single-season home run record with 61 homers in 1961. (Courtesy Transcendental Graphics)

a low fast ball from the Orioles' righty, on a 2–1 count, and put it into orbit. The ball cleared the 14-foot wire fence at the 380-foot mark in right center field and settled into the bleachers for #59, making Roger the #2 man of all time, behind Ruth. Dick Hall, a crafty veteran who relieved Pappas in the third, when the Yanks went up 4–0, fanned the Yankee slugger in the fourth. In the seventh, after smashing a long foul down the right field line, Maris hit a fly ball to right center field, that Earl Robinson hauled in near the fence. The courageous left handed slugger had one chance left, but he had to face Baltimore's butterfly artist, Hoyt Wilhelm. Wilhelm fed Maris nothing but junk in the ninth, and Roger, off balance most of the time, couldn't handle it. He tried to check his swing on an 0–1 count and dribbled the ball down the first base line for an easy out. His wife Patricia, watching the game on television in Kansas City, cried, "What did you swing at that pitch for, Roger?"

    Afterwards, in the clubhouse, Maris seemed relieved that it was over. As he said in *Season of Glory*, "I tried … I tried hard all night, but I only got one. I wanted to go out swinging, but I never did get a chance to swing good against Wilhelm." Responding to a question about Commissioner Ford Frick's asterisk ruling, Maris replied, "The Commissioner makes the rules. If he says all I'm entitled to is an asterisk, that's all right with me. I'm happy with what I got."

There was a celebration going on elsewhere in the clubhouse, but with very little media coverage. The New York Yankees had just clinched the American League pennant with their 104th victory of the season, a workmanlike 4–2 four-hitter by Terry.

Ralph Houk's warriors traveled to Beantown for a two-game set against Pinky Higgins' Red Sox after the celebration in Baltimore ended. Mickey Mantle returned to the lineup and socked his 54th and last home run of the year in the first game of the series. Maris was shut out in both games.

The team returned home on September 26th, to play the last five games of the season. On Tuesday night, before a disappointing Yankee Stadium gathering of 19,000, Roger Maris faced off against Jack Fisher (10–13), another of Baltimore's Baby Brigade. In the third inning, he caught up with one of Fisher's fast balls and hit it into the third deck of the right field stands, for #60. Reluctantly, the shy slugger emerged from the darkness of the dugout to tip his hat to the roaring crowd. It was an exciting moment for the 27-year-old outfielder.

An even more exciting moment was yet to come. After sitting out one game, Roger Maris returned to the lineup for the final three-game set with Boston. He was unable to connect against either Bill Monbouquette or Don Schwall in the first two games.

The Sunday finale was his last chance to break Babe Ruth's magic 60 home run mark, even if it was with an asterisk. The temperature was in the low 70s, with some clouds, as the Yanks and Red Sox locked horns for the last time in 1961. An embarrassingly small crowd of 23,154 people took advantage of the weather to come to the park to root for Maris. Tracy Stallard, a tall, husky right hander, toed the rubber for the Sox. Bill Stafford, gunning for his 14th win, was manager Houk's choice to close out the season. The two teams were scoreless after 3½ innings. In the bottom of the fourth, with a count of 2–0, Maris picked out a waist high fast ball and sent a high fly ball to right field. It came to rest in the lower deck, about 360 feet from home plate, for home run #61. An obviously happy Maris made a triumphant trip around the bases, after finally laying the ghost of Babe Ruth to rest beneath the Yankee Stadium sod. Roger's teammates pushed the smiling slugger back up the dugout steps to acknowledge the screams of the crowd. A smiling Maris doffed his cap to the crowd four times before retreating into the peace and quiet of the dugout. As Joseph Reichler and Jack Clary reported in *Baseball's Greatest Moments*, Maris finally felt fulfilled. "If I never hit another home run," he said with deep satisfaction, "this is one they can never take away from me."

Roger Maris' 61st homer was the only run of the game as New York blanked Boston 1–0.

The powerhouse 1961 New York Yankees, arguably one of the greatest teams of all time, buried the Cincinnati Reds in the World Series, four games to one, and outscored their National League opponents, 27 runs to 13. Roger Maris, obviously physically and emotionally drained after his pressure-packed season, batted only .105 in the Series, with one home run. But the Yanks didn't need him this time. Blanchard (.400 with two home runs), Richardson (.391), Skowron (.353), and Lopez (.333), more than took care of the offense. And on the hill, Whitey Ford (2–0), building on his 1960 performance, tossed 14 consecutive shutout innings. In the 1962 World Series he would throw another 1⅔ innings before yielding a run, giving him a total of 32⅔ consecutive scoreless World Series innings, breaking the record of Babe Ruth, set with the Boston Red Sox in 1916 and 1918.

Roger Maris won his second consecutive Most Valuable Player trophy for his history-making season.

The Yankee slugger had another outstanding year in 1962, batting .256 with 33 home runs and 100 runs batted in, but it wasn't up to his 1961 performance, and the fickle New York fans didn't let him forget that. He played four more years in the big city, then was traded to St. Louis, where he helped the Cardinals win two National League pennants and one World Championship. In all, Roger Maris played in the major leagues for 12 years, hammering 275 home runs and driving in 851 runs, with a .260 batting average. Combining his offensive tools with his exceptional glovework, made him one of the major league's best all around players of his era. His contributions to his teams resulted in seven league pennants and three World Championships in just 12 years.

Roger Maris was a winner.

7. The 1960s to the 1990s— An Historical Perspective

Patriotism blanketed the land during the 1940s. Eager young men entered military service to defend their country from foreign enemies. Their wives and sweethearts kissed them good-bye, then went to work in defense plants. Some women even joined the service themselves, serving as nurses, pilots, and administrators.

After World War II ended, the birth rate exploded as returning veterans and their girl friends got married and began raising families. The feeling of patriotism the country had during World War II continued into the '50s with the Korean conflict once again uniting the people against a common foe.

Times were good in the United States in the late '40s and '50s. The economy boomed, and the standard of living improved for most Americans. New automobiles, television sets, and homes became accessible, not only to the wealthy, but also to blue collar workers. The G.I. Bill, available to all military veterans, made it possible for thousands of young men to obtain a college education.

As the '60s approached, however, a cloud descended over the country. Psychologists introduced the philosophy of "permissiveness" into the society. Parents were taught that disciplining their children was bad and that reasoning with young children was the only acceptable method of raising a child. Children grew up without adult discipline as their parents concentrated on making money. More and more women joined the work force, leaving the children home unsupervised. Teenage pregnancies and suicides increased dramatically over the next two decades, as the family structure and scholastic discipline both eroded significantly.

The 1960s and '70s were a turbulent period in the country. Civil rights for all people was the top priority for the 48 states in the early '60s.

Integration was the law of the land, bringing with it the concomitant white backlash, as well as civil rights demonstrations by blacks demanding equal treatment in all phases of American life.

School integration was a major part of the civil rights program initiated by President John F. Kennedy after his election in 1960. On September 30, 1962, James A. Meredith made history when he became the first black to attend the University of Mississippi. The enrollment was not without incident. Two men died in rioting in the university town of Oxford, while many others were injured. More than 300 Federal Marshals guarding Meredith were attacked with stones and bottles. Federal troops occupied the town.

On June 11, 1963, Alabama governor George C. Wallace stood in the doorway of the University of Alabama, trying to block a black student from entering the building. He lost the fight when President Kennedy called in the National Guard to enforce the integration order.

Violence was the law of the land during the '60s. On November 22, 1963, President John Fitzgerald Kennedy was killed by an assassin's bullet in Dallas, Texas, as he rode through the city in a motorcade. Five years later, civil rights leader, Reverend Martin Luther King was assassinated on a motel balcony in Memphis, Tennessee. Within months, Robert F. Kennedy, the president's brother, was assassinated in a hotel kitchen in Los Angeles, while on a presidential election campaign.

Civil rights demonstrations and riots in black inner-city ghettos dominated the news of the nation in the mid–'60s. In 1965, 30 people were killed, over 1000 were injured, and 4000 were arrested in a riot in the Watts section of Los Angeles. In 1967, a rash of summer riots caused havoc in Newark, New Jersey, and Detroit, Michigan. More than 65 people were killed in the two cities, and property damage was in the millions of dollars.

A civil rights "Freedom March," from Selma, Alabama, to the state capitol at Montgomery, went off without incident on March 27, 1965. Twenty-five thousand marchers, both black and white, completed the peaceful demonstration under the watchful eyes of the U.S. Army and the Alabama National Guard.

During the mid–'60s, the United States became embroiled in another land confrontation, this one in Vietnam. It was an unpopular action from the beginning, involving the country in a civil war between North and South Vietnam. Anti–war demonstrators, called "Yippies" (Youth International Party), battled police in Chicago during the 1968 Democratic Party Convention. Thousands of young men fled the country rather than allow themselves to be drafted into military service.

Thousands of other young people, children of the Baby Boomer generation, "dropped out" of society, living in communes, falling under the influence of drugs like heroin, cocaine and LSD, practicing free sex and, in general, ignoring the mores of the society. In August 1969, thousands of so-called hippies descended on Woodstock, New York, for a rock concert and a weekend of hedonistic revelry.

Richard M. Nixon was elected the 37th president of the United States in 1968 and was re-elected in 1972. The most positive historic event of his administration occurred on July 20, 1969, when astronaut Neil Armstrong walked on the surface of the moon, completing a space project initiated by John F. Kennedy.

Four years later, President Nixon threw in the towel in Vietnam, agreeing to withdraw American troops and American sympathizers from the country, prior to a North Vietnamese occupation of the country. It was one of the darkest moments in American history.

In 1974, another humiliating event tossed the country into depression. President Nixon, admitting to a coverup of a Republican break-in at the Democratic Party National Headquarters in the Watergate Hotel in Washington, D.C., resigned his office of president rather than face a certain impeachment.

Baseball during the '60s, '70s, and '80s became the legacy of the "Baby Boomer" generation and post–"Baby Boomer" generation. It was and continues to be turbulent and chaotic. Expansion continued unabated. Sixteen major league teams in 1960 became 20 teams in 1962, 24 teams in 1969, 26 teams in 1977, 28 teams in 1993, and 30 teams in 1998.

Some significant rule changes were made to major league baseball during the 1970s. The American League adopted the designated hitter in 1973, but the National League did not follow suit. It is likely that the designated hitter will be discarded in the near future. In 1975, in one of the most disastrous decisions in major league history, Peter Seitz, the chairman of a three-man mediation panel, ruled that players who perform one year without a signed contract automatically become free agents. Pitcher Andy Messersmith of the Los Angeles Dodgers was the first major leaguer to test the free agent market. When he signed with the Atlanta Braves for the 1976 season, his salary jumped up from $115,000 a year to $333,000 a year. Free agency has been a Pandora's box ever since, with salaries skyrocketing into the sublime, then the ridiculous. Babe Ruth was the first $80,000 a year player in 1930. Joe DiMaggio was the first to top $100,000 in 1949. Nolan Ryan, a benefactor of free agency, became the first $1,000,000 man in 1980. By 2000, the top salary rose to $22,000,000 when the Texas Rangers signed free agent Alex Rodriguez. The major leagues are being split into the Haves and Have-nots. The wealthy teams in large markets, such as New York, Los Angeles, and Atlanta, can spend freely to obtain the players necessary to make them contenders. Small market teams, like Montreal and Pittsburgh, cannot afford to spend the money necessary to compete.

Another negative aspect of modern major league baseball has been player-management labor relations. Over the past 20 years, strikes, the threat of strikes, and the threat of lockouts have dismayed the paying public. The situation came to a head in 1994 when the players went on strike, canceling the baseball season after playing just 115 games. The World Series fell victim to the strike also and, when a settlement was finally reached in March 1995, 18 games had to be cut off that season as well. The strike had an adverse effect on attendance as fans, bitter at the greed on both sides of the bargaining table, stayed away from major league parks in droves. It wasn't until Mark McGwire and Sammy Sosa put on their pyrotechnic displays in 1998 that attendance came back to the 1993 level.

The batting philosophy in the major leagues changed after the Maris year. The change actually started with Mickey Mantle in the '50s and '60s. The Mick was the guru of the "new breed" of sluggers, a free swinging group that believed home runs and strikeouts went hand in hand. The handsome Oklahoman averaged 116 strikeouts a year during his 18-year career, with 36 home runs. Prior to that, Babe Ruth was the major leagues' strikeout king, with 87 strikeouts a year, to go along with 50 home runs. Jimmie Foxx, another early slugger, piled up 89 strikeouts a year, with 36 home runs.

During the 1970s and '80s, sluggers actually carried the Mantle philosophy to the extreme, striking out more, and watching their batting averages plummet as they strove for more and more home runs. Batters waved futilely at pitch after pitch, hoping to make contact. "Guess hitting" became a way of life. Rather than waiting on a pitch, to see what kind of pitch it was, and where it would cross the plate, as the players of previous generations had done, the "guess" hitter committed his swing as soon as the pitcher released the ball, trying to guess the type of pitch and the location. It is a philosophy that has never worked, but it is still popular today.

History has proven that more strikeouts do not mean significantly more home runs. More strikeouts generally mean lower batting averages. Babe Ruth, with 50 home runs and just 87 strikeouts, had a career batting average of .342. Jimmie Foxx, with 89 strikeouts, batted .325. At the other end of the spectrum, Reggie Jackson, with his 145 strikeouts, had a career batting average of .262, and Dave Kingman, with his 150 K's, could hit no higher than .236. No major league player, with a minimum of ten years experience, who struck out more than 100 times a year, has had a career batting average over .300. Most .300 hitters, in fact, have struck out less than 60–70 times a year.

There were only six 50-plus home run seasons between 1950 and 1990 in the major leagues, including Roger Maris' fantastic 61 home run year. The other historic seasons were Mickey Mantle's 52 homers in 1956 and 54 homers in 1961, Willie Mays' 51 homers in 1955 and 52 homers in 1965, and George Foster's 52 homers in 1977. No one challenged Maris' record until 1994.

8. Sammy Sosa—
The Early Years

Samuel (Sammy) Sosa was born Samuel Montero in the sugar mill company town of Ingenio Consuelo, to Bautista Montero and his wife Lucrecia, on November 12, 1968. The family moved to nearby San Pedro de Macoris when Sammy, or Mayki as he was called, was five years old. Their home, which was located on Calle Cincumbacion, in Jarro Sucio Barrio (Dirty Jar district), a poor section of the town, was a cramped, two-room, tangerine-colored, stucco apartment that was part of an abandoned hospital. Sammy slept on a wafer-thin mattress on a dirt floor. The house had no indoor plumbing, so baths had to be taken by collecting rain water in a drum or by washing in the sea. Open trenches and outhouses served as the barrio's sanitary facilities.

The dirt streets and alleys of Jarro Sucio, where the barefooted children played baseball, were strewn with garbage and refuse. Down the street from the Sosa house was a hard-packed dirt baseball field where many Dominican major leaguers began their careers. Along the right field line, across the street from the field, was the local prison.

When Sammy was seven years old, his father, who worked in the fields and on the highways, was struck down by an aneurysm. He died at age 42, leaving the family destitute. Sammy's mother Lucrecia, although a young widow, was a strong-willed, very religious lady, who was determined to raise her six children, ages two to 14, by herself. She worked as a maid, and also sold sandwiches to workers in the nearby factories. The three oldest boys (Luis Emilio age 14, Sammy, and Juan age 12) worked at odd jobs after school to help make ends meet. Sonia and Raquel helped their mother and took care of two-year-old Jose, called Nino (The Kid). Luis had a fruit stand in Parque Duarte, the town plaza, where he sold oranges for ten cents apiece. Sammy was a shoe shine boy. He lugged his tools of the trade to the plaza, after school, where he shined shoes for about seven cents a pair. Two of his customers were major league baseball players Joachin Andujar and George Bell. He also washed cars occasionally. On a good day, he would bring home about $2.00. One Mother's Day, Sammy tried unsuccessfully to earn money to buy his mother a present. All he came up with was one cent. He used it to buy her one Monte Carlo cigarette. It was probably the best present Lucrecia Sosa ever received. Once, reminiscing about those days, Sosa said, "I never had a childhood. I went from a little boy to a man overnight."

By the time Sammy Sosa was 11 or 12 years old, he had his heart set on a boxing career. He made boxing gloves out of socks stuffed with rags, and he fought with other neighborhood kids whenever he could. He also played baseball but not in an organized league. He played ball in the dirt streets of the barrio, in his bare feet, with a milk carton as a glove, stuffed rags for a ball, and an old stick or sugar cane for a bat.

Lucrecia and Luis, watching Sammy play baseball, realized that his exceptional baseball talent could carry him to a successful professional career if he could channel his energies in the right direction. At the age of 14, the eighth-grade dropout (education was mandatory only until the age of 14 in the Dominican Republic), urged on by his big brother Luis, began his baseball education. His first teacher was a former member of the Dominican Junior Team, 21-year-old Hector Paguero. The dirt expanses of the field known as "Mexico" became Sammy's school for the next two years, as he struggled to master the fundamentals of hitting. It was the same baseball field that had nurtured such major league talents as Julio Franco, Alfredo Griffin, and George Bell. San Pedro de Macoris, strangely enough, has sent more baseball players to the major leagues, per capita, than any city in the world. At one time, during the 1980s, six of the 26 major league shortstops were born in San Pedro de Macoris. A sign on the outskirts of the city reads, "San Pedro de Macoris, the Birthplace of Major League Shortstops."

Sosa and Paguero worked on Sammy's game four to six hours a day. The first thing Paguero taught Sammy was to swing big, and swing with bad intentions. The big, looping swing Sammy developed was full of holes, but it did make him into a long ball hitter which, in turn, attracted professional scouts.

Omar Minaya, a scout for the Texas Rangers, stationed in Florida, received glowing reports about the young slugger, and invited him to a tryout camp in the northern port city of Puerto Plata. Sammy Sosa arrived in camp, after a four hour bus ride, wearing a borrowed uniform and borrowed shoes, determined to impress Ranger officials with his superior baseball abilities. Although Sosa's skills were crude and unrefined, and even though he looked badly undernourished, the 5'10", 145-pound dynamo had certain qualities that caught Minaya's eye. He was outgoing, energetic, aggressive, and optimistic. He gave 110 percent all the time. He had an outstanding throwing arm, a quick bat, and good power. On the negative side, he had only average speed and a looping swing full of holes. He didn't know the slightest thing about baseball fundamentals—he had no concept of the strike zone, didn't know how to run the bases, where to throw the ball on hits to the outfield, how to charge a ball, or how to hit the cutoff man.

Still, on the recommendation of Minaya, the Texas Rangers offered the 16-year-old Sosa a professional baseball contract, with a signing bonus of $3500. He bought himself a bike, then gave the rest of the money, which was almost two years' wages, to his mother. The Rangers, in order to prepare young Dominicans for the culture shock of living and playing baseball in the United States, had them attend a baseball academy at the University of Santo Domingo during their first year. Sammy and the other boys played baseball at the academy, learned rudimentary English, and were taught hygiene, how to use a knife and fork, and other intricacies of everyday living in America.

The next year, 1986, Sammy was assigned to the Sarasota Rangers in the Gulf Coast League. When he arrived in Florida, he still didn't know much English, but he knew how to get ahead. First, he latched on to some Puerto Rican players, like Juan Gonzalez, Rey Sanchez, and Bernie Williams, who could help him with his English. Then he followed the American players, like Dean Palmer, to the local fast food restaurants, ordering what they ordered, until he understood the language better.

Sammy Sosa had his ups and downs during the season, but overall his debut was a great success. The right-handed slugger batted .275, with a league-leading 19 doubles, four home runs, and 11 stolen bases, in 61 games. His 96 total bases also led the league. By comparison, teammate Dean Palmer, now entering his tenth year in the major leagues, batted an anemic .209 with no home runs. Bernie Williams of the Sarasota Yankees, hit .270 with two home runs and a league-leading 45 runs scored in 61 games, and Juan Gonzalez, who has twice led the American League in home runs and has hit more than 40 home runs in a season, five times in ten years, hit .240 with no home runs.

Sosa struck out 51 times in 229 at bats, but as Omar Minaya explained later, "Dominican players know only one way to get to the major leagues, by putting up big numbers. And you can't put up big numbers unless you swing the bat."

Early in his career, Sammy Sosa was known as a "hot dog." He was flamboyant, enthusiastic, overly aggressive, and swaggered when he walked. At the plate, one coach noted, "He never saw a pitch he didn't like." On the bases, he ran with abandon, regardless of the pitch count or the game situation. His selfish pursuit of his own statistics would bring him considerable criticism for almost a decade. But it was all a learning experience for the youngster from the Dominican Republic. And he was still only 17 years old.

In 1987, Sammy Sosa played with Gastonia in the Class A South Atlantic League. The Rangers did not have a very good club that year, finishing fifth in a six-team division. Their record of 52–82 left them 33½ games behind the Asheville Tourists.

Sosa batted .279 with 11 home runs and 59 RBIs in 129 games, and was elected to the mid-season all-star team. He led the club with 73 runs scored, but also struck out 123 times in 519 at bats. Dean Palmer batted .215 with nine homers, while Juan Gonzalez hit .265 with 14 homers and 74 RBIs.

The Texas trio of Sosa, Palmer, and Gonzalez stayed in Class A ball in '88, playing with Charlotte in the Florida State League. Sosa's batting average nosedived with Charlotte, as he hit only .229, but he continued to develop in other areas. He showed good power, leading the league with 12 triples, to go along with 13 doubles and nine home runs. He set a personal high with 42 stolen bases, reduced his strikeouts to 106, and was charged with only seven outfield errors. Unfortunately, he was still having trouble taking pitches, as evidenced by his 35 bases on balls.

Nineteen eighty nine was a momentous year in the life of 20-year-old Sammy Sosa. He began the year with Tulsa in the AA Texas League and, for the first time, he began to realize his hidden potential. In 66 games with the Drillers, the right-handed power hitter, now a muscular 175 pounds, smashed 33 extra base hits including 15 doubles, four triples, and seven home runs. He drove in 31 runners, and stole 16 bases, while hitting a solid .297. On June 15, Sosa was called up to the big club for his first taste of major league pitching.

It was reported that, when Sammy Sosa received his first major league check of $18,000, he cashed it, threw the money on the bed, and rolled around on it for several minutes. Then he excitedly telephoned his mother in San Pedro de Macoris to tell her the good news. "Mommy, we're rich."

Even though Sosa got off to a good start by pounding out a single and double against Andy Hawkins of the Yankees in his first game, slugging a home run off Roger Clemens five days later, and enjoying a four-hit game, it was obvious he was in over his head. He batted only

.238 in 25 games, with just three runs batted in, in 84 at bats, and he struck out 20 times—with no walks. Tom Grieve, the general manager of the Rangers, later admitted they may have called the 20-year-old Sosa up too soon.

Texas farmed Sosa out to Oklahoma City in the AAA American Association, for more experience but, after playing just ten games for the 89ers, he was traded to the Chicago White Sox for Harold Baines and was subsequently sent to Vancouver in the Pacific Coast League. Sammy played 13 games with the Canadians and whacked the ball at a sizzling .367 clip, prompting the last-place Chi-Sox to recall him. He finished the season in Chicago, the fifth team he had played on, in a hectic, confusing year. In his first game, Sammy Sosa went three for three, with a two-run homer, against the Minnesota Twins. He played in 33 games for Chicago, batting a respectable .273. In 99 at bats, the kid from San Pedro pounded out five doubles and three home runs, with ten runs batted in and seven stolen bases. It was a good debut.

Over the winter of 1989-90, after his dizzying season in the United States, Sosa went home to the Dominican Republic to be with his family and to relax and unwind. He played 37 games for Escogido in the Winter League, batting .285 with two homers and 19 RBIs. One night, while listening to the merengue music at a disco in Santo Domingo, Sammy noticed a beautiful, olive-skinned, red-haired girl across the dance floor, and was immediately attracted to her. Her name was Sonia. She was 17 years old, and was a singer and dancer on Dominican television. As reported by Michael Bamberger in *Sports Illustrated*, "He had a waiter bring her a note: 'If you will do the honor of having one dance with me, it will be the start of a beautiful friendship....'" She had no idea that Sammy was a baseball player, but he had other qualities. 'I like guys who are big, tall and dark,' she says. 'I looked at him and said, 'Oh, wow—what a man.'"

That first dance did indeed become the start of a beautiful friendship. In fact, Sammy and Sonia were married within a year. Keysha, born in 1992, was the first addition to the family. Later, Sammy and Sonia were blessed with Kenia (1994), Sammy Jr. (1996), and Michael (1997).

Sammy Sosa spent the entire 1990 season in the major leagues, with mixed results. In spite of optimism in the White Sox camp, the experts still predicted a last-place finish for Jeff Torborg's team. The experts were wrong. Chicago surprised everyone with a second-place finish. They won a total of 94 games, an improvement of 25 games over '89, and just finished nine games behind the Oakland Athletics. The experts also called Sosa an exciting addition to the Chicago outfield. In this case, they were correct. He played in 153 games for the White Sox and, although he batted only .233, he hit 25 doubles, 10 triples and 15 home runs, with 70 runs batted in. He was the only American League player to reach double figures in all three categories. He also stole 32 bases, joining Ivan Calderon (32)and Lance Johnson (36) in becoming the first White Sox trio in almost 90 years, to steal 30 bases in one year.

Sosa got off the mark quickly in '91, pounding out two home runs and driving in five runners, against Baltimore, but by late July his world had collapsed completely. He was batting an anemic .200, with just 51 hits in 255 at bats, and was on his way to Vancouver. Sosa's immaturity may also have led to his downfall. He, like many other young major league players, succumbed to the demon of too much money and too much celebrity, too soon. He slicked his hair down with gel, bought gaudy gold trinkets, and became part of the night scene.

Sosa spent a month in Vancouver, where he played resonably well, then was recalled to Chicago to finish out the season. His final numbers (.203 batting average, ten homers and 33 RBIs) were easily forgettable. He couldn't even find his batting stroke in the Dominican Winter League, hitting just .248. He did, however, lead the league in home runs, with four. Sammy's Winter League career essentially ended that year. He would play just three more games in succeeding years.

Sammy's big break came on March 29, 1992, when he was traded to the Chicago Cubs. It was the real beginning of his major league career. Manager Jim Lefebvre and batting coach Billy Williams were thrilled to get such a talent, and they went to work immediately to restore the young slugger's confidence.

The team got off to a slow start in '92, winning just 12 of their first 31 games, and falling into the cellar. Sosa was one of the reasons for their poor showing, as he hit just .211, with one RBI, in the first 24 games. He finally hit his first Cubs' homer, off Ryan Bowen of the Houston Astros, on May 7. After he was moved down from leadoff man to #6 in the batting order, he started to hit, banging out four homers in ten games, from May 31 to June 10. Then, just when he seemed to be getting untracked, he went down with an injury. On June 12, Sosa suffered a broken right hand after being hit by Montreal's Dennis Martinez.

He was out of action for almost seven weeks. When he returned to the lineup, he jumped on Doug Drabek's first pitch, homering off the Pittsburgh ace. Four days later, he excited the crowd by scoring all the way from first base on a pitchout, when Mets catcher Mickey Sasser threw the ball into center field on a stolen base attempt. Sammy Sosa whacked the ball at a torrid .385 clip (15 for 39), with three homers and nine RBIs

Sammy Sosa played for the Chicago White Sox for three years, before being traded to the Chicago Cubs in 1992. (Brace photo)

after coming off the disabled list, but his season came to a disappointing end in his tenth game back, when he fouled a pitch off his left ankle, fracturing it.

The season was not a complete loss for Sosa. He found a home with the Cubs. He liked his new manager and his new batting coach. And he got his swing back. In just 67 games, the right-handed slugger hit an acceptable .260, with eight home runs and 25 runs batted in. It was a season to build on. From now on, it would be onward and upward.

In 1993, Sosa began to live up to his potential, although he was still a raw talent. He swung at pitches in the dirt, and pitches over his head. He stole bases at inopportune times. In the outfield, he was still a threat to the health of his teammates. The other outfielders dove for cover whenever Sosa came in their direction. Cutoff men never grew tall enough to reach his throw-ins. And he was still considered to be a selfish player, more interested in his own statistics than in the welfare of the team.

The Chicago Cubs, coming off fourth-place finishes in 1991 and '92, hoped to work their way back to the top, and Sammy Sosa was one of the important cogs in the wheel. Sosa, now wearing #21 on his uniform in honor of his idol Roberto Clemente, got off to a fast start, leading the Cactus League in home runs in spring training. He continued his blasting when the season started. On April 23, the right-handed bomber ripped two homers with five RBIs, as the Cubbies whipped the Cincinnati Reds 7–4. Eleven days later he went 5–6 with two more homers. His three-run, two-out shot in the bottom of the ninth brought the Cubs back from a 10–5 deficit to a ten all tie. The Rockies pushed across four runs in the top of the 11th to beat Lefebvre's cohorts 14–13 in wind-swept Wrigley Field. Sosa's two-run homer in the bottom of the 11th was too little, too late.

Sammy Sosa had another two-homer game against the St. Louis Cardinals on June 17, then hit two more in San Diego, on the 30th of the month. The big slugger went six for six against the Rockies in hitter-friendly Mile High Stadium, on July 2, giving him nine consecutive base hits, to establish a new Chicago Cubs record. The Cubs won the game 11–8.

Chicago's new hitting sensation was selected as the National League's Player of the Week for June 28–July 4, hitting .538 in six games, with two homers and six RBIs.

The cannonading continued into August and September. He put up another two-homer day against the St. Louis Cardinals on August 6. He hit his 30th home run of the season on September 2, driving one off Josias Manzanillo of the New York Mets. And he stole his 30th base of the year on September 15th in 3 Com Park in San Francisco.

It was a good year for Sammy Sosa, but not a good year for the Cubs. They once again finished in fourth place, their 84–78 record leaving them 13 games behind the Phillies. Chicago's poor showing spelled finish for manager Jim Lefebvre, who was replaced by Tom Trebelhorn.

Sosa put up some outstanding numbers. He played in 159 games, batting .261 with 33 home runs and 93 runs batted in. His flying feet enabled him to steal 36 bases, making him the Cubs' first 30–30 man (home runs and stolen bases). In the outfield, he improved immensely. His powerful right throwing arm shot down 17 ambitious base runners, making him the #2 man in the National League in assists. He still needed to become more familiar with the strike zone however, as evidenced by his 135 strikeouts in 598 at bats. He drew just 38 bases on balls.

The 1993 season was a satisfying one for Sammy Sosa in many respects, but it was far from perfect. Many people still looked upon him as a selfish player. And his occasional mental lapses brought more criticism from fans and media types alike. One Chicago radio personality called him "Roberto Clemente without a brain." Manager Jim Lefebvre called the comments on his selfishness, jealousy on the part of some players, who could not understand a potential superstar like Sosa. Lefebvre admitted that when Sosa was in a groove, he could hit homers in bunches, but when he was in a slump, he piled up many strikeouts.

There was one thing everyone agreed with. Sammy Sosa came to the ballpark ready to play every day. And he gave his team and his manager a 110-percent effort every day. Sammy's physical game still needed refinement. And Sammy's mental approach still needed to be fine-tuned. But his enthusiasm and his dedication were above reproach.

Sosa, celebrating his outstanding 1993 campaign, arrived at spring training camp in Mesa, Arizona, flaunting a heavy, gold necklace adorned with two crossed bats and a large gaudy "30–30" inlaid with diamonds. The weight of his jewelry apparently didn't affect his swing, however, as he picked up where he left off in '93. Although he hit well in spring training, the Cubs' right fielder went into a slump as soon as the bell tolled to start the regular season. He hit a paltry .225 in April and that, along with first baseman Mark Grace's slump, contributed to the Cubs' painful 12-game losing streak. In an attempt to end the jinx, the Cubs brought a lucky billy goat onto the field. Manager Trebelhorn also moved Sosa up into the leadoff spot. The Cubs won, and the jinx was lifted—temporarily.

Sammy Sosa went on to have an outstanding month in May. On the 4th of the month, batting leadoff, he homered off Tom Browning of Cincinnati. He tripled in four straight games from May 14 to 17. And he homered again leading off, this time against Tom Glavine of the Atlanta Braves on May 29. For the month, the big slugger batted .317 with 11 home runs and 23 runs batted in.

He batted .339 over the team's last 53 games, before the players went out on strike, ending the season after only 113 games. It was none too soon for Chicago, who finished in the cellar with a sorry record of 49–64.

Sammy's overall totals showed a solid .300 batting average, 25 homers, 70 RBIs, and 22 stolen bases. He struck out 92 times and walked 25 times, in 426 at bats.

The 1995 season was also an abbreviated season, as the strike, which was finally settled in March, reduced the playing schedule by 18 games. When the season finally began in late April, Sammy Sosa was ready—and happy. He had just signed a one-year contract for $4.3 million. This would be his "coming out" year, when he would begin to realize his almost unlimited potential. The undernourished kid from a third world country had grown into a 6', 190-pound slugger with immense shoulders and anvil-like arms, and he was ready to explode. Through the first 31 games, Jim Riggleman's overachieving troops racked up a 20–11 record, sparked by Sosa who hit .315 with ten homers.

On May 14, Sosa reached his first milestone when he homered off Trevor Hofman of the San Diego Padres for his 100th career home run. One week later, the free-swinging Sosa homered in the top of the 13th inning in Los Angeles to give the Cubbies a 2–1 victory over the Dodgers. It was Chicago's 9000th major league victory, going back to 1876.

The Cubs, who had only a few bonafide major leaguers, such as Sosa, Shawon Dunston, and Mark Grace, slowly drifted back into the pack. By July 2, their record stood at 30–31. Sammy Sosa, on his way to his first All-Star game, was hitting .289, with 15 homers and 52 RBIs in 61 games. His strikeouts and walks were still out of whack however, with 56 K's and only 16 walks.

During August, the Cubs' right fielder went on a home run hitting spree. From August 10 to August 24, he smashed nine homers, with 27 RBIs, in 14 games. He hit seven of the homers and drove in 18 of the runs, between the 17th and 24th. In one span, from the 17th to the 20th, he homered in four straight games. From August 13 to September 2, he hit 13 homers in 20 games, driving in 32 runs. Included in the barrage, were a trio of two-homer games. On August 14, he hit a memorable home run off the Dodgers' Tom Candiotti, the 10,000th home run in Chicago history.

When the season ended, the Cubs had settled into third place, with a record of 73–71, a full 12 games out of first. Sammy Sosa, on the other hand, had an outstanding year. He was selected as the National League Player of the Week, twice. He won his first Silver Slugger Award, and was named to The Sporting News National League all-star team.

On September 24th, Sosa stole third base in a 3–2 win over the Pittsburgh Pirates, making him a 30–30 man for the second time. Only five other men in major league history have been 30–30 men more than once.

For the year, Sosa batted .268, with 36 home runs, 119 runs batted in, and 34 stolen bases. Nineteen ninety-five marked the first of four successive years that Sosa would rack up 30 or more homers and 100 or more RBIs. He continued to impress baseball experts with his outstanding arm, as he finished with 13 outfield assists, #2 in the National League. He was also the first Chicago player in the twentieth century to lead the team in home runs and steals in three successive seasons.

The big topic of conversation in the States over the winter was expansion. It was announced that two new teams would be added to the major leagues in 1998, Tampa Bay in the American League and Arizona in the National League. Almost immediately, speculation began about the possibility of someone breaking Roger Maris' home run record. In 1994, before the disgraceful players' strike almost destroyed the game, several players were on track to challenge the most visible of all records. No fewer than six players, three in each league, were threatening to hit more than 50 home runs, and one player, Matt Williams of the San Francisco Giants, was on track to match Maris' record of 61 homers. The other big boomers included Ken Griffey, Albert Belle, Frank Thomas, Jeff Bagwell, and Barry Bonds.

The 1996 season was another step forward for Sammy Sosa, but a big disappointment for Jim Riggleman's Chicago Cubs. The Cubbies, who were hoping to improve on their 73–71 showing in '95, had a more mature, confident Sammy Sosa in right field. The right-handed bomber, now 27 years old, had discarded his flashy jewelry and was concentrating on being a good person, a devoted family man, and a dangerous clean-up hitter.

The Chicago Cubs stumbled coming out of the starting gate. On Monday, May 13, their record stood at 18–20, leaving them, surprisingly enough, in a flat-footed tie with the Cincinnati Reds, for first place in the weak Central Division. The team was mediocre in all aspects of the game. Sosa was hitting a barely visible .233, but he had hit 11 home runs with 27 RBIs, to lead the team in both categories.

On May 16, Sammy Sosa became the first player in Cubs history to hit two homers in one inning. Facing Jeff Tabaka of the Houston Astros in the seventh inning, the Chicago slugger hit a leadoff homer. Later in the inning, he hit a two-run shot off Jim Dougherty.

Three weeks later, on June 5, the pride of the Dominican Republic slammed three home runs against the Philadelphia Phillies, in a 9–6 Cubs victory. He slammed two home runs off Terry Mulholland, and one off Russ Springer. Sosa's second homer was the 150th of his career.

At the All-Star break, Jim Riggleman's crew had slipped into fourth place, their 41–46 record leaving them five games behind the St. Louis Cardinals. Sammy Sosa, after a slow start, enjoyed the warm weather and had his average up to .258. His 27 homers led the National League, while his 63 RBIs were near the top.

Sosa continued hot during July, winning the Player of the Month Award for his .358 batting average, ten homers and 29 RBIs. He was on his way to a potential 50 home run season when disaster struck. He was leading the league with 40 home runs on August 21, when an errant pitch from Florida's Mark Hutton broke his right hand, shelving him for the balance of the season. The injury ended a consecutive games–played streak of 304 for Sosa.

The Cubs, who had worked their way back into contention in the National League Central Division, could not compensate for Sosa's loss. They dropped 14 of their last 16 games, and finished the season in fourth place with a disappointing 76–86 record.

Overall, Sammy Sosa had a successful year. Even though he missed the last 38 games of the season, he hit .273 with 40 homers and 100 runs batted in. More important, Sonia Sosa gave birth to a baby boy in October, Sammy Jr. He joined sisters Keysha, age four, and Kenia, age two.

When spring training got underway at HoHoKam Park in Mesa, Arizona, in February 1997, manager Jim Riggleman was faced with many problems, not the least of which was to find a strong bat to hit behind, and protect, Sammy Sosa. The search would prove to be fruitless.

The major leagues were coming off a sensational home run explosion in 1996, when the 28 teams hit a total of 4962 home runs, an average of 2.19 per game, and 22 percent higher than 1995. Eight teams hit more than 200 homers. Seventeen players hit 40 or more homers, with Oakland A's slugger Mark McGwire rattling the fences for 52 home runs, and Baltimore Oriole outfielder Brady Anderson topping out at 50. The reasons for the home run surge are many. Colorado's new Coors Field, at an altitude of more than 5000 feet, produced 70 percent more circuit blows than the average major league field. Other reasons given include smaller ballparks, expansion, and bigger, stronger players who utilize weight training to the fullest. The experts continued to focus on the 1998 season when two new expansion teams would be admitted into the major leagues. They felt that Rogers Maris' record would be in jeopardy, particularly from the likes of McGwire, Ken Griffey, Albert Belle, and Frank Thomas. Sammy Sosa's name never came up in the predictions.

The Cubs were picked to finish third in the Central division in 1997. They had strengthened their pitching staff with the addition of closer Mel Rojas and starters Kevin Tapani and Terry Mulholland, but they were still weak offensively, with just three dependable bats—Sosa, Mark Grace, and Brian McRae.

The season opened, fittingly enough, on April Fools Day. Playing in Florida, Chicago dropped a 4–2 decision to Jim Leyland's eventual World Champion Marlins. Terry Mulholland was rapped around for four runs and seven hits in 4⅔ innings. Sosa went 0–4, Grace had 1–3, and McRae was hitless in two at bats. On the 13th of the month, the Cubs were beaten at home by the Atlanta Braves, 6–4, for their tenth straight loss. The team had an anemic .169 batting average and a poor 4.39 earned run average. Sammy Sosa was hitting .200 with one homer and three RBIs. One week later, on the 20th, Chicago met the New York Mets in a doubleheader. They dropped the opener 8–2 as Bobby Jones tossed a five-hitter at them. Sammy Sosa, after another 0-for-four, saw his batting average plummet to .157. Finally, in game two, behind a strong pitching performance by Kevin Foster, Jim Riggleman's embattled troops broke into the win column, with a 4–3 victory.

The Cubs' 0–14 start was the worst in National League history, topping the ten game skein by the 1988 Atlanta Braves. The Baltimore Orioles hold the major league record with a 0–21 start, also in 1988.

On Friday, April 25, the Cubs' anemic offense finally came to life. They pounded out 14 hits in an 11–1 laugher against the Pittsburgh Pirates. Sammy Sosa, with three hits including his third home run, drove in five runs and raised his batting average 27 points to .224. The next day they beat Pittsburgh again 7–6, behind another 14-hit attack. Doug Glanville drove in three runs, and Ryne Sandberg hit a homer to pace the attack.

By the end of April, Harry Caray's favorite team had settled into the cellar with a dismal 6–19 record, but May was a turnaround month for the Windy City boys. Sammy Sosa, who was unhappy at the start of the year, partly because he was playing the last year of his contract and negotiations between his agent and Chicago management had dragged on into the season, picked up his offensive production in May. He was named Player of the Week for the week ending May 18, thanks to a .348 batting average, with four homers, two triples and 12 RBIs in six games. On May 16, he went 4–4 with a triple, a home run, and a career high six runs batted in, against the San Diego Padres. Four days later, he slammed two home runs off San Francisco Giant pitching (the 22nd multi-homer game of his career), as the Cubs won 5–3. And on the 26th of the month, he hit his first inside-the-park home run, in Pittsburgh, sparking another Chicago victory, 2–1.

Surprisingly, as May ended, the Cubs were only five games out of first place, their 15–13 month bringing their overall record up to 21–32. For the month, Sammy Sosa scorched the ball at a .339 clip, with eight doubles, two triples, ten homers, and 28 RBIs. Mark Grace was batting .302, Shawon Dunston .301, Jose Hernandez .319, and Doug Glanville .302.

In June and July, two important things happened that would have a significant effect on Sosa's baseball career. On June 27, the Dominican slugger signed a four-year deal worth $42.5 million, making him the third highest paid player in the major leagues. The signing took a big load off Sammy's mind. As he said, "Talking about a contract in the middle of the season is hard." Manager Jim Riggleman, in an attempt to get better pitches for Sosa to look at, moved him up to third place in the batting order, just ahead of Mark Grace.

Then, on July 14, batting coach Tony Muser left to become manager of Kansas City and was replaced by Jeff Pentland, a New York Mets minor league batting instructor. Pentland and Sosa grew close over the next few months, and began to work together to fine-tune Sosa's batting style. Pentland basically worked on just two important things with Sosa, a way to shift his weight so he would be ready for any kind of pitch, and a lowering of Sosa's hands, allowing him to be more relaxed when he swung.

The changes in Sosa's batting stance wouldn't be evident until 1998. In the meantime, the 1997 season continued on its downward spiral. The Cubs went 11–17 in June and 11–17 again in July to fall back into the cellar, a distant 16½ games behind the Houston Astros. Sosa was limping along at .251, but had 49 extra base hits including 21 homers and 77 RBIs. His continued disdain for the strike zone (120 strikeouts and only 32 bases on balls) continued to concern Riggleman and Pentland.

The season finally came to a merciful end, none too soon, on September 28, with Chicago dropping a tight 2–1 decision to Tony LaRussa's Redbirds at Busch Stadium. Sosa struck out as a pinch hitter in the ninth, while St. Louis' new addition, Mark McGwire, hit a home run off Steve Trachsel in the sixth inning. It was an omen of things to come for Trachsel. McGwire would hit his record-breaking 62nd homer off the Chicago righty in the same park on September 8, 1998. Sammy Sosa's numbers for the year showed a .251 batting average, 36 home runs, 119 RBI's, and 22 stolen bases. He struck out 174 times, a new Chicago record, while drawing only 45 walks in 642 at bats.

9. Mark McGwire — The Early Years

Mark McGwire was a big kid who grew into a big man. The entire family was big. His father stood 6'3" tall, and his four brothers went between 6'3" and 6'8". John McGwire, the family patriarch, had his dreams of athletic excellence snatched away from him when he was just seven years old. He collapsed at his home in Spokane, Washington, one day in 1944, with poliomyelitis. It was ten years before the Salk polio vaccine was available, and the disease was thought to be contagious. John spent seven months isolated in a hospital ward. The only contact he had with his family was when a hospital attendant would roll his bed over to the window so he could look out and wave to them. It was a torturous time in the life of a young boy.

Polio was a setback for John McGwire, not a defeat. He grew into a strong, 225-pound athlete, who became a top bicyclist and an outstanding golfer who, at one time, had an eight handicap.

He attended the University of Washington in Seattle, where he studied predentistry and met his future wife. Ginger was a nurse for two university doctors.

John and Ginger McGwire settled in Claremont, a small community of about 35,000 people, 35 miles east of Los Angeles. John opened a dental office in Claremont, while Ginger became a homemaker, mother, and community volunteer.

Mark David McGwire was born in Pomona, California, on October 1, 1963, the second of five McGwire boys.

He was a big, pudgy kid when he was 8–12 years old, with thick glasses, red hair, and freckles. Although his size made him look threatening, he was actually a gentle, shy boy who wanted everyone to like him. Since the five McGwire boys lived on a cul-de-sac, all the neighborhood kids hung out at their house, rapping and watching TV inside, and playing games like tennis baseball and touch football in the street. Mark, whose size and flaming red locks brought to mind the giant redwoods of Northern California, was called "Tree," a nickname he carried through La Puerta Middle School.

About the time he started playing baseball, John and Ginger McGwire noticed that eight-year-old Mark squinted a lot. He always sat close to the screen when he watched television. He had difficulty reading street signs. And one day, when his father sent him out to play shortstop, he complained that the ball looked fuzzy. Mark was quickly whisked off to an optometrist, who diagnosed his problem as nearsightedness, a condition that would leave his vision at 20/500 by the time he reached the major leagues. The freckle-faced youngster wore thick glasses for five years until contact lenses became popular.

In 1974, in his first official at bat with the Claremont Athletics, the big right-handed basher hit the ball over the 175-foot chicken wire fence in right field, for a home run. His grandmother was there to see the historic blast, but his parents missed it. They were on a cruise. Mark went on to hit 13 home runs in the Claremont Little League, a single season record that stood for 20 years. Although he was a long ball threat, he considered himself to be, first and foremost, a pitcher. Standing almost 6' tall, he was an intimidating presence on the mound. He never lost a game he pitched in Little League, according to his father. Mark was primarily a pitcher for the next ten years, until he was finally converted into a slugging first baseman in his junior year in college.

McGwire pitched on his high school baseball team for two years and, as a senior, he won five games against three losses, with a 1.90 earned run average. He also banged out five homers and batted .359. During the winter, he played center on the basketball team. Now a full 6'5" tall, he was a force to be reckoned with on the hardwood. Unfortunately, he never reached his potential because he wasn't a good jumper.

He was drafted by the Montreal Expos out of high school as a pitcher, and was offered an $8,500 signing bonus. He was also recruited by several colleges, including Arizona State and USC. He was offered a full baseball scholarship at USC, which he figured was worth about $50,000. He accepted the scholarship.

McGwire entered the University of Southern California at Los Angeles in the fall of 1981. His primary interest in college was to play baseball and to prepare himself for a professional career. He majored in Public Administration because he thought he might like to be a police officer if he didn't make it in baseball. Mark was an average student, graduating from Damien with a B average, and carrying a C average at USC.

The next spring, at a pre-season baseball breakfast, Mark met a striking brunette. Her name was Kathy Hughes, and she was one of the team's bat girls. Over the next few months, the big redhead and the beautiful bat girl became an item. Less than four years later, they would be married.

During Mark's freshman year at USC, he got into 29 games for the Trojans, most of them as a pitcher. The big right-hander compiled a 4–4 record, with a 3.04 ERA. He struck out 31 batters in 47 innings. At the plate, he hit only .200 but showed some power with three home runs in 75 at bats.

Mark's biggest asset throughout his career was his dedicated work ethic. He had the talent to become a major league player, and he had the discipline to work hard to perfect that talent.

In his sophomore season, Mark told coach Rod Dedeaux he wanted to play first base. Dedeaux still wanted him to pitch, but after the Claremont Clubber hit a couple of early-season home runs, the USC coach reconsidered and put him on first base. Mark responded brilliantly, with a tough .319 batting average, 19 home runs and 59 RBIs. His 19 homers broke the USC single-season home run record of 17, held jointly by Kent Hadley and Dave Hostettler.

He still pitched occasionally, winning three games against a single loss, with a 2.78 earned run average.

During the summer, Mark played baseball for the pre–Olympic National Baseball Federation team. The team visited Japan and China, and played against Japan and South Korea in the U.S. They also played in the International Cup Tournament in Belgium and the Pan American Games in Venezuela. McGwire slugged the ball at a .454 clip, with six homers in just 33 at bats. The U.S. team came in second in the Pan Am Games, losing to Cuba in the finals, 8–1. Mark's experience in Venezuela was not a happy one. The sheltered middle-class American teenager couldn't eat the food and couldn't adjust to the primitive living conditions in the South American country, causing him to lose almost 15 pounds.

The next year, the big redhead's bat sizzled to the tune of .387, with a whopping 32 homers and 80 runs batted in. The 32 homers broke his own USC record and set a new Pac-10 Conference record. It also led all NCAA schools in 1983. His 54 career home runs set a new USC career home run record. His slugging feats earned him the *Sporting News* College Player of the Year award, as well as a spot on the *Sporting News*

College All-America team. His three-year totals at USC included 54 home runs in 503 at bats, a frequency of 59 homers for every 550 at bats.

Mark tried out for, and made, the United States Olympic Team in 1984, a talented team that included future major leaguers Barry Larkin, Billy Swift, Cory Snyder, and B.J. Surhoff. Prior to the Olympics, the team traveled the country, playing a strenuous schedule. They played 35 games in 33 cities in five weeks. They played in several major league parks, including Shea Stadium and Fenway Park. Once again, Mark's bat was on fire. His .391 batting average included 13 doubles and six home runs in 110 at bats. He didn't fare as well in the Olympics however. He was held to four singles in 21 at bats as the U.S. team won the silver medal. After dumping Taipei 2–1, Italy 16–1, the Dominican Republic 12–0, and South Korea 5–2, they came out on the short end of the game with Japan 6–3, after having defeated Japan six times in seven previous meetings.

After the Olympics, Mark decided to forgo his senior year at USC and enter the baseball draft on June 4, 1984. He was selected in the first round, by the Oakland Athletics, and received a $125,000 signing bonus. As soon as the draft was over, he proposed marriage to Kathy Hughes. They were married in December.

Mark was sent to Modesto in the Class A California League. It was wakeup time for the immature teenager, and it almost beat him. The A's had a decent team that year, finishing second to the Redwood Pioneers, with an 83–56 record. The young first baseman didn't contribute much however, as he batted a barely visible .200, with three homers and 11 RBIs in 75 at bats. The next year, back with Modesto, he got off to another horrible start. According to Rick Reilly, Mark was ready to give up. Kathy said Mark would often lie in bed in the middle of the night saying, "I can't hit the baseball anymore. I'm done. I've lost it. I've got to quit."

Mark didn't quit however, and he eventually regained his stroke. He finished the year with a respectable .274 batting average, with 24 dingers and 106 RBIs in just 489 at bats.

From there it was onwards and upwards. In 1986, the big slugger started the season with Huntsville in the AA Southern League, moved up to Tacoma in the AAA Pacific Coast League, and was called up by the Oakland Athletics at the end of the season. He hit .303 with ten homers and 53 RBIs in 195 at bats with Huntsville, and followed that up with a .318 average, 13 homers and another 53 RBIs, in 280 at bats with Tacoma.

Mark McGwire became a major leaguer on August 22, 1986. After going 0–6 in his first two games, Mark broke out with three base hits on the 24th. The first two hits, a single and a double, were off Tommy John, and Oakland beat the Yankees 11–4. The next day he clipped Detroit's Walt Terrell for his first major league home run, a 450-foot bomb over the center field wall. He finished the season with a batting average of just .189, but he impressed manager Tony LaRussa with his power, hitting three homers with nine RBIs in 53 at bats.

The 1987 season catapulted Mark McGwire into the national spotlight, but in some ways it was a year he would rather forget. On the field, it was a thrilling introduction to the big time. Off the field, it was a self-destructive descent into hedonism. His baseball career survived. His marriage didn't. Mark had an outstanding spring in Scottsdale, Arizona, but sputtered coming out of the starting gate. He was hitting only .136 after three weeks, with a single home run, but he clocked #2 on April 21 and took off from there.

After finishing April with just four home runs, the 215-pound slugger clocked 15 in May, one less than Mickey Mantle's major league record for the month. He followed that up with eight more in June and another six through the All-Star break on July 14. His 33 homers at the All-Star break were just four behind Reggie Jackson's record 37 set in 1969.

American League All-Star manager, John McNamara of Boston, selected the big first baseman as one of his reserves. The game was played in Oakland-Alameda County Stadium on the 14th, and McGwire played about half the game, going 0–3 against National League pitching. The Nationals won the game on a two-run triple by Tim Raines in the top of the thirteenth inning.

As the second half of the season got underway, the McGwire watch was focused on the rookie home run records. Al Rosen of the Cleveland Indians held the American League mark with 37 homers in 1950, while Wally Berger of the Boston Braves (1930) and Frank Robinson of the Cincinnati Reds (1956) were tied for the major league lead with 38.

Mark finished July with 37 home runs, then went ten days without another one. He finally smashed #38 against Mike Moore of Seattle on August 11, to break the American League record and tie the major league mark. Three days later, he became the major league's rookie home run champion, hitting #39 against curve ball artist Don Sutton of the California Angels.

The new celebrity status had Mark's head spinning, as newspapermen suddenly descended on his locker after every game to question him about his record breaking home run feats. All the attention overwhelmed the claustrophobic slugger, but he bravely confronted it head on. He also received good advice, from time to time, from Oakland coach Reggie Jackson, who had more than his share of media attention over the years.

Mark was less than successful in dealing with his off-field celebrity. He started accompanying his teammates out on the town after games, and was soon engulfed by adoring fans and by groupies of every age and description. The sheltered youngster from Claremont soon succumbed to the fame, fortune, and revelry. From that point on, Mark's marriage began to dissolve as Kathy could not compete with the excitement of the night club scene. Mark would later say that he and Kathy just got married too young, and that, if he knew then what he learned over the next ten years, the marriage would probably have lasted. In 1987, 23-year-old Mark McGwire was too immature to deal with it.

The Oakland bomber slowed down slightly after setting a new rookie home run record, hitting only two more homers over the last 17 days of August. He finished the month with 40 homers, a tremendous achievement for a raw rookie, and he was not done yet. On September 15, Mark hit two homers against the Texas Rangers, bringing his total to 45. He hit #46 at Kansas City on the 20th, then tied Reggie Jackson's Oakland mark with a dinger against the White Sox four days later. The next day he broke Jackson's record with #48 off Chicago's 6'3" closer, Bobby Thigpen. Number 49 left his bat on the 29th, leaving him just one homer short of the magic 50, with five games remaining on the schedule.

He looked like a cinch to become just the 18th player in major league history to hit 50 or more home runs in one season, but fate decided otherwise. Mark's wife Kathy was pregnant with their first child and was due any day. The two of them had discussed the matter in some detail and had decided that if the pennant didn't depend on it, Mark would leave the team to be with her when she went into labor. Mark received manager Tony LaRussa's permission to do just that.

Mark went homerless in the final two games against Cleveland, then accompanied the team to Chicago for the final three games against the White Sox. The big slugger failed to connect in the first two games of the series, and before the last game of the season was played, Kathy went into labor. Mark jumped the next plane west, and the potential 50-homer season went down the drain. But a bigger reward awaited Mark in Oakland when Kathy gave birth to a son. Matthew was a far greater thrill than 50 home runs.

Mark and Kathy tried to salvage their shaky marriage after the birth of Matthew, without success. They separated for a period of time, tried to get back together again during the 1988 season, then split for good just before the '88 World Series.

The Oakland Athletics had finished in third place in 1987, just four games behind the Minnesota Twins. The A's strengthened their club over the winter, picking up slugging outfielders Dave Henderson and Dave Parker, as well as 15-game winner Bob Welch. And they inserted rookie Walt Weiss at shortstop. They already had a great nucleus in pitchers Dave Stewart and Dennis Eckersley, and sluggers Jose Canseco and Carney Lansford.

The 1988 season opened on April 7, with Oakland hosting Seattle. Dave Stewart, the ace of manager Tony LaRussa's staff, handcuffed the Mariners for 8⅓ innings en route to a 4–1 victory. Canseco and Henderson sparked the attack with home runs. Mark McGwire hit his first of the season on the 7th as the A's crushed California 8–2. Jose Canseco hit his second.

Canseco had hit 31 homers in 1987 after banging 33 in his rookie season. He and McGwire had become known as the "Bash Brothers" in 1987 for their habit of bashing forearms with their teammates after hitting a home run. They "bashed" 80 times between them in '87 and would do it another 74 times in '88.

Mark McGwire hit his sixth home run of the year on April 27 as Oakland topped the Toronto Blue Jays, 5–3. Dave Henderson chipped in with his third round tripper. Canseco hit his eighth home run on the 30th to finish the month two ahead of McGwire. Oakland had run up a record of 16–7 through April 30, giving them a four-game bulge over the Chicago White Sox.

Dave Stewart dropped a 4–1 decision to the Baltimore Orioles on May 13, saddling him with his first loss of the season after eight wins. Mark McGwire hit a leadoff home run in the second inning in Baltimore on May 15 to give Tony LaRussa's boys a 1–0 lead. Weiss homered in the fifth and Canseco hit one out with a man on in the eighth as Oakland won 7–4. The A's were streaking, their 10–3 record in May good enough for a seven game lead. By the end of the month, after winning nine of the next 14 games, they had opened up a nine-game lead over the Minnesota Twins.

McGwire's big bat went silent in June as he put only two home runs on the board. Canseco struggled to keep the team afloat, but his eight dingers were not enough to protect their lead. It dwindled to five games over the Twins by month's end.

The attack continued to sputter through July 10 when, mercifully, the All-Star break gave LaRussa's boys time to relax and regroup. One of the few bright spots in early July occurred on the 3rd, when the A's outslugged the Blue Jays 9–8 in 16 innings. Mark McGwire belted his 14th homer of the season in the top of the 16th to win the game. But Jose Canseco was the star of the game with three homers and six runs batted in. The 240 pound Cuban left the yard in the first, sixth, and 12th innings.

By July 17, the Oakland lead was down to just three games as they dropped three of four to Toronto, with Luis Polonia hitting the only Oakland home run of the series. Dave Stewart, who was shut out 1–0 by Jimmy Key, was 4–8 after his sizzling 8–0 start.

The next day, the Oakland Athletics met the Cleveland Indians in Oakland. It was just the tonic the A's needed. They took three of four from Doc Edwards' team, with Canseco homering in game one and McGwire going yard in both games of a double-header. Big Mac's two-run shot in the bottom of the first inning of game one was

Mark McGwire and his Oakland teammate, Jose Canseco, were known as "The Bash Brothers" in the late 1980s. (Brace photo)

the game winner. In game two, his three-run dinger in the fifth brought his team back from a 6–4 deficit, the A's winning 9–6.

By the end of July, the Oakland lead was back up to 5½ games, and by August 14 it was a healthy 8½ games. From July 18 to August 14, the A's won 20 games against only seven losses while the Twins went 14–12. McGwire hit nine homers in 27 games, and Canseco chipped in with 7.

Oakland maintained their lead for the rest of the season, finishing with a record of 104–58, a full 13 games ahead of Minnesota. Jose Canseco was the big story of the year. He hit his 40th home run of the year on September 18. Then, on the 23rd, he stole two bases to become the first player in major league history to hit 40 home runs and steal 40 bases in the same year.

For the season, Canseco led the league with 42 homers and 124 RBIs, while hitting .307. His "Bash Brother" Mark McGwire batted .260 with

32 homers and 99 runs batted in. Dave Stewart won 21 games while Bob Welch won 17. Dennis Eckersley led the league in saves with 45.

The A's swept the Eastern Division champion Boston Red Sox in four games to advance to the World Series. Their opponents in the Series were the improbable Los Angeles Dodgers. Tommy Lasorda's team won the National League west with a .584 winning percentage. They beat the New York Mets in the Championship Series, four games to three, thanks to brilliant pitching by Orel Hershiser and key home runs by Mike Scioscia and Kirk Gibson.

Oakland was an overwhelming favorite to take the World Series against one of the weakest teams ever to play in the fall classic. But in 1988 L.A. was a team of destiny. Kirk Gibson's dramatic home run in the bottom of the ninth inning off Dennis Eckersley, giving the Dodgers a 5–4 victory in game one, set the tone for the Series. The Dodgers went on to win the World Championship in five games. The A's only bright spot came in game three when Mark McGwire picked out a Jay Howell fastball to his liking and deposited it into the left center field stands with two men out in the bottom of the ninth inning to win the game, 2–1. It was Mark's only hit of the Series as he went one for 17. His Bash Brother, Jose Canseco, was just as ineffective, going one for 19 with five RBIs. Jose's only hit was a grand slam homer in game one.

Mark McGwire's life was in the pits as the 1989 season got underway. His marriage was in a shambles, on its way to the divorce courts, and he was having trouble reconciling his new lifestyle with his personal values. His off-the-field problems carried over onto the field, and his career began to slip away before his eyes.

In 1989, the Oakland Athletics repeated as American League Western Division champions, crushed the Toronto Blue Jays in the A.L. Championship Series four games to one, and whipped the San Francisco Giants in the World Series, in a four-game sweep. But for McGwire it was a subpar year. Shortly after the season opened, McGwire pulled something in his back and went on the disabled list for two weeks. There were numerous distractions from the media and the fans hounding him for autographs, all of which carried over onto the field. His batting average dropped 29 points from 1988 to an embarrassing .231, although he still managed to hit 33 home runs with 95 runs batted in. One of his few pleasant moments during the year occurred on July 5 when he hit his 100th major league home run off Charlie Leibrandt of the Kansas City Royals. His 100 homers came in just 1,400 at bats, the second fastest time in major league history. Ralph Kiner hit 100 homers in 1,351 at bats back in 1948.

The next year was more of the same. The A's took the A.L. west by nine games with a record of 103–59. McGwire hit just .235 for the season but slammed 39 home runs and drove in 108 runs. He became the first player to hit 30 or more home runs in his first four seasons. He also won a Golden Glove Award in appreciation of his defensive play around first base. Unfortunately, Mark had another dismal postseason. He was two for 13 with no home runs in the Championship Series as the A's once again routed the Red Sox four games to none. In the World Series, he hit just .214 with no homers and no RBIs as the A's were stunned by the Cincinnati Reds four games to none.

In 1991, the Oakland A's collapsed, and so did Mark McGwire's world. Oakland dropped to fourth place, 11 games behind the pennant-winning Minnesota Twins, and the big first baseman hit rock bottom at the plate, nudging the ball at a barely visible .201 clip, with just 22 homers and 75 RBIs. McGwire's private life was in complete disarray, and he lost confidence in his ability to hit a baseball. He once remarked, "I must have gotten 100 suggestions, and I listened to 90 of them." He got off the mark slowly when the season opened, and by July 26 he was bottomed out at .187. He didn't hit it off with the A's new batting coach, Rick Burleson, either, which added to his confusion. Things got so bad that he asked manager Tony LaRussa to bench him for the last game of the season, in fear that his average would drop below .200.

Mark McGwire's collapse was more noticeable in his batting average than in his other statistics. From 1986 to 1988, Mark averaged 40 home runs a year, with 107 RBIs, while batting .271. In the three-year period from 1989 to 1991, he still hit 35 homers a year with 102 RBIs, but his batting average plummeted 48 points to .223.

When the season ended, McGwire cleaned out his locker and began the 380-mile drive back to his home near Los Angeles. He spent the five-hour drive analyzing his life, and where it had gone awry. He came to the conclusion that he needed outside help, both physically and mentally. He couldn't do it by himself. When he got back to Long Beach, he contacted a therapist, beginning a relationship that would continue through the decade. The therapy not only dealt with his personal life as a bachelor, but also touched on his relationship with the media and the fans. Mark's brother J.J., a physical trainer, moved in with him and began a program to build up Mark's body. The weight lifting, aerobics, and running, combined with a regimen of nutritional supplements, continued daily through the winter.

By the time spring training began in Scottsdale, Arizona, Mark McGwire was ready to resume his baseball career. He was more focused mentally and better able to deal with the off-field distractions. The Oakland A's bounced back also, capturing the Western Division by six games over Minnesota. The big first baseman, now with 20 pounds of additional muscle at 235, crashed 42 homers, drove in 104 runs, and batted a decent .268. His .385 on base percentage was the highest of his career, and his .585 slugging average was his second highest. He reached another milestone on June 10 when he hit his 200th major league home run off Chris Bosio of the Milwaukee Brewers.

Oakland couldn't maintain its momentum in the postseason, losing the Championship Series to the Toronto Blue Jays four games to two. Mark McGwire's two-run homer in the top of the second inning of game one, got the A's off running, and they won the game 4–3. But after that, it was all downhill. The Jays took the next three, on their way to becoming World Champions. Mark McGwire had a dismal series, finishing with a batting average of .150 on a three for 20 performance.

All in all, it was a good year for the man from Claremont. His mind was back on track, and his bat was as quick as ever. Unfortunately, his body was about to self destruct. The 1993, '94, and '95 seasons were three years Mark McGwire would rather forget. He was on the disabled list a total of six times, including the beginning of the '96 season, from March 31 to April 23. He had three surgeries over that period.

He suffered a severe heel injury on May 14, 1993, which was originally diagnosed as a bruised heel. It turned out to be much more serious—a partial tear of the fascia, the tissue that supports the arch. He was on the disabled list for almost four months, returning to action on September 3. He played only 27 games in 1993 and 47 games in 1994. In addition to the foot problems, he was also sidelined with another back injury in 1995.

When he was able to play, Mark McGwire was a terror at the plate. Although limited to a total of 317 games (out of a possible 583 games) from 1992 to 1995, he pounded the ball at a .273 pace, averaging 54 home runs and driving in 133 runners for every 550 at bats. In 1995, in just 317 at bats, the big slugger ripped 39 homers, an average of 68 homers for every 550 at bats. It was the best single-season average in major league history. Using his new J.J.-built muscular frame, his long-distance bombarding gave him an average distance of 418 feet for every home run. His .685 slugging average was his personal best, and his .441 on-base percentage was the second highest in Oakland history.

McGwire's injuries had some unexpected positive results. They made him a better hitter. He put the time on the bench to good use, studying the pitchers, talking to the coaches and scouts, and sitting behind the plate to analyze each pitcher's delivery. He stopped being a guess hitter and started to develop his mental faculties, concentrating on getting into a "zone" prior to going to the plate. The newly acquired mental aspect of his game was one of the primary reasons he was able to break Roger Maris' home run record in 1998.

Mark McGwire hit .333 in 27 games in 1993, .252 in 47 games in '94, and .274 in 104 games in '95, with 9, 9, and 39 homers respectively. In 1996, he played in 130 games and finally began to realize his full potential. Although the A's, who were now in decline, finished third in a four-team division under first-year manager, Art Howe, the rugged red head, now a Bunyonesque 250 pounds, put on one long-distance show after another for the fans around the league.

After coming off the disabled list on April 23, he started to drive the ball with authority.

Some of McGwire's home runs were titanic blasts, such as the one he hit in Toronto's Skydome in late July. It traveled an estimated 488 feet before landing in row seven of the fifth deck of the left field stands.

On September 14th, in just his 119th game of the year, Mark McGwire blasted a home run off Chad Ogea of the Cleveland Indians for his 50th home run of the year. No one in baseball history had ever before hit 50 home runs in less than 140 games. It was a satisfying year for the big first baseman. He played in 130 games and hit a career high .312 with 52 home runs and 113 RBIs.

The good times continued in 1997, although there were constant trade rumors as the Oakland management restructured the team to go with young players. They had brought Jose Canseco back to team up with the 34-year-old McGwire, in hopes that the "Bash Brothers" could lead a young team into the playoffs. Failing that, they intended to trade McGwire to a contender before the end of the season, since he was on the last year of a contract and would become a free agent after the season ended.

When spring training got underway, the veteran slugger was the center of media attention. There was speculation that Roger Maris' 37-year-old single-season home run record would fall by the wayside, based on the fact that home run production was up 30 percent in '96, over previous years' outputs. The most likely candidates to break the record were McGwire (52 homers in '96), Ken Griffey Jr.(49 homers in '96), Albert Belle (50 homers in '95), and Frank Thomas (40 homers in '96).

When asked about his chances to hit 61, McGwire said it was possible, but that it would take a perfect year with no injuries and no prolonged slumps. He also said it was foolish to speculate about it so early in the season. If he entered September with 50 home runs, then he would have a shot at the record.

When the season opened on April 2, McGwire was ready. He had a double and three RBIs in an opening day 9–7 loss to Cleveland, then smashed a double and a homer and drove in two more runs in a 5–4 win over the Indians. By the end of April, the 6'5" slugger had 11 home runs and 25 RBIs, and was hitting a lusty .322. The A's were in third place in their division, 2½ games behind Seattle, with a 13–13 record.

Mark McGwire banged out another nine homers in May, giving him 19 for the year, but the Athletics won only nine games against 21 losses to fall into the Western Division cellar, a full nine games behind the Seattle Mariners.

McGwire and Canseco tried to keep the team afloat, but it was a losing battle. By the end of June, Oakland had sunk 14 games out of first place after going 12–15 during the month. While Canseco was bogged down with 17 home runs and a .240 batting average, the kid from Claremont was hitting a respectable .279 with 63 runs batted in. His 29 home runs in 83 games still had him in contention for the home run title. Ken Griffey, Jr., and Tino Martinez of the New York Yankees also had 29 homers, making it a three-man race through June 30. No one in the National League was even close.

Mark had one memorable home run on June 24. In a game against the Seattle Mariners, facing fireballer Randy Johnson in the fifth inning, he hit a shot into deep left center field, that landed high up in the upper deck of the Kingdome. It was measured at 538 feet, one of the longest home runs ever measured. Johnson said later that McGwire hit it so far, he ought to get credit for two homers.

As the second half of the season got underway, with Oakland's hopes dashed for another year, the trade rumors regarding Mark McGwire heated up. Since the big first baseman had to approve a trade, and since he preferred playing in Southern California if possible, it was expected he would end up in either Los Angeles or Anaheim. But fate ruled otherwise. The Dodgers and Angels took themselves out of the running, while the St. Louis Cardinals moved to the front of the pack. Since McGwire would be a free agent at the end of the season, able to negotiate with all teams, he decided to approve a trade to St. Louis if it could be made. Cardinal general manager Walt Jocketty, realizing the risk he was taking, felt he could re-sign McGwire once Mark got to know and appreciate the St. Louis management, the team, the city and, most of all, the fans.

The trade was completed just before the trading deadline for post-season play, on July 31. Mark joined the Cardinals on August 1 in Philadelphia and drew the collar in three trips to the plate as St. Louis fell 4–1. By the time the Cardinals returned to Busch Stadium seven days later, McGwire was mired in a 2–25 slump with no home runs. In his first home game, however, before a welcoming committee of 38,300 screaming fans, the big red head slammed a one out homer off Mark Leiter of the Phillies in the bottom of the third inning. The Cards won 6–1, and McGwire was on his way to becoming a St. Louis legend.

Unfortunately, the trade may have inadvertently cost the handsome slugger a new home run record. His 35 home runs as of August 8 had him on a pace to hit 52 for the year. He had been on a record pace only three weeks earlier, but the distractions of the trade rumors, followed by the adjustment to the National League, took its toll. He went through a long drought, going homerless over his last 13 games in Oakland and his first seven games in St. Louis. From July 16 to August 8, he went 71 at bats without going yard.

After ten games in which the Cards went 2–8, Big Mac was hitting a paltry .088 with just one homer and one RBI. He gradually settled in over the rest of the season. He hit eight homers over the next 15 games and drove in 17 runs in the process. By the end of the month he had his average up to .211.

McGwire continued to punish the ball down the stretch although he couldn't pull the Cards out of the doldrums. On September 10, in San Francisco, he hit a 446-foot blast into the left field stands against southpaw Shawn Estes. It was his 50th home run of the year, making him the only player (other than Babe Ruth) to hit 50 or more home runs in two successive seasons. In the season finale against the Chicago Cubs, he homered in the bottom of the sixth, and the Cards went on to win 2–1. Still, it was just their 22nd victory with McGwire. They lost 33 times. Over his last 41 games, McGwire hit a tough .293, with 23 homers and 41 runs batted in. In all, his Cardinal totals were .253, 24, 42.

His overall record for 1997, with both Oakland and St. Louis, showed a .274 batting average with 58 home runs and 123 RBIs. The 1997 season showed that Mark McGwire had reached a new level in his baseball career. He was now a world class slugger, capable of competing with any of the mythical giants in baseball history, including the mighty Babe Ruth. His 58 home runs in '97 were the most home runs in a season since Roger Maris pounded out 61 in 1961. Since his injury-plagued seasons of '93–'94, when he was forced to sit on the bench and just observe, he had become a much more dangerous hitter. From 1987 through 1994, he batted .250 and averaged 39 home runs for every 550 times at bat. From 1995 through 1997, Big Mac ripped the ball at a .287 clip and averaged a mind-boggling 67 home runs a year!

On September 16, Jocketty announced that Mark McGwire had signed a $28.5 million contract to play for the St. Louis Cardinals through the year 2001, with an option for a fourth year.

10. The Great Home Run Race of 1998

The 1998 baseball season got underway with unbridled expectations on the part of the baseball community. Fans everywhere were holding their collective breaths, wondering, "Will this be the year Roger Maris' home run record will fall?" The media began speculating about that possibility as far back as 1996 when it was announced that two new teams would be admitted into the major leagues in '98. There were indications as early as 1994 that the single-season home run record was in jeopardy.

During that season, several players made a run at the record, only to be derailed by the heinous players' strike. When the season ended prematurely on August 11, Matt Williams of the San Francisco Giants was on track to tie Maris with 61 homers. Ken Griffey, Jr., would have hit 58, with Frank Thomas at 54, and Albert Belle at 52. Overall major league home run production in 1994 was up more than 23 percent over the previous 30-year average.

In 1995, Albert Belle hit 50 homers in another strike-shortened season of 144 games. The next year, Brady Anderson of the Baltimore Orioles hit 50 homers and Mark McGwire banged out 52. In 1997, it was more of the same. Mark McGwire, the new "Monster of the Midway," crushed 58 homers while Ken Griffey, Jr., hit 56. Albert Belle chipped in with 48.

The overall home run output stayed at the new higher level established in 1994. The average home runs per team from 1994 through 1997, calculated on a base point 154-game schedule, was 162. The average home runs per team from 1967 through 1993 was 120.

It seemed to be just a matter of time before the record would fall. There were many reasons given for the increased home run production, including:

• In 1994, major league baseballs began to be manufactured in Costa Rica. They had been manufactured in Haiti since 1980. The new "Costa Rican" balls seemed to be livelier.

• In 1993, the major leagues expanded from 26 to 28 teams, with the addition of the Florida Marlins and the Colorado Rockies. In 1998, the Tampa Bay Devil Rays and the Arizona Diamondbacks joined the majors.

Every time a new team is added to a league, it dilutes the quality of the pitching by about 7 percent. In 1998, there were approximately two dozen pitchers in the major leagues who would have pitched in the minors under the 1992 alignment.

• The players of the 1990s were bigger, stronger, and better conditioned. Weight training and dietary supplements added extra muscle to the modern-day sluggers.

As soon as spring training opened, writers and sportscasters descended on Florida and Arizona in record numbers, interviewing Griffey, Belle, Thomas, and McGwire, about the home run record. Sammy Sosa was not considered to be a threat to Maris' record at the time. When McGwire was asked if he thought the record would be broken, he repeated what he had said in 1997, it would take a perfect season to do it. He also reiterated that if he could get 50 homers by September 1, he would have a chance. One reporter asked him if he could hit 70, to which McGwire replied, "If I hit 70, I'll retire."

Mark McGwire was the odds-on favorite to break the record since he had hit over 50 homers in each of the two preceding seasons and had averaged 64 homers for every 550 at bats, over the last three years.

The 1998 season opened with a bang on March 31, with the Cards hosting the Los Angeles Dodgers, one of the pre-season favorites to win a division title. In the fifth inning of a scoreless game, Mark McGwire stepped to the plate with the bases loaded. He promptly sent a 1-0 changeup from Ramon Martinez into moon orbit. It finally came down and settled into the left field stands, 364 feet from home plate. The grand slam sparked the Cards to a 6-0 opening day victory.

The next day the Dodgers and Cardinals were locked in 5–5 game in the 12th inning when Mighty Mac stepped to the plate again, this time with two on and two out. He crushed a Frank Lankford serve 368 feet into the left center field stands for the game-winning homer.

When McGwire also homered in games three and four, the newspaper headlines said, "McGwire on a pace to hit 162 home runs." His four home runs tied Willie May's record of homering in the first four games of the season.

Ken Griffey, Jr., kept pace with McGwire on March 31 by homering off Charles Nagy of the Cleveland Indians in the fifth inning, but the Indians prevailed 10–9. The smooth-swinging left hander homered again on April 3rd and April 4th, giving him three homers for the year, one behind McGwire. Sammy Sosa hit his first 1998 home run on April 4, a game-winning homer as Chicago beat Montreal 3–1.

The McGwire blitzkrieg continued unabated through the month of April. Number four was a monstrous 430-foot shot off Don Wengert of San Diego; #5 a 424-foot sizzler to left field off Jeff Suppan of the Arizona Diamondbacks, #6 a mini-homer, 347 feet off Suppan again, #7 a titanic 462-foot blast off Barry Manuel of the Diamondbacks, his third homer of the game, #8 a 410-foot drive to left off Matt Whiteside of the Phillies, #9 a long 440-foot homer off Trey Moore of the Expos in Exposition Park, #10 a 410-foot dinger off Jerry Spradlin of Philadelphia, and #11 a 380-foot chip shot into the left center field stands at Wrigley Field. McGwire finished the month with 11 homers and 36 RBIs in 27 games.

Sammy Sosa hit just six home runs in April, but Griffey was on fire, matching the St. Louis bomber homer for homer. He hit three bombs against the Boston Red Sox, two against Cleveland, one each against Minnesota and Kansas City, and one against Mike Stanton of the Yankees, on April 29. When he stroked two out of the park against David Wells in Yankee Stadium on April 30, it gave him 11 for the year. The Maris watchers were ecstatic, since Roger hit only one in April. McGwire and Griffey were a full 30 days ahead of the Yankee record holder and 23 days ahead of Babe Ruth.

Mark McGwire put on a pyrotechnics display in May that left his closest competitor far in arrears. On May 1, in Chicago, the St. Louis slugger took Rod Beck downtown in the ninth inning with a man on base. The 362-foot homer

Mark McGwire blossomed into the world's deadliest slugger when he joined the St. Louis Cardinals in 1997.

to left center field brought the Cards to within one run of the Cubs, but Beck settled down to retire Gaetti and preserve a 6–5 victory.

Seven days later, McGwire reached another milestone when he crushed his 400th career homer off Rick Reed of the New York Mets. The 358 foot dinger came in McGwire's 4,726 at bat, 128 fewer at bats than it took Babe Ruth to reach the magic plateau. He is just the 26th player in baseball history to hit 400 homers. No other active player has reached that mark.

McGwire's theatrics through the first 34 games brought increased media pressure. His 13 homers put him nine games ahead of Ruth and 13 games ahead of Maris. The baseball world eagerly awaited each day's TV sports news or daily newspaper to see if their hero had hit another one. Writers, reporters, and cameramen, by the dozen, began to descend on the Cardinals' locker room before and after every game to obtain a story for the next edition or TV spot. For McGwire, a naturally shy, claustrophobic individual, the interviews affected him emotionally. They would continue to irritate him until Sammy Sosa came to his rescue and showed him how to enjoy the attention.

The off-field difficulties, fortunately, did not carry over onto the field. Mark McGwire was loose and relaxed once the game started.

On May 12, Big Mac hit a towering blast, 527 feet into the upper deck in left center field, a Busch Stadium record. It came in the fifth inning off Paul Wagner of Milwaukee, and gave the Cards a 4–3 lead in a game they eventually won 6–5 in ten innings. Two days later, he hit #15 against Atlanta, and on the 16th he reached the pinnacle. Batting against Livan Hernandez of the Florida Marlins at home, he guessed right on a pitch and crushed it. The ball traveled on a high arc to straightaway center field, finally coming to rest just below the luxury boxes, 550 feet from home plate. As McGwire said later, "I don't think I can hit a ball any better than that."

At the park, Mark McGwire, somewhat of a "neatnik" at home, had a definite routine he went through every day. He arrived at the clubhouse at the same time, visited the trainer's room, did loosening up exercises, put his clothes on in the same order, and socialized with his teammates. On the field he signed autographs (mostly for children) and took batting practice. It never varied from day to day. When the game started, he had other routines he followed, on deck and at the plate—adjustments to his glove, putting rosin on his bat, stretching, digging in at the plate, and staring into space as he attempted to reach "the zone."

McGwire's punishment of opposing pitchers continued through the month. Eleven more home runs left his bat over the next two weeks, including several tape measure jobs. Two days after he punished Livan Hernandez, the right-handed bomber hit a 478-foot shot off Hernandez' teammate, Jesus Sanchez. He went on to hit nine homers in the next eight days. On the 19th, he hit three titanic homers, totaling 1,362 feet, against the Philadelphia Phillies. The first one was a 440-foot jolt against Tyler Green, the second a mighty blast of 471 feet against Green again, and the third a 451-foot zinger against Wayne Gomes. His third homer, in the eighth inning with a man on, proved to be the game winner for the Cards, 10–8.

McGwire hit a 425-foot bomb against Mark Gardner of the Giants on the 22nd and followed that with a two-homer game the next day. Homer #1 was a 366-foot chip shot off Rich Rodriguez, while #2 was a towering drive of 477 feet into the upper deck in left center field at Busch Stadium. As in his three-homer game four days earlier, the Cards needed both of McGwire's homers to win. His second of the game, with two men on base in the fifth inning, was the eventual game winner, 11–10.

When the sun set on May 23rd, Mark McGwire's 23 homers in 47 games put him on a course to hit 79 home runs for the season. He was 13 games ahead of Ruth and 14 games ahead of Maris. He had opened up a big lead on the other challengers. Ken Griffey, Jr., was stuck at 17 homers, having hit just six in May and three in the last 12 games. Surprisingly, Griffey's teammate, shortstop Alex Rodriguez, was McGwire's closest competitor with 18 home runs. The 22-year-old potential superstar had clocked nine homers in each of the first two months. Albert Belle, the White Sox anti-social left fielder, had nine homers, and Frank Thomas had seven. Sammy Sosa, also with nine homers, was lurking in the back of the pack but was ready to explode.

When the month ended, the tally sheet showed McGwire with 27 home runs, Rodriguez with 20, Griffey with 19, and Sosa with 13.

As June got underway, Sosa trailed Big Mac by 14 home runs, but things were about to get interesting. The happy-go-lucky Dominican bruiser tattooed 17 different pitchers for home runs in June to break the record of 15 home runs in June, held jointly by Babe Ruth, Bob Johnson, and Roger Maris, and to break the record of 18 home runs in a single month, set by Rudy York in August 1937.

Sosa started right in on June 1st with a two-homer game against the Florida Marlins. His first homer was a 430-foot blast against Ryan Dempster, the second a 410 footer against Oscar Henriquez, both to left center field. The Cubs won the game easily, 10–2. The 6', 200-pound slugger homered again on the 3rd, the 5th, the 6th, the 7th, and the 8th, bringing his total to 20 in 62 games, not world class stuff, but getting closer.

After hitting his 21st homer in a 10–8 Cubs win over the Phillies on the 13th, Sammy went on another homer spree two days later. In a 6–5 Chicago victory over Milwaukee, he went yard three times, all against the Brewers' Cal Eldred. A crowd of 37,903 screaming Sosa fanatics cheered as he put the first ball into the right field stands, then chipped the next two to the legion of fans waiting on Waveland Avenue. Sammy himself celebrated each homer with his own special routine. First, after the ball left the bat, he hopped sideways toward first base, then skipped before he started his home run trot. After crossing the plate, he touched his lips with two fingers, then

Sammy Sosa finally realized his "superstar" potential in 1998. (Brace photo)

his chest, then threw a kiss skyward as he mouthed the words, "I love you momma." Another kiss was sent to mothers in Chicago as well as the Dominican Republic. And he finished with a "V" for victory sign to his guardian angel, Harry Caray, who died on February 18. Caray had been a beloved figure in Chicago, as well as the Cubs' play-by-play broadcaster for 16 years. His famous oversized glasses and his raspy seventh-inning stretch rendition of "Take Me Out to the Ballgame" are Cubs legends.

Sammy Sosa trailed Mark McGwire by only seven home runs after his demolition of Eldred. The Cardinal first baseman took Jose Lima of Houston downtown on the 17th, but Sosa kept pace with a shot off Milwaukee's Bronswell Patrick. Another multi-homer game against Philadelphia, his fifth of the season, brought his home run total to 27. The next night the amazing 29-year-old slugger ripped two more homers against the Phils, with 39,761 Cubs fans looking on. The first one was a pitching wedge of 366 feet that barely carried into the left field seats. The second homer, off side-wheeling Toby Borland, came in the sixth inning with two men on base and gave the Cubs a 9–4 victory. It was the longest homer of Sosa's career, a 500-foot rocket that disappeared over the left field wall, sailed over Waveland Avenue, and landed on the roof of a three-story apartment building, scattering 60 guests who were attending a party. It was Sammy's 16th homer of the month, which broke the record for home runs in June—and there were still ten days left in the month.

The 6' strong man hit #30 against Tyler Green of the Phils on June 21, pulling him within three homers of Mark McGwire. Now the race was on in earnest. And as he would do several times over the next three months, Mr. McGwire would answer the challenge. First, he punished Jared Wright of the Cleveland Indians with #34, a 433-foot blazer in Jacobs Field. He followed that up with a gigantic shot of 461 feet. The ball would have left the park completely if it hadn't hit a beam attached to the scoreboard. McGwire's 35th was followed by Sosa's 32nd, hit against the Tigers' Brian Moehler. It was Sammy's 12th homer in 13 games.

The Cardinal slugger hit #36 on the 27th and #37 on the 30th to close out the month of June with ten homers for the month, and a total of 37 for the year. Sosa's last blast on the 30th was his 20th of the month and his 33rd of the year. It established a new record for the most homers in a month, breaking the old record by two. Ken Griffey, Jr., was still in the race with 33 home runs of his own after a big month in which he hit 14 homers. Alex Rodriguez had dropped out of contention after hitting for just seven homers in June. Albert Belle with 17 homers, and Frank Thomas with 14, were never factors in the race.

The media circus finally caught up with Mark McGwire in June. After months of literally living in a goldfish bowl, constantly surrounded by cameramen, reporters, writers, and fans of every size and description, he put his foot down, saying he felt as if he was in a cage. The before-and-after game interviews became a thing of the past. For the rest of the season, on the road, the St. Louis slugger would hold a pre-game interview before the first game of the series. No other interviews would be scheduled. At home he would hold a post-game interview, discussing only the day's game. Other interviews would have to be scheduled in advance.

In the pennant races, the Chicago Cubs were hanging tough in the Central Division race. Their 43–39 record had them in third place, just one game behind Milwaukee for the wild card berth. They were seven games behind the front-running Houston Astros. The Cardinals, on the other hand, were 10½ games out of first and 4½ games out of second, despite McGwire's heroics.

With the home run race turning into a three-man contest, the media vultures began to circle the Chicago clubhouse, looking for the Cubs' gift to major league baseball. They began to corral Sosa before and after every game, similar to the treatment being given McGwire. Unlike the St. Louis strongman however, Sosa never saw a camera he didn't like. He reveled in the media attention and, over the course of the summer, developed a routine that fascinated and entertained the viewing public. His one-liners even captivated the writers. His favorite expressions included, "To tell you the truth," "I'm not gonna lie to you," "Believe me when I tell you," "I love this country," and "You don't wanna know, buddy."

Sammy Sosa, had a few superstitions, that the media began to focus on. Before every game, Sammy carried a cup of coffee into the dugout, then proceeded to bless the area around the bat rack, in three equal pours. Several times during a game, the trainer brought Sammy a cup of water, which Sammy splashed on his face to cool down. When he walked up to the plate, he crossed himself, then gently tapped the catcher on the back of the leg with his bat as a sign of respect.

During the summer of 1998, Sammy Sosa and Mark McGwire brought class and dignity back to major league baseball. After years of watching egocentric ballplayers behaving like clowns after hitting a home run, it was refreshing to see two players act professionally on a baseball field, doing what they were being paid to do, without creating a circus atmosphere.

July was a slow month for all the sluggers as they appeared to be getting their second wind for the stretch run. The All-Star break on July 7 gave them a chance to relax for a few days. Ken Griffey, Jr., was the only challenger to hit any home runs prior to the break. He slugged #34 off Mike Saipe of the Colorado Rockies on the first of the month, then punished Darryl Kile of the same team the next day to close within two of McGwire.

When action resumed on July 9, Griffey went downtown again, this time against Pep Harris of Anaheim. The same day, Sammy Sosa lugged his big black bat to the plate against Jeff Juden of the Milwaukee Brewers and promptly sent a 432-foot dinger into orbit at County Stadium for #34. The Chicago bomber hit another one the next day, a 450-foot laser off Scott Karl of Milwaukee. Big Mac didn't hit his first home run of the month until the 11th when he connected for #38 off Billy Wagner of Houston. He added seven more by the end of July to give him 45 for the year. Home run #41 was a monstrous blast of 511 feet into Busch Stadium's upper deck against Brian Bohanon of the Dodgers on July 17. He homered off Antonio Osuna in the same game, a 425-foot shot to left field. At month's end, Big Mac's 45 home runs put him 12 games ahead of Roger Maris and 27 games ahead of Babe Ruth. Sosa trailed with 42 homers and Griffey with 41.

In the pennant races, the Chicago Cubs held down the second spot in the Central Division with a 61–48 record after a torrid 18–9 run in July. They were just 3½ games behind the Astros. McGwire's Cards were rapidly fading from contention in fourth place 13½ games out of first.

The baseball world was buzzing with anticipation as August got underway. McGwire needed just 17 homers in his last 57 games to break Maris' record. His home run frequency was 69 through July. He only needed to average 48 the rest of the way to break the record. Most fans thought it was a lock.

Mark McGwire's life was no longer his own, either on the field or off. He was rapidly becoming a legend in his own time because of his outlandish destruction of official National League baseballs. Batting practice was a spectacle in itself. Fans pushed their way into the ballpark two hours before game time just to see the 6'5" behemoth tee off against batting practice pitcher, Dave McKay, who estimated he had thrown the big redhead about 8,000 B.P. home runs. When the Cardinals arrived in Chicago for a three-game series with the Cubs beginning on August 7, hundreds of fans congregated on Waveland Avenue behind the left field fence in hopes of catching a Mark McGwire blast. And it wasn't just the fans who were mesmerized by the exhibition. Players from both teams stationed themselves around the batting cage to watch in awe as one ball after another sailed out of the park. The batting practice show actually went back to spring training in Jupiter, Florida, where crowds of people stood transfixed behind the batting cage in Roger Dean Stadium, watching one moon-shot after another disappear over the left field fence and explode against the building behind it.

One of the turning points of the season took place on August 18 in Chicago when the Cubs hosted the Cardinals. Mark McGwire had hit only two homers during the first 17 days of the month and was bogged down at 47 homers. Sammy Sosa was on a roll. When he homered off the Astros' Sean Bergman on the 16th, a 360-foot shot to right field, it was his 47th of the year, putting him in a tie with Big Mac.

As the happy-go-lucky Dominican bomber stepped onto the field before the game, he spied McGwire stretching in front of the dugout. He walked over, grabbed Mark's hand, pulled him up, and gave him a giant bear hug. It was his way of letting the Cardinal slugger know that the home run chase and all the media attention was an experience to be enjoyed, not a chore to be dreaded. Whether that meeting changed Mark McGwire's attitude is not known. What is known is that Big Mac seemed to loosen up after the meeting with Sosa and appeared to enjoy the rest of the season. He captivated the fans with his calm demeanor and his class down the stretch.

Chicago took the opener of the series 4–1, with both sluggers taking the collar. The next night, before a wild Wrigley Field gathering of 39,689, Sosa was the first to act. He hit into the left field stands with a man on in the fifth inning to give the Cubs a 6–2 lead. It was his 48th dinger of the season and gave him the home run lead—a lead that lasted less than one hour. Mark McGwire's 48th, a 430-foot shot onto Waveland Avenue in the top of the eighth, tied the game at 6–6, and his 49th in the tenth won it for Tony La Russa's club, 10–8. The rest of the season would be nip and tuck as the two adversaries jockeyed for position. Twice over the final six weeks, Sammy Sosa would grab the lead, only to see McGwire regain it within an hour. Three times they would be tied for the lead in the most exciting home run race in baseball history.

The Chicago management, after watching the media circus in the Cubs locker room with 50 reporters hounding Sosa at his locker while the rest of the team was trying to relax, decided the interviews were a disruption to the team at a time when they were fighting for a playoff spot. They subsequently moved the interviews to an old storage room down the hall. Sosa, seated behind a table, answered questions from the floor for about 20 minutes after every game.

The charismatic Chicago right fielder captivated the fans with his boyish demeanor. When asked whether he expected to finish ahead of McGwire in the home run race, he replied, "Mark's the Man. I'm just a little boy." When he was asked how he was handling the pressure, he said, "What pressure? Pressure is shining shoes when you're seven years old, trying to earn enough money to put food on the table."

On August 22, tabloid journalism reared its ugly head right on schedule, clouding the home run chase. Steve Wilstein, an Associated Press reporter, wrote an article stating that McGwire was taking androstenedione, a testosterone-producing substance that is banned by the NFL, NCAA, and the Olympics but is legal in the major leagues. Dozens of big league players, in addition to Mark McGwire, take andro and similar supplements as a regular part of their conditioning regimen.

The furor over McGwire's taking a legal substance seemed to be a continuation of the media's "build 'em up, tear 'em down" philosophy of sensationalism, designed to sell more newspapers and magazines. As Mark said, the story resulted from someone "snooping in his locker."

According to McGwire, he started taking androstenedione less than two years ago. That being the case, two facts are indisputable. In 1996, "before andro," Mark McGwire averaged 418 feet for each of his 52 home runs. His 1998 average was 423 feet. Also, in 1995 and '96, again "before andro," McGwire averaged 68 home runs for every 550 at bats. His '97–'98 average was 67 home runs.

Obviously, Big Mac didn't need andro to break the record.

Sammy Sosa injected a little humor into the controversy, noting that he took Flintstone chewable vitamins on a routine basis. He said Barney and Fred gave him all the energy he needed.

The home run race went on in spite of the media's attempts to disrupt it. McGwire had hit homers 50 and 51 on August 20 against the Mets in New York before the androstenedione exposé. He hit another on the 22nd, a 477-foot rocket to right field at Three Rivers Stadium off Francisco Cordova. It was one of only three home runs hit to right field by McGwire during the entire season. The big redhead hit three more homers between August 23 and the end of the month. Number 54 was a 509-foot shot to dead center field while #55 traveled 501 feet in the same direction.

Sammy Sosa kept pace. He homered on the 21st, then took two downtown on the 23rd, his 50th and 51st of the year. Both were hit off Jose Lima of the Houston Astros at Wrigley Field. The first one was a 440 footer onto Waveland Avenue in the fifth inning. The second one landed in the left field bleachers, 380 feet from home plate. Three days later, Sosa homered against the Reds into the upper deck in Cinergy Field. That was followed by #53 against John Thomson of the Colorado Rockies in Coors Field on the 28th.

The slugging spray hitter from the North Side crushed a 482 foot bomb off Darryl Kyle of the Rockies, high up in the left center field stands, on the 30th, and finished out the month with a 364-foot pitching wedge at Wrigley. It was Sosa's 55th home run of the season, once again tying him with Mark McGwire. When Sammy's mother Lucrecia was interviewed by A.P. sports writer, R.B. Fallstrom, about her son's home run achievements, she said, "What I know is that my son will get as many home runs as God wants, not one more or one less."

The month's totals revealed what everyone already knew. The Maris chase was now a two-man race. Ken Griffey, Jr., the remaining challenger, with only six homers in August, was bogged down at 47 with little chance of catching the leaders. The individual stats showed Sammy Sosa at 55 homers, 136 RBIs and a .313 batting average. He had his Cubs three games in front of the New York Mets for the wild card spot in the playoffs. The Cardinals were a distant 21½ games out of first and were just counting the days until they could go fishing. All except McGwire, that is. Big Mac was stinging the ball at a .293 clip with 55 homers and 119 runs batted in.

Sammy Sosa continued to light up the post-game interviews with lines like, "Every day is a holiday for me. What a country" and "I won't lie to you man. I love this country."

Mark McGwire took off like a man trying to catch a train, in September. He ripped two home runs on the first, no's 56 & 57. He tomahawked a fastball by Livan Hernandez of the Marlins in the seventh inning and sent it whistling into the center field stands in Pro Player Stadium, 450 feet from home plate. Two innings later, he hit a longer one, sending a Donn Pall serve in the same direction—only 22 feet farther. The Cards won going away, 7–1.

The next day, in the Friendly Confines of Wrigley Field, Sosa hit his 56th, a 370-foot shot to right center field. The crowds attending the games now, realizing they were on the verge of witnessing history, stood and cheered after each home run until Sosa came out of the dugout for a curtain call. Fans attending the Cardinal games did the same thing to McGwire.

In spite of his heroics, Sammy Sosa lost ground in the home run race. Big Mac crushed numbers 58 and 59 in a 14–4 rout of Florida. His first homer was a mammoth 497-foot clout off Brian Edmondson in the seventh inning, giving St. Louis a comfortable 9–0 lead. He finished his day's work in the eighth, smashing a 458-foot blast to left center field off Rob Stanifer.

When the games resumed on September fourth, the bombardment continued. Sosa hit his fifth homer in six games, a 387 footer in Three Rivers Stadium in the first inning, sparking the Cubs to a 5–2 victory. It was the Dominican dandy's 57th, breaking Hack Wilson's Chicago Cubs record of 56 home runs. It also gave the Cubs a three-game bulge over the New York Mets in the wild card race.

September 5, however, belonged to Mark McGwire. In the first inning, with a man on base, the 6'5" pull hitter jumped on a low fast ball from southpaw Dennis Reyes of Cincinnati and drove it into the left field seats, 381 feet from home plate. Busch Stadium exploded in a colorful fireworks display that brightened the evening sky, and an exuberant crowd of 47,994 shook the park to its rafters until the shy Californian came out of the dugout to acknowledge their cheers. Mark joined Babe Ruth and Roger Maris as the only players in the baseball history to hit 60 or more home runs in a single season. And Mark had hit 60 in just 142 games, putting him a stunning 12 games ahead of Ruth and 18 games ahead of Maris.

Mark McGwire drew the collar the next day, then dined with his parents in the evening. His father John was celebrating his 61st birthday the following day, and he said to Mark, "If I can do 61, so can you."

Monday, September 7, was Labor Day, and the festive holiday atmosphere carried over into the 32-year-old stadium along Spruce Street and

Stadium Plaza, where Tony La Russa's troops were hosting Jim Riggleman's Chicago Cubs. Mark McGwire's parents were in the stands. So were Roger Maris' children, Mark's former wife Kathy and her husband Tom Williamson, and Baseball Commissioner Bud Selig. Maris' wife Pat was unable to attend the game. She watched from her hotel room after being hospitalized with an irregular heartbeat. Mark's ten-year-old son was the Cardinal batboy, as he had been a number of times since May. Young Matt had seen his father hit several of his tape measure home runs during the season, including no.'s 50, 55, 56, and 57, and he got to keep #50. Now he was about to witness his father's most historic achievement.

McGwire and Sosa held a widely televised, pre-game press conference before 700 media members two hours before the game. It was a light-hearted session with both players thoroughly enjoying themselves. Sammy, as usual, was absolutely giddy, at one point exclaiming in a mock Spanish accent imitating a television comedian, "Baseball has been berry, berry good to me." When asked about the home run race, he replied smiling, "Mark is The Man in United States. I am The Man in Dominican Republic." He laughed. Mark McGwire applauded, then replied, "God bless America."

The game started on a more serious note, with the Cubs still battling for a playoff berth (they held a slim, one-game lead over the Mets as play started). When McGwire stepped to the plate in the first inning, the clock said 1:21 P.M. With a count of 1–1, the 6'5" slugger drilled a Mike Morgan fast ball 430 feet into the left field stands, for home run #61, tying him with Roger Maris for the most home runs in major league history. A sellout crowd of 50,530 red-shirted Cardinal fans leaped to their feet, screaming and hollering. Big Mac received high fives from Chicago first baseman Mark Grace and third baseman and former teammate Gary Gaetti. Sammy Sosa in right field thrilled for his buddy, pumped his fist in the air, then clapped quietly into his glove. Heading home, the big redhead pointed to the sky in tribute to Roger Maris. After he crossed home plate, he exchanged punches with Ray Lankford, then grabbed his son in a big bear hug and lifted him high in the air, in celebration. He also pointed to his father in the stands, mouthing the words "Happy birthday, Dad," then saluted the Maris family in the stands, tapping his heart, pointing his finger to the sky and blowing the Maris clan a kiss. It was a tender moment at the climax of a most amazing quest. Later in the game, Sammy Sosa, after reaching first base on a single, gave Mark a hug, and said, "Congratulations. But don't get too far ahead. Wait for me."

The Cardinals won the game 3–2, temporarily stalling the Cubs' playoff chase.

If Monday was exciting, Tuesday was absolutely crazy. Busch Stadium welcomed 43,688 Cardinal and Cubs fans to continue the McGwire-Sosa watch. The score stood, Mark 61—Sammy 58, with much more excitement to come. Before the game, McGwire rubbed Roger Maris' 61st home run bat for good luck. When the game started, the Cubs pushed across two runs in the top of the first. Mark grounded out meekly on a 3–0 pitch in the bottom of the inning, as St. Louis put nothing but goose-eggs on the scoreboard through the first three innings. In the fourth, McGwire sat in the dugout caressing his bat, his eyes closed in meditation as he tried to visualize his next at bat. It was the same ritual he had practiced all year, to put himself mentally "in a zone." With two men out and the bases empty, the St. Louis strongman stepped to the plate to face Steve Trachsel, Chicago's 14-game winner. He lashed out at Trachsel's first pitch and hit a low line drive down the left field line. As 44,000 pairs of eyes stared in wonder, the ball barely cleared the left field wall at the 341 foot mark. It was McGwire's shortest home run of the year but his most important. It was #62, setting him apart from every other baseball player who ever played the game. And he accomplished it in 145 games, eliminating the need for an asterisk of any kind. He was now in uncharted territory, and he still had 17 games left to add to his total.

Mark McGwire was in a daze as he began his home run trot. He missed first base and had to be sent back to touch it by first base coach Dave McKay. He got high fives from all the Chicago infielders, plus a big hug from catcher Scott Servais. His teammates mobbed him at home plate as the entire ballpark went ballistic. He gave his favorite batboy another sky high bear hug, then climbed into the stands to hug all the Maris children—Susan Ann, Roger Jr., Kevin, Randy, Richard, and Sandra. Pat Maris missed the historic event, as she was back in the hospital with a case of nerves. After about 11 minutes, Mark McGwire addressed the fans over the PA system, thanking everyone from the Maris family, to the Cubs, his family, and the Cardinals.

Sammy rushed in to give McGwire a big hug. Big Mac picked the 200-pound outfielder off the ground as if he were a little kid and squeezed him tightly. Sosa pounded McGwire on the back and ruffled his hair. After the hug they high-fived each other and exchanged McGwire's famous solar plexus punch.

McGwire's homer cut the Cubs lead to 2–1. The Redbirds put a big five-spot on the board in the sixth, three runs coming on Ray Lankford's 27th homer of the year. They went on to defeat Chicago again, 6–3, dropping the Cubs into a tie with New York and San Francisco for the National League wild card berth.

Once all the furor over the historic event had settled down, the season continued. Mark McGwire relaxed after his unique achievement. Over the next five games, he went 1–14 with six strikeouts. In the meantime, Sammy Sosa was making hay, banging out home run number 59 on the 11th (a 464 footer), and number 60 on the 12th (a 430 footer), against the Milwaukee Brewers. On September 13, the Brewers closed out their season series with the Cubs, in Wrigley Field. The first two games were both slugfests, the Brewers winning 13–11 on Friday and the Cubs taking the Saturday game 15–12. Between them, they had pounded out 68 hits, including 13 home runs. Sunday was no different. Eight more balls left the Friendly Confines before the sun went down. The Brewers drew first blood with single runs in the first and the third for a 2–0 lead. Jim Riggleman's bombers drove Milwaukee starter Brad Woodall to cover under a six-run barrage in the third. A Sammy Sosa home run, a mighty 480-foot blast onto Waveland Avenue, with a man on, brought the score to 8–3, but the Brew Crew was not ready to call it a day. They scored seven runs over the next four innings to take a 10 8 lead into the bottom of the ninth. With one out, Sosa stepped to the plate to face righthander Eric Plunk. The 220-pound fireballer tried to blow a fastball past the Cub slugger, but Sosa was ready for it, and he crushed it, sending it on a high arc toward left field. It landed on Waveland Avenue, 480 feet from home plate, near the spot the first ball landed.

It was #62 and put Sammy Sosa in the history books, alongside Mark McGwire, as the only two players in baseball history to hit as many as 62 home runs in one season. It was a dramatic moment for the former shoeshine boy from the Dominican Republic as the ecstatic Chicago fans called him out of the dugout for three curtain calls. He said later, according to AP, "I have to say what I did was for the people of Chicago, for America, for my mother, for my wife, my kids, and the people I have around me. My team.... I don't usually cry, but I cry inside. I was blowing kisses to my mother. I was crying a little bit." When Mark McGwire heard the news, he said, "It's awesome, outstanding."

Sammy's fans back home got to see the historic home runs on TV, as Television Dominicana began broadcasting the Cubs games on September 10th. When number 62 left the yard, the entire island nation exploded in celebration. Parties were underway in Santo Domingo. In San Pedro de Macoris, it seemed as if the whole town spilled out into the streets to dance and party. Kids raced through the street screaming "sesenta y dos" (62). The 30-30 Plaza was sheer bedlam. The crowd watching the game on TV outside the Juancito Sports Shop toasted their hero again and again. When one man was asked how popular Sammy Sosa was in the Dominican Republic, he said, "I think he's leading the Pope right now."

Chicago eventually tied the game in the bottom of the ninth, then won it in the tenth on a Mark Grace home run. The final score was 11–10.

Two days later McGwire recaptured the lead with a 385-foot dinger to left field off Pittsburgh's Jason Christiansen at Three Rivers Stadium. Sosa tied it again in a 6–3 Cubbies victory when he took the Padres' Brian Boehringer down town, in San Diego's Qualcomm Stadium. Mark McGwire answered. He hit number 64 on the 18th and number 65 on the 20th, giving him a two-homer lead over his Chicago adversary, with just five games left in the season.

On the same day in Wrigley Field, 40,117 Chicago fans honored their hero with Sammy Sosa Day. The invited guests included Sammy's family, his business advisor and surrogate father, Bill Chase, Baseball Commissioner Bud Selig, Dominican Republic President Leonel Fernandez, Hall-of-Fame pitcher Juan Marichal, and Chicago General Manager Ed Lynch. Sosa received numerous gifts including a Plymouth Prowler and a painting of himself. After the speeches were completed, Sammy made a tour of the big park, paying special attention to his "bleacher bums" in right field.

Sammy and Sonia Sosa entertained over a dozen guests in their luxury apartment in downtown Chicago overlooking Lake Michigan during the last week of the season. The gathering on the 55th floor above exclusive Lakeshore Drive included Sammy's mother, his four brothers, two sisters, two step-brothers, and an aunt.

While McGwire was putting another ball in orbit, and Sosa was being feted in Chicago, baseball history of another kind was made in Baltimore, Maryland. Cal Ripken, Jr., benched himself, ending a consecutive-games-played streak of 2,632, 502 more than Lou Gehrig. The streak began on May 30, 1982, and lasted more than 16 years. Ryan Minor, who was eight years old when the streak began, when told he would start in place of Ripken at third base, asked, "Does he know?" As soon as the Orioles took the field without Cal Ripken, the New York Yankee players came to the top of the dugout steps to applaud a record that might last forever. Certainly it will last at least another 14 years because Albert Belle has the next longest active streak at 327 games. Ripken came out of the dugout, waved to the crowd, took a bow, then retreated back into the darkness.

Cincinnati swept the three-game weekend series against the Cubs, including the Sunday Sammy Sosa Day game, putting a damper on the day's festivities. The Dominican slugger went 0–13 over the weekend and would see his slump reach 0–21 before he broke out of it. But, like the gentleman he is, he graciously attended every press conference and answered every embarrassing question thrown at him by the aggressive media representatives. All he could say regarding his streak was, "When this happens to me, I know I'm doing something wrong. I just try to relax when I hit. I've got to keep swinging."

On September 23, Sammy Sosa broke out of his slump and closed the gap again, tying Mark McGwire at 65 home runs apiece. Playing in Milwaukee, the 200-pound spray hitter cracked a fifth-inning homer off Rafael Roque, a 344-foot shot down the right field line in County Stadium. In the next inning, he crushed a 410-foot rocket into the center field stands, giving the Cubs a commanding 7–0 lead at that point. Sosa's 65th was his 11th multi-homer game of the season, breaking Hank Greenberg's mark of ten, set in 1938.

On Friday, September 25th, the Chicago Cubs visited the Houston Astros in a night game. In the fourth inning, leading off against countryman Jose Lima, Sammy Sosa hit a titanic blast, 462 feet into the left field seats at the Astrodome. It was his 66th home run of the year, and it gave him the lead over Mark McGwire for just the second time during the season. The first lead, on August 19, lasted 58 minutes. This one disappeared in just 45 minutes as Mark McGwire, playing at home against the Montreal Expos, hit a 375-foot dinger off Shayne Bennett in the fifth inning, sparking the Cardinals to a 6–5 win. The Cubs were beaten 6–2, leaving them in a flat-footed tie with San Francisco and New York for the wild card spot.

In the most memorable home run chase in major league baseball history, the two combatants were deadlocked at an incomprehensible 66 home runs apiece, with just two games remaining in the season.

But, just as suddenly as the race began, it was over. The Chicago Cubs split their two-game set with the Houston Astros to finish the season tied with the San Francisco Giants. Sosa went 4–9 in the series, all singles. The Cubs met the Giants in a one-game playoff for the National League wild card berth in the Windy City on the Monday after the regular season ended. Chicago's finest took the measure of Dusty Baker's troops, 5–3. Sammy Sosa had two hits in four at bats, and scored two big runs. In the Division Series, the Atlanta Braves swept Jim Riggleman's crew three straight, ending Sammy Sosa's season.

Meanwhile, in St. Louis over the final weekend of the season, the redheaded bomber from California absolutely destroyed Montreal manager Felipe Alou's pitching staff. Counting his last two at bats on Friday, Mark McGwire smashed an unbelievable five home runs in his last 11 at bats. On Saturday, September 26, with 48,212 wild-eyed Cardinal fans looking on, he jumped on a first pitch fast ball from Dustin Hermanson

Mark McGwire set a new home run record when he smashed an unbelieveable 70 homers in 1998.

and sent it on a line into the left field seats. The 403-foot homer put McGwire in the driver's seat again, 67 to 66. Just two innings later, he crushed a 1–1 serve from Kirk Bullinger and put it into the center field stands, 435 feet from home plate.

On the final Sunday, Mark McGwire was at it again. He took a Mike Thurman fast ball downtown in his second at bat, in the third inning. The 377-foot chip shot into the left field seats, #69 of the year, came with the bases empty and gave St. Louis a 3–2 lead. In the seventh inning, with two men out and two men on base, in a tie game, the home run king hit a 370–foot line drive into the left field seats for home run #70. It was the game winner.

When interviewed after the game, Mark McGwire put it in perspective when he said, "It's unbelievable for anyone to hit 70 home runs. I'm in awe of myself."

Reflecting on the season, Sammy Sosa said, "I'm proud of myself because of where I came from—the guy I used to be—the guy I am now." As reported by Tim Keown in *ESPN Magazine*, Sammy also said, "That boy shining shoes is still who I am. That's why I'm so friendly and nice to people. I believe in God, and God says you have to be a nice person."

The season ended as explosively as it began. Beginning on March 31, Mark McGwire went seven for 16 in his first four games, with a double, four home runs, and 12 runs batted in. In his last 11 at bats of the season, over a 3½ game span, the 6'5" slugger went six for ten, with five home runs and nine RBIs. It was the kind of season that legends are made from.

The game of baseball desperately needed a hero after the 1994 debacle. Thanks to a poor kid from the Dominican Republic and a big red-head from California, it got two.

11. The Home Run
War Continues

The great home run race did not end with the final pitch of the 1998 season. It continued to rage throughout the following year, as Mark McGwire and Sammy Sosa once again matched round trippers, in another epic struggle for home run supremacy. And their homers had added significance, as the pre-season prognosticators picked Tony La Russa's Redbirds to battle Jim Riggleman's Chicago Cubs and Larry Dierker's Houston Astros for the National League Central Division crown. St. Louis had strengthened its team over the winter months with the acquisition of shortstop Edgar Renteria and second baseman Carlos Baerga, and the maturation of players like J.D. Drew, Placido Polanco, and Eli Marrero. The Cubs had an aging team, but one that had a core of talented players. Sosa would be protected by the likes of Glenallen Hill, Jose Hernandez, and Mark Grace, giving him many opportunities to put good wood on the ball.

The media, fresh off the 1998 pyrotechnics, immediately began to chart Mark McGwire's race for the all-time career home run record. His thunderous demolition of National League pitchers in '98 left him with a total of 457 home runs. At 35 years of age, the big redhead could eclipse Hammerin' Hank's mark by 2003, averaging a modest 50 homers a year. Fate, however, wasn't kind to the kid from Clairmont, California. He had just one more outstanding season in his war chest, blasting the ball at a .278 clip in '99, and leading the National League in both home runs and runs batted in, with 65 and 147 respectively.

Early in the season, the three pre-season favorites filled the top spots, with Houston on top followed by St. Louis and Chicago. By the end of April, the Astros held a ½ game lead over the Cards, with the Cubs two games out. In the home run race, Matt Williams of the Arizona

Diamondbacks had charged to the front of the pack with ten dingers in 26 games, Mark McGwire was way back in the pack with five, and Sammy Sosa trailed him by one.

As the weather began to warm, so too did Sosa's bat. The affable slugger from the Dominican Republic suddenly caught fire in May, sending 13 balls over the friendly wall of Wrigley Field, sparking his team to a 17–10 record for the month, and moving them into second place, one game behind Houston. The Cardinals, in spite of Big Mac's ten home runs, could do no better than 12–15, leaving them gasping for air in fifth place in the division, four games out of the top spot. And the situation deteriorated even more as the days passed. They slipped 7½ games behind in June, and finished July 11½ games out, in third place. By that time however, Riggleman's Windy City Boys had passed them going in the wrong direction, plummeting to the basement, with 14 games separating them from the front running Astros. The Cubs' demise can be traced to their pitching, which showed an embarrassing 5.38 earned-run-average, a full run worse than the league average. Kerry Wood went down for the season in early April with a bad elbow, Terry Mulholland was traded to Atlanta, along with his 5.15 ERA, Steve Trachsel was mired in a 3–14 morass, and the bullpen blew 18 games in 42 opportunities.

As far as the Cardinals and Cubs were concerned, any thoughts of a division title had disappeared by early August. Now all attention shifted to the home run race. Sammy Sosa moved to the front of the pack, by hitting 13 home runs in June and ten in July, giving him 40 home runs in 101 games, a pace that would bring him to 64 homers for the year. Still, he could not shake the big Cardinal first baseman, who lurked close behind, with 39 homers for the year. Still, he could not shake the big Cardinal first baseman, who lurked close behind, with 39 homers. Following the All-Star game, the 250 pound behemoth went on a tear, smashing 16 homers in 20 games, including six in seven games leading up to his historic 500th. On Thursday, August 5, in St. Louis, Mark McGwire passed that milestone when he sent two balls into the evening sky, giving him 501 for his career.

Some of the most exciting games remaining on the baseball schedule were those that pitted St. Louis against Chicago. The first series took place in Busch Stadium the weekend of August 13. In the opener, on Friday, the Redbirds romped to an easy 7–1 victory, with McGwire pounding out numbers 45 and 46, and driving in five of the runs. Sosa drew the collar in two trips to the plate. The next day, the St. Louis slugger propelled #47 over the vines with two on, but Sammy matched it with a three run shot of his own in the eighth inning, giving the Cubs a hard fought

9–7 victory. This was drama at its best, with two gargantuan gladiators standing face to face and battling it out. The series ended on Sunday with the Cards eking out another close victory, this one by a 6–5 count. McGwire contributed a run-scoring double to the Redbird attack, while Sosa knocked in four of the Cubs five runs, with two home runs and nine runs batted in, while Sosa had four hits in eleven at-bats, with three homers and seven RBIs. It was a show well worth the cost of a ticket.

St. Louis finished the month of August with a disappointing 64–69 record, leaving them resting in fourth place in the Central Division, 14½ games our of first. But that was good compared to the Chicago Cubs predicament. They had just finished the worst month in Chicago history, winning just five of 29 games. The previous worst month was way back in 1921 when they went 8–21.

The home run race had long ago turned into a two man race. The early season leader, Matt Williams, was out of sight, with 31 home runs. Jeff Bagwell and Chipper Jones were the nearest players to the dynamic duo, and they had 40. The next to last meeting between the two sluggers took place on September 21–23, in St. Louis. As the two teams took the field under the lights, the score stood at Sosa 61–McGwire 58. The Chicago strongman came into the series on a tear, having hit home runs #60 and 61 the previous day, in an 8–7 victory over the Milwaukee Brewers. It was also the Cubs' first two-game win streak in two months. But, as in the previous meeting between the two teams, La Russa's cohorts took the opener, 7–2. And McGwire took John Lieber deep in the seventh inning, to narrow Sosa's lead to two. The Cub right hander entered the seventh inning in a scoreless tie, but was raked for six big runs before Rodney Myers could put the fire out.

In game two, the Cardinals prevailed again by a 7–2 score, as both McGwire and Sosa took the collar gracefully. In the get-away game, the Chicago Cubs prevented a St. Louis sweep with a 5–3 win, as once again, the two sluggers went o-fer. Four days later, the kid from California joined Sosa in the 60 home-run club, by slamming a round tripper off Scott Sullivan of the Cincinnati Reds, in an 8–7 loss.

As he had done the year before, Mark McGwire finished strong, hitting five home runs in the last seven games, giving him 65 for the season, and another home run title. Sammy Sosa, the perennial bridesmaid, hit two in five games, finishing with 63 for the year.

The pennant races ended pretty much as expected. Atlanta, Houston, and Arizona were the National League Division winners, with the New York Mets pulling down the wild card slot. In the American League, the Yankees, Indians, and Rangers captured the top spots, with the Boston

Red Sox still in the hunt for the October flag. Bobby Cox's Braves and Joe Torre's Bronx Bombers took care of their league challengers rather easily, and met in the 95th World Series, with a titanic struggle for the baseball world supremacy expected. But it was not to be. The feisty New Yorkers steamrolled their southern neighbors in a four game sweep, taking the first two games on enemy soil. Torre's bombers jumped on Greg Maddux for four runs in the top of the eighth, in support of Orlando Hernandez, who stifled the Braves on one hit over eight innings. The final score was 4–1. The next day, they chased Kevin Millwood in two-plus innings, en route to a 7–2 laugher. Back home, they closed out the National League champs quickly, winning game three, 6–5 in ten innings, after pounding Atlanta ace Tom Glavine for five runs in seven innings. They completed the sweep with a 4–1 win in game four.

Mark McGwire's career home run total now stood at a lofty 522, and at the age of 36, he was favored to break Hank Aaron's record of 755 career home runs before he reached the age of 41. But just when the future looked bright, McGwire's luck ran out. As the 2000 season got underway, fans were anticipating another stirring home run battle between McGwire and his energetic challenger, Sammy Sosa. And for awhile the battle raged. As July got underway, Tony LaRussa's Redbirds had a big ten game lead in the National League Central Division, while the poor Cubs were mired in fifth place, 17 games behind. The only thing making life bearable for Cub fans was the home run race, but even that was against them, as McGwire held a 30 to 23 lead over their boy, Sosa.

Then fate interceded. The big Redhead went down with a knee injury, and was essentially finished for the year. He batted only 15 more times during the season, finishing with 32 home runs. The Dominican dandy continued his pummeling of opposing pitchers, and captured the home run title with 50 circuit blows.

The year 2001 didn't treat the St. Louis slugger any more kindly. He was still recovering from knee surgery when the season got underway, and he was put on an every-other-day playing schedule by La Russa, to protect his knee during the long, hot summer. Even the light playing schedule didn't keep McGwire off the disabled list, however. After going 2–21, with one home run in seven games, the big slugger's tender knee forced him to the sidelines once again. He missed six weeks, finally returning to the lineup on May 28. He celebrated his return with a sixth inning home run off Milwaukee's Paul Rigdon, as the Cards dumped the Brewers, 6–2.

McGwire came back just in time, as his Redbirds were tied for the lead with Sosa's Cubs, both with a record of 29–20, giving them a four game bulge over Milwaukee. Barry Bonds of the San Francisco Giants had the home run lead with an amazing 26 home runs in just 51 games, a pace that would give him 82 homers over a 162 game season. Sosa was back in the pack, with 14 homers.

As the summer wore on, the wear and tear on McGwire's knee left him in constant pain, and with limited mobility. The big slugger suffered through an 0–29 drought in early July, leaving him in pain and very discouraged. And without him being completely healthy and productive, the Cardinals fell into third place, seven games behind Sammy's Cubbies. In early August, McGwire suffered through another hitless streak, going 0-for-15 before homering off Glendon Rusch of the New York Mets, sparking the Cardinals to a 6–3 victory.

It was a painful summer for Mark McGwire. He finally got his home runs up to 21 on August 12, but his batting average was a barely visible .192. His home run buddy, Sammy Sosa, was having a typical Sosa year, with 41 home runs in 114 games. But he wasn't in the home run race this year either. Barry Bonds had slammed 50 round trippers in 118 games.

As August ground to a close, Bonds was leading the National League in home runs with 56, and Sammy Sosa was still in the hunt with 52. Mark McGwire was on the outside looking in this time, with just 22 round trippers. With the home run race now over as far as McGwire was concerned, the kid from Claremont could concentrate on the more important task at hand, helping his team capture the Central Division title. But that wouldn't be an easy task either. The Houston Astros held a four game lead over Chicago and a six game lead over St. Louis, with just 28 games to play.

One month later, Sosa's Cubs were essentially out of the race, trailing Houston by six games with just six games left in the season. But the Cardinals came on like Gangbusters, picking up four games on Houston over the final ten days of the season, and ending in a dead heat for the top spot. In the playoffs, the Arizona Diamondbacks ended the St. Louis Cardinals' season, winning their playoff series, three games to two. Mark McGwire managed just one single in 11 at-bats.

The Diamondbacks went on to capture the National League Championship with a win over the Atlanta Braves, then shocked the baseball world by knocking off the New York Yankees in seven games, to capture the World Championship.

Barry Bonds broke the single season home run title, by blasting 73 round trippers in just 476 official at-bats. Sammy Sosa came in a respectable second with 64, thereby becoming the first man ever to hit 60 or more home runs in three different seasons. On a sadder note, Mark McGwire decided to call it a career after a disappointing season in which he hit just .187 with 29 home runs and 64 RBIs in 97 games. As Big Mac said, "The thing I'm feeling now is my age."

When McGwire's retirement plans were made known late in the season, the popular slugger was honored in every city the team visited over the last two months. Baseball fans and the handsome first baseman had had a love affair long before 1998, but that year made him a legend. When the 2001 season ended, McGwire cashed in his chips, and became just another fan. He left behind some impressive numbers, that should give him a free pass through the portals of the National Baseball Hall of Fame five years from now. In 16 big league seasons, the California strongboy smashed 583 home runs, number five on the all-time list. He also knocked in 1414 runs, to go along with a .263 career batting average. His electrifying long distance clouts will be sorely missed by baseball fans everywhere. No one ever hit the ball any farther than Mark McGwire.

12. Barry Bonds— The Early Years

Barry Bonds came into the world blessed with extraordinary athletic genes, compliments of his talented father, Bobby Lee Bonds, who was born in Riverside, California, on March 15, 1946. The older Bonds, after graduating from high school, signed a professional baseball contract with the upstate San Francisco Giants. The date was August 4, 1964, only 11 days after the birth of his first son, Barry Lamar Bonds.

Bobby Bonds spent less than four years in the Giants' minor league system before joining the big team. As a 19-year-old rookie, he distinguished himself with Lexington in the Class A Western Carolina League, batting .323, with 25 home runs in just 418 at-bats. Four years later he terrorized pitchers all around the Pacific Coast League, slamming the ball at a .370 clip, with 31 extra base hits in 219 at-bats, before joining San Francisco on June 25, 1968. His major league debut was memorable. Coming to bat in the seventh inning against the Los Angeles Dodgers in Candlestick Park, the rangy right-handed slugger hit a grand slam home run off Jack Purdin, becoming the first player ever to hit a grand slam homer in his first major league at-bat.

The 22-year-old outfielder joined a perennial pennant contender, the Giants having finished in the first division every year since 1961, and in second place each of the previous three years. He shared the outfield with his son's godfather, Willie Mays, and Jesus Alou. The powerful San Franciscans also boasted such talented players as Willie McCovey, Juan Marichal, and Gaylord Perry, but they still couldn't capture the coveted top spot. They finished second again, trailing the league-leading St. Louis Cardinals by nine games.

Bobby Bonds went on to have an outstanding major league career, compiling 1886 hits over 14 years, with 332 home runs (number 72 all-time) and 461 stolen bases (number 43). Yet the general consensus among baseball experts was that Bonds never lived up to his potential. He brought Hall-of-Fame talent to the table. He had exceptional power and dazzling speed, but his lack of discipline at the plate resulted in 1,757 career strikeouts, a figure exceeded by only seven men. He set a single season strikeout record in 1969 when he fanned 187 times. Then he broke his own record the following year, going down on strikes 189 times.

For all his talent, Bobby Bonds seemed to wear out his welcome quickly. He spent seven productive years in San Francisco, then was shuttled off to the New York Yankees, and the merry-go-round began. He played for seven teams over the last seven years of his career.

Barry Lamar Bonds was born to Bobby and Patricia Bonds in Riverside, California, on July 24, 1964. When Bobby Bonds joined the San Francisco Giants in 1968, the family relocated to northern California. They settled in San Carlos, an affluent middle class community of 20,000, located 20 miles south of San Francisco, one of the big city's "bedroom communities." Young Barry developed into an outstanding athlete, helped by the expert instructions he received from his father and from godfather Willie Mays, arguably the greatest all-around baseball player in history, as well as by other members of the San Francisco ball club.

From the time Barry was 4 years old, until he reached the age of 10, he was a frequent visitor to Candlestick Park, either sitting in the stands with his mother, his two brothers and his sister, or in the clubhouse, talking to and playing catch with the likes of Jesus Alou, Willie McCovey, and Mays. The San Francisco Giant clubhouse became Barry Bonds' classroom. He had the unique opportunity of being able to observe the camaraderie of a professional baseball team up close. He saw how Hall-of-Famers like Mays, Perry, and Marichal handled the suffocating pressure of a pennant race. And he watched with fascination the daily give-and-take between the players and the aggressive (and often annoying) sportswriters and television reporters. This experience would help form Barry's approach to the game in later years, when he participated in stifling pennant races, and when he challenged Mark McGwire's single season home run record.

Barry received on-the-field pointers at Candlestick Park that most kids would sell their souls for. The youngster was allowed on the field during pre-game practice, where he would play catch with one of the players or just watch his father take batting practice. When he got older, he was permitted to stand in the outfield during pre-game drills, shagging flies and listening to his father and Mays. Over the years, the "Say Hey Kid" coached young Barry in baseball fundamentals, such as the proper way to catch a ball and how to hit with power. It's difficult to imagine any other boy receiving the quality of instruction that Barry Bonds received as a child. He was groomed to be the best, by the best.

The youngster, not surprisingly, became infatuated with the game of baseball. As he told James Panter, "I grew up in my family playing baseball, along with my brothers and my dad. I was brought up loving the game, and it must be in my blood, because it's in my genes. It came natural to me." Young Barry couldn't get enough baseball. When he wasn't at the park, he was swinging a bat in his backyard. His father occasionally brought him bats from the clubhouse, and Barry would practice batting for hours on end. But being a little fellow, standing a shade over five feet tall and weighing about 80 pounds, he had difficulty handling a big leaguer's bat, so he had to choke halfway up the handle in order to swing it.

Barry played in the San Carlos Little League for several years. Then in 1978 he entered Junipero Serra High School, an all-boys prep school located in nearby San Mateo. The school was noted for its rich athletic history, having sent many notable athletes into the professional ranks, including Lynn Swann, the great Hall-of-Fame receiver of the Pittsburgh Steelers; Gregg Jeffries, former New York Met second baseman; and Tom Brady, the 24-year-old quarterback of the 2002 Super Bowl Champion New England Patriots. Bonds' natural athletic instincts blossomed at Serra, and he lettered in three sports—baseball, basketball, and football. But baseball was by far his favorite sport. The tall, skinny outfielder had both power and speed, leading the Padres in home runs, total bases, and stolen bases each of his three years on the team. He also hit for average, banging the ball at a .350 clip in his sophomore year and .395 the following year. He capped off his high school career with a sizzling .467 average as a senior. Not surprisingly, he was an all-state selection every year, as he led the Padres to three successive conference titles.

Barry Bonds was a talented athlete, but even as a youngster he had a chip on his shoulder that may have been partly due to his being the son of a famous father. He spent his childhood, and a good part of his adult life, being known as "Bobby Bonds' son," an epithet he detested. It took him more than thirty years to get out from under his father's shadow and establish his own identity.

When he graduated from high school, the San Francisco Giants drafted him in the second round of the amateur draft, and they recruited him vigorously. Unfortunately, the two sides couldn't reach an agreement, and the young slugger opted to attend college, receiving a full scholarship to Arizona State University, one of the country's top "baseball factories." Rick Monday and Reggie Jackson preceded Bonds through the portals of ASU, where they refined their natural baseball skills. Monday, a 19-year major league star, is best remembered for two exploits. In 1976 the Chicago Cub outfielder and former marine intercepted two men who were trying to burn an American flag in the outfield at Dodger Stadium. Five years later, as a member of the Dodgers, Monday hit a pennant-winning home run off Montreal Expos ace Steve Rogers in the ninth inning of the final game of the National League Championship Series. Reggie Jackson, the ultimate "hot dog," cavorted around major league outfields for 21 years, catching some balls and missing others. His Hall-of-Fame credentials were strictly power numbers. He hit 563 career home runs, with 1702 RBIs, but he also set a major league record with 2597 strike-outs. Jackson earned the nickname "Mr. October" by slamming 10 home runs in 27 World Series games, including three off three different Dodger pitchers in the sixth game of the 1977 classic.

Bonds arrived in Tempe in the fall of 1982, carrying the baggage of real or imagined wounds. Still striving to erase the stigma of "Bobby Bonds' son," he dedicated himself to achieving individual excellence on the baseball diamond. In his freshman year the physical education major batted a respectable .306 for the Sun Devils, with 11 home runs, 54 runs batted in, and a .568 slugging percentage in 64 games. He made eyes pop in the NCAA West II Regional Tournament by launching a towering home run over the "Green Monster," ASU's center field fence, one of only 18 players to accomplish that feat in 12 years. He walked off with MVP honors for the tournament, then capped off his freshman year by hitting two home runs in the College World Series.

Barry Bonds' prodigious home run blasts were all the more amazing when his slender build was taken into account. The 19-year-old outfielder stood just over six feet tall and weighed 160 pounds. He looked and ran like a greyhound, but hit like a slugger. He choked up on the bat about ¾ inch, and whipped the barrel of the bat through the strike zone with blinding speed. His quick wrists and short, compact swing generated surprising power.

During the summer he made the trek to Alaska to play in the Alaskan Summer League, a collegiate training ground where major league hopefuls cultivated their skills. Tom Seaver, Mark McGwire, and Tim Leary were some of the big leaguers who made their mark in the northland. Bonds joined the Alaska Goldpanners in Fairbanks but played in only six games, going 4 for 18, with one double and two RBIs.

Back at Arizona State for his sophomore year, the 6'2" slugger stepped it up a bit, hitting .360, with 20 doubles, 11 homers, 55 RBIs,

Barry Bonds was a 165-pound speedster when he entered Arizona State University. (Courtesy ASU Sports Information)

and 30 stolen bases in 70 games. He sparked the Maroon and Gold to the Pacific Ten Conference championship, and was selected to the All-Pac-10 all-star team. In postseason play he tied an NCAA record with seven consecutive hits in the College World Series, and was named ESPN amateur athlete of the week for his performance.

As a junior, Barry Bonds led his team once again, with a .368 average, 23 home runs, and 66 runs batted in. The slim speedster hit into only one double play during the season, while banging out six game-winning hits. As former teammate Don Wakamatsu recalled, "He wasn't as physical a player then.... He was a frail kid with a quick bat, 165–170 [pounds], max." His outfield partners were also future major league stars, Oddibe McDowell and Mike Devereaux.

Nineteen-eighty-five was Bonds' last year at Arizona State. He was drafted by the Pittsburgh Pirates in the first round of the major league baseball draft, and left school to follow his dream. His three-year totals with the Sun Devils showed a composite .347 batting average, with 45 home runs, 175 RBIs, and 57 stolen bases in 711 at-bats. He finished number three on the ASU career home run list, behind Bob Horner of the Atlanta Braves, who slammed 56 round trippers, and major league outfielder Mike Kelly, who hit 46.

Barry Bonds began his professional baseball career with Prince William of the Class A Carolina League. The Pirates, under manager Ed Ott, crawled home in last place, their 65–74 record leaving them 29½ games behind the Lynchburg Mets. Bonds' debut was relatively quiet, as he hit a respectable .299, with 13 home runs in 254 at-bats.

That earned him a raise for 1986, upping his salary to $60,000. He also moved up two classifications, joining the Hawaii Islanders of the Pacific Coast League. He was not overwhelmed by the rarefied air of AAA ball, hitting a hard .311 in 44 games, with seven home runs. In less than two months he was called up to the parent club, which was holding down last place in the National League East and was in desperate need of help. The 24-year-old outfielder arrived at Forbes Field with a reputation of having decent power and blinding speed—and an attitude problem. He was immediately inserted into the leadoff spot by manager Jim Leyland,

Bob Horner is number three on the all-time ASU career home run list, with 45. (Courtesy William F. McNeil)

Bonds is number three on the all-time ASU career home run list, with 45. (Courtesy ASU Sports Information)

in hopes of injecting some badly needed offense into his team's feeble attack. Barry made his major league debut on May 30, 1986, wearing number 24 in honor of his godfather and idol, Willie Mays. But he didn't make the fans forget the "Say Hey Kid" immediately. Bonds struggled at the plate in his rookie season, hitting a barely visible .223, but he did show flashes of power by putting 16 balls into orbit in 413 at-bats. Under the guidance of the patient Jim Leyland, the California native slowly developed into a full-fledged major leaguer.

Unfortunately, the Pirate manager was unable to curb Bonds' vocal outbursts. Even as a rookie, he was arrogant and difficult to get along with. He verbally attacked photographers on the field, and complained about his slugging talents being wasted in the leadoff position. He refused to talk to the press, and hardly spoke to his teammates. Sometimes players brought him a baseball to sign, and he wouldn't sign it.

In 1987 Barry Bonds was joined on the Pirates by Bobby Bonilla (a young third baseman who was picked up in a trade with the Chicago White Sox), hard hitting outfielder Andy Van Slyke, and pitchers Doug Drabek and John Smiley. Slowly but steadily the Pirates made their way up the Eastern Division ladder. Bonds, playing his first full major league season, responded with 25 home runs, 99 runs scored, and 32 stolen bases to go along with a .261 batting average. Bonilla batted .300 with 15 home runs; Van Slyke chipped in with 21 homers and a .293 average; Drabek was 11–12 in his first full season as a starter; and Smiley went 7–5 in 63 games out of the bullpen. The team finished in fourth place, a jump of two spots in the standings.

The 1988 season opened in Philadelphia, matching the fourth place Pirates against the fifth place Phils. The Bucs got off the mark quickly, capturing the opener 5–3 behind right hander Mike Dunne, who went 13–6 in 1987. Bonds rapped out three hits in five times at bat, including his first home run of the season. The next day they dropped a heartbreaking 6–5, 14-inning thriller to Lee Elia's team. Bonds had two singles in six at-bats, and Bobby Bonilla hit two homers; but Mike Schmidt's two home runs sent the game into extra innings, and Juan Samuel's two-out double, followed by Milt Thompson's single, sent the Steel City boys down to defeat.

Pittsburgh was 3–2 after five games; then they got hot, running up 14 wins in their next 18 games, to take a ½ game lead over the New York Mets in the Eastern Division. Bobby Bonilla led the barrage with seven home runs, followed by Barry Bonds with five. Bob Walk paced the pitching staff with a 4–1 record.

May was a lukewarm month for the Pirate crew, as they went 14–14, and dropped 3½ games behind the Mets, with a 30–20 record. Bonilla (13) and Bonds (12) still led the offense, and Doug Drabek (5–3) and Bob Walk (5–3) showed the way on the mound. But the overall pitching was erratic and the hitting was mediocre. Barry Bonds had too many 0-fers to be a productive leadoff man. A 13–14 slate in June dropped Jim Leyland's boys even farther behind the Mets, who opened up a 5½ game lead.

The young Bucs made a push early in July, running up 12 victories in 13 games to close the gap between them and the New Yorkers to a slim ½ game. After dropping a tough 4–3, 10-inning game to San Diego on the fourth of July, Leyland's contingent won the next day, 3–2, behind the fine pitching of Bob Walk, who had 13 base runners but allowed only two of them to score. Andy Van Slyke was the star of the game, hitting an eventual game-winning home run in the top of the seventh inning, then throwing out the potential tying run at the plate in the bottom of the ninth. When the All-Star break came five days later, the Pirates had run off another four victories, thanks to some great pitching by Smiley, Drabek, Dunne, and Walk.

Surprisingly, the General Managers in the National League made Andy Van Slyke their second choice in the outfield, behind Darryl Strawberry of the Mets. Bobby Bonilla was a unanimous choice at third base, but Barry Bonds had to watch this one on TV. Bob Walk, who was 10–4 at the break, was also on the team. The Americans edged the Nationals 2–1 in a classic pitching duel, with Frank Viola besting Dwight Gooden.

When the second half of the season got underway on July 14, the red hot Pittsburgh crew ran off another seven wins in eight games. During the streak, Barry Bonds hit a torrid .439, with six doubles, four homers, and 10 runs batted in. Andy Van Slyke, in addition to playing a sensational right field, pounded the ball at a .355 clip, with two doubles, two triples, three homers, and 12 RBIs. Bobby Bonilla hit only .244, with four RBIs. Bob Walk and Doug Drabek both had 3–0 records during the streak.

That was as close as the young Pirates could get. They dropped seven of their next nine games, finishing the month with a record of 58–45, a full five games behind New York. The Mets continued to stretch the lead through August and September, and when the final curtain came down, they owned a solid 15 game bulge over Pittsburgh. But there was a lot of optimism in the Steel City over the winter, as fans witnessed the development of two future stars, Barry Bonds and Bobby Bonilla. Bonds finished with a .283 average, with 24 home runs (ninth in the National League). Bonilla tied him in homers, and knocked in 100 runs to go along with a .274 average. Pittsburgh also had one of the game's premier center fielders. Andy Van Slyke not only patrolled the spacious middle garden at Three Rivers Stadium with grace and speed, he also excelled at the plate, leading the league with 15 triples, slamming 25 homers, driving in 100 runs, stealing 30 bases, and hitting a dangerous .288. He finished fourth in the Most Valuable Player voting, and was selected by baseball experts as one of the top four or five outfielders in the game. The Pirates also had the nucleus of an outstanding pitching staff, with Doug Drabek (15–7), John Smiley (13–11), Bob Walk (12–10),and Jim Gott (6–6, with 34 saves).

Springtime optimism turned quickly to despair in 1989, as nothing went right for Pittsburgh. The team couldn't get untracked, finishing at 74–88, 19 games behind the pennant-winning Chicago Cubs. Barry Bonds slipped to .248 and hit just 19 homers, with 58 runs batted in. Van Slyke's numbers plummeted. Plagued by injuries, he missed 32 games, and when he did play he was mediocre, hitting only nine home runs, driving in 53 runners, and batting .237. Bobby Bonilla had another productive year with the bat, but was a defensive liability at the hot corner, booting 35 balls. Their closer, Jim Gott, pitched in one game, then went on the disabled list and missed the rest of the season.

Barry Bonds' poor season didn't help his attitude any. One time he got into a shouting match with Jim Leyland, screaming, "No one's gonna tell me what to do." The Pirate manager responded by saying, "I'm the manager of this team, and I'm going to run it my way. If someone doesn't like it, they can go play somewhere else."

Things were a little more peaceful outside Pittsburgh, especially in Arlington, Texas, where the most exciting event of the year took place. There, on August 22, the Texas Rangers' flame-throwing right hander, Nolan Ryan, fanned his 5000th batter, establishing a strikeout record that may last forever. Entering the game against the Oakland Athletics, the 42-year-old graybeard had 4994 scalps on his belt. He added number 5000 in the fifth inning when he threw a 92 mile-per-hour fast ball past Rickey Henderson. Seven more A's went down before his high hard one before the game ended, but his effort was wasted, as Bob Welch blanked the Rangers, 2–0.

The other notable event of the year was more somber. Pete Rose, known to his fans as "Charlie Hustle," was banned from baseball for life by Commissioner Bart Giamatti for betting on baseball games. Rose, who is the all-time leader in career base hits, with 4,256, is not only barred from participating in the great American game in any official capacity, he is also ineligible for induction into the National Baseball Hall of Fame in Cooperstown, New York.

Nineteen-hundred-and-ninety was another year, and Jim Leyland had his boys ready to make their move to the top of the pack. Where everything went wrong the previous year, things came together this time, giving the Pittsburgh contingent the National League Eastern Division crown. In a close pennant race with the Montreal Expos, the Pirates came out on top, finishing with a 95–67 record, 21 games better than 1989 and good enough for a four game cushion over the second place Canadians. Barry Bonds burst upon the major league scene in 1990, a 26-year-old superstar with both speed and power. He hit .301, slammed 33 home runs, drove in 114 runs, stole 52 bases, and walked off with the league's Most Valuable Player award. He also won a Gold Glove and was voted the Sporting News Major League Player of the Year. His all-around play brought him a lucrative $2.3 million contract in 1991, an increase of $1.45 million over his previous salary.

Bobby Bonilla, having moved to the outfield, backed up Bonds admirably, hitting .280, with 32 homers and 120 RBIs. Andy Van Slyke bounced back from a dismal '89, but nagging injuries limited his playing time to just 136 games. When he was healthy, he contributed 17 homers and 77 RBIs to go along with a .284 batting average. Jose Lind and Jay Bell anchored the middle of the infield and gave the Pirates an exceptional double play combination. Jeff King played a solid third base, and Sid Bream was his usual reliable self on first (15 homers, 67 RBIs, .270 average). Doug Drabek won a league-leading 22 games (against only six losses) to capture the Cy Young award.

The Pittsburgh Pirates faced a fired-up Cincinnati Reds team under the direction of Lou Pinella in the National League Championship Series, and went down to defeat, four games to two. Bob Walk took the opener for the Pirates, 4–3, but they then dropped three in a row before bouncing back to take game five, 3–2 behind Doug Drabek. The Big Red Machine closed out the series with a 2–1 win in game six, leaving Leyland's futile warriors with just 15 runs scored in six games. Barry Bonds was held to three singles in 18 at-bats. His slugging counterpart, Bobby Bonilla, was not much better, going four for 21.

The Pirates were back again the next year, as the deadly duo of Bonds and Bonilla led the team to another division title—by a whopping 14 games over the St. Louis Cardinals. Bonds was now holding down fifth place in the batting order, with Van Slyke batting third and Bonilla hitting cleanup. The season got off to a slow start when Doug Drabek lost his first three games and Barry Bonds hurt his knee sliding into a wall trying to catch a foul ball in Wrigley Field. Bob Walk pulled a groin muscle and went on the D.L. But Leyland's crew righted the ship, and by the end of April they were sitting in first place, with a 13–7 record, good enough for a half-game lead over the St. Louis Cardinals. One of the more exciting games of the month was played in Three Rivers Stadium on April 21. Pittsburgh trailed the Chicago Cubs 3–2 after seven innings. In the top of the eighth, the Cubs padded their lead to 7–2, but the plucky Pirates bounced back with a four-spot of their own to narrow the margin to 7–6. Then, in the bottom of the ninth, they tied the game at 7–7, sending it into extra innings. Andre Dawson, the Cubs' slugging outfielder, slammed a grand slam home run in the top of the 11th inning, giving his team an apparently insurmountable 11–7 lead. But Pittsburgh stormed back one more time and scored five runs in the bottom of the inning, winning 13–12 before a small Sunday crowd of only 10,860 delirious fans. Merced, Bell, Bonilla, and Slaught knocked in two runs apiece. Bobby Bonilla led the attack with a double and a home run.

Barry Bonds was bogged down with a .177 batting average at the end of April, but he had driven in 10 runs in 16 games. Andy Van Slyke was hitting just .254, but his four home runs were good for 16 RBIs. And Bobby Bonilla was hitting .315, with three homers and 17 RBIs.

May was a big month for Jim Leyland's Pittsburgh Pirates as they captured 17 of 25 games and widened their lead over the second place New York Mets to four games. On May 14 Barry Bonds went zero for five against Houston, dropping his average to .177. The next day he punched out two hits in four at-bats, and he was off and running. By the end of the month he had his average up to .236, and four days later he was batting .259. He had seven home runs in 44 games, with 32 RBIs. John Smiley, a big left hander, was leading the pitching brigade with an 8–1 record. Zane Smith, another tall southpaw with pinpoint control, stood at 7–3, with a 2.66 ERA. He had walked only nine men in 74 innings.

The summer passed quickly for the Pittsburgh players, who were thoroughly enjoying their success. Early in the year the press reported turmoil in Pirate-land, with Barry Bonds and Bobby Bonilla the main culprits. But once the season got underway, Jim Leyland had all his players pulling in the same direction, and he had private meetings with both Bonds and Bonilla to clear the air. It must have worked because, even though Bonds was hitting only .236 through May, Van Slyke was hitting .235, and the ace of the pitching staff, Doug Drabek, was mired at 3–7, the Bucs ruled the roost in the National League East.

The anonymous players, plus Bonilla (.311, six homers, 34 RBIs), picked up the superstars. First baseman Orlando Merced was hitting .323, catcher Mike Lavalliere had 15 runs batted in, and Smiley and Smith were almost unbeatable on the mound, as noted earlier.

When the final bell rang, Jim Leyland's team had a comfortable 14 game lead over Joe Torre's Cardinals. Bonds finished with 25 homers, 116 RBIs, and a .292 batting average, while the big, rugged right fielder was 18 and 100, with a .302 average and a league-leading 44 doubles. Van Slyke was 17 and 83, with a .265 average. John Smiley had a career season, with 20 wins against eight losses; Zane Smith went 16–10; and Drabek finished at 15–14. This time Pittsburgh had to face the Atlanta Braves, the Cinderella team of the National League, who had gone from last place to first place in just one season. Unknown to the fans at the time, Bobby Cox's charges were embarking on a decade-long domination of the National League. Pittsburgh fought the upstart Braves tooth and nail before finally succumbing in game seven. Once again, Pittsburgh took the opener, 5–1 behind Drabek's five-hitter and Andy Van Slyke's double and home run. Atlanta came back to take game two 1–0, as Steve Avery out dueled Zane Smith. Bonds and Bonilla were a collective zero for eight. The Braves kept the pressure on the next day, pounding John Smiley and four relievers, 10–3. Pittsburgh knotted the series at 2–2 with a pressure packed 3–2, 10-inning victory. A walk to Van Slyke, a stolen base, and a pinch single by Mike Lavalliere brought in the game winner. After winning game five 1–0 behind Zane Smith, Pittsburgh took the hose in games six and seven, losing by scores of 1–0 and 4–0. Jim Leyland's crew seemed mesmerized to be in post-season play once again. This time they scored a measly 12 runs in seven games, an average of 1.7 runs per game. And, once again, Barry Bonds came up short, batting .148 on a four for 27 performance, with one run scored and no RBIs.

The seemingly ageless wonder, Nolan Ryan, continued to amaze the baseball world in 1991. The 44-year-old Texas Ranger pitcher tossed his 7th no-hitter on May 1 when he blanked the Toronto Blue Jays 3–0 in a game liberally sprinkled with 16 strikeouts. The modest, native-born Texan would finally retire in '93, leaving behind some unbelievable strikeout and no-hit records. His final tally, after 27 years of pitching in the Big Time, included 324 victories against 292 losses, 5386 strikeouts, and, of course, the seven no-no's.

Pittsburgh made it a three-peat in 1992, taking the East by nine games over Montreal, but the handwriting was on the wall for the Steel City nine. Pirate management had developed two potential Hall-of-Fame players over the previous six years, Barry Bonds and Bobby Bonilla, but they couldn't afford to keep them. They were unable to compete with the enormous salaries doled out by the big market teams like the Yankees, Mets, and Dodgers. Bonilla became a free agent after the 1991 season, and he jumped ship, signing a lucrative contract with the New York Mets.

Barry Bonds would become a free agent as soon as the '92 post-season ended, and he was expected to bid adieu to the team also, essentially ending any thoughts of a Pirate dynasty.

Barry Bonds had a sensational year in 1992. He broke into the thirty home run bracket for the second time in three years, slamming 34 round trippers into the far reaches of National League parks, with 19 of them coming on the road. He led the league with 109 runs scored, drove in 103 runs, and stole 39 bases to go along with a .311 batting average, earning him his second National League MVP award. He joined his father, Bobby, as one of the few 30–30 players in major league baseball. In future years he would join his father as the only five-time 30–30 players in history.

When playoff time rolled around, the Braves were waiting to meet Jim Leyland's boys in the National League Championship Series once again; and the Atlantans had too much of everything for the Pittsburgh crew to contend with. The Pirates did stretch it out to seven games, but came up short for the third straight time. After throwing eight blanks at Bobby Cox's boys in game seven, Drabek weakened in the ninth, loading the bases on a double, an error, and a walk. Two outs later, Francisco Cabrera, a journeyman catcher who had only ten at-bats during the regular season, hit a pennant-winning two-run single to left, leaving the Pirates talking to themselves. Barry Bonds hit a more respectable .261 this time, but batted in just one run. It was a far cry from his regular season marks.

During the off-season, Bonds became a free agent, and he signed with his father's old team, the San Francisco Giants, who were striving for respect in the National League's Western Division. Not too many people in the Pittsburgh organization were sorry to see Barry Bonds leave. One of his few friends on the Pirates had been Bobby Bonilla, another player with a chip on his shoulder. And Bonilla had jumped the club the previous year. Some people didn't think the talented left fielder gave 100 percent in every game. Others thought he was a "choker." Former teammate Sid Bream, who played with Barry from 1986 through 1990, told an ESPN reporter that everyone on the team wanted to hit him sometime during the season.

Barry Bonds signed a seven year, $43.75 million contract, tying him to the West Coast team until at least the year 2000. The first thing Bonds had to do upon joining the Giants was to get a new uniform number, since number 24, Willie Mays' number, had been retired. Bonds selected number 25, his father's old number.

Owner Bob Lurie and General Manager Al Rosen not only signed a new superstar, they also hired a new manager. Dusty Baker, who had been

Bonds could relax after signing a seven year, $43.75 million contract in 1993. (Courtesy James R. Madden, Jr.)

a bench coach with the Giants since 1988, was signed to manage the team in 1993. He inherited a club that had finished fifth in the six-team National League Western Division the previous year. But he had the nucleus of a good ball club, with players like Will Clark, Matt Williams, and Willie McGee. He also had strong pitching with John Burkett (13–9), Billy Swift (10–4), and closer Rod Beck (65 games, a 1.76 ERA, and 17 saves). With the addition of Bonds, and expected comebacks from key veteran players, the Giants were hoping to make their move to the top. Matt Williams had had an off year in '92, batting .227, with 20 homers and 66 runs batted in. Both Darren Lewis (who hit a meager .231) and rookie Royce Clayton (who hit just .224) were expected to be more productive in '93. And Robby Thompson was ready to improve on his .260 average.

Nineteen-ninety-three was an expansion year in the National League, with the addition of two new teams, the Florida Marlins and the Colorado Rockies. The league maintained its two-division structure in '93, with seven teams in each division, but in 1994 the league would present a three-division format, with the addition of a Central Division.

The San Francisco Giants gave their fans more thrills than they expected in 1993, but some of the experiences were very painful. They jumped out on top early, and as All-Star time approached they held a healthy nine game lead over the Atlanta Braves. The Astros and Dodgers were a distant 12 games out. Robby Thompson, who was having a career year, was red hot in early July. He had two five-hit games in two weeks, and two consecutive two-homer games, pacing the league's second basemen with a .328 batting average, eight home runs, and 36 RBIs in 66 games. Barry Bonds was living up to his press notices, with a torrid .357 average, 21 homers and 60 RBIs in 74 games. Matt Williams was at 21 and 64, with a .290 average; while Willie McGee was batting .328, Kirt Manwaring was at .289, and Royce Clayton was at .286. John Burkett was leading the mound corps with an 11–2 record, followed by Billy Swift (10–4), Bud Black (7–1), and Rod Beck (1.49 ERA and 22 saves).

By July 22 the Atlanta Braves had fallen ten games behind the spurting Giants, and were, for all intents and purposes, out of the race. But baseball is a funny game, and strange things happen on the way to a division title. The dog days of summer occasionally turn into the spine-tingling days of fall. And for the Giants and Braves, the season didn't begin until after Labor Day.

Atlanta General Manager John Schuerholz made a key move in mid–July by obtaining slugging first baseman Fred McGriff from the San Diego Padres, and the Braves' fortunes took an immediate turn upward. In his Atlanta debut, the 6'3", 215-pound southpaw swinger homered to spark an eight run rally that brought his team back from a 5–0 deficit to a thrilling 8–5 victory.

At the same time the Braves were beginning to peak, the Giants went into a slump. The Los Angeles Dodgers traveled up the coast to San Francisco in late July and took two out of three from Dusty Baker's boys, by scores of 15–1 and 2–1. The Giants won the middle game 3–2.

After winning 15 of 17 games during July, San Francisco went stone cold in August, and their once insurmountable lead began to dwindle, one game at a time. Atlanta, who had kept pace with the Giants in July, with a 19–9 record, ran off a nine game winning streak in early August before being derailed by the Dodgers, 7–5. A critical three game series between the two contenders took place in San Francisco August 23–25. In the opener, Steve Avery beat Dusty Baker's Bay Area Bombers 5–3 to cut the Giant lead to a mere 6½ games. On the 24th, Tom Glavine won 6–4, backed by home runs by Terry Pendleton, David Justice, and Ron Gant. And in the getaway game, Greg Maddux captured his 15th game, 9–1, behind a six-homer barrage.

August had been a month to forget for the San Francisco Giants, and September was just as bad. On September 10 the Braves beat the San

Diego Padres and moved into a first place tie with the rapidly fading Giants. Six days later the Atlanta lead had widened to four games; but just when it looked like the Giants were dead, they got their second wind and sent their fans into delirium once again. San Francisco roared down the stretch, going 14–3, to get back into the race. On September 26 the Orange and Black won their 100th game and moved back into a tie for the lead, with five games remaining.

The two teams were still deadlocked after 161 games, with 103 victories apiece. On the final Sunday the Braves hosted the Colorado Rockies, while the Giants visited their arch enemies in Los Angeles. In Atlanta, Dave Justice clubbed his 40th home run, and Tom Glavine won his 22nd game, 5–3. Later in the day, with the result of the Braves game staring at them from the Diamond Vision scoreboard, Dusty Baker's warriors met their fate. Tommy Lasorda's team jumped on Giant starter Salomon Torres for two runs in the bottom of the third and a singleton in the fourth, as 54,340 Giant-haters screamed with delight. For the Giants, it was all downhill after that. L.A. added a three-spot in the fifth, a run in the sixth, and a final five in the bottom of the eighth. Mike Piazza led the Dodger onslaught with two home runs and four runs batted in. San Francisco was held by Kevin Gross to just six hits, with Barry Bonds drawing the collar in four trips to the plate.

The season ended badly for the Giants, but they had a few individual honors to keep them warm over the winter. Barry Bonds, who was now a superstar with unlimited potential, captured his third National League Most Valuable Player award after batting .336 and leading the league in both home runs (46) and runs batted in (123). Matt Williams bounced back with a fine .294 season, with 38 homers and 110 RBIs. Robby Thompson hit .312, Willie McGee hit .301, and Mark Carreon hit .327 in limited service. John Burkett (22–7), Billy Swift (21–8), and Rod Beck (48 saves) anchored a strong pitching corps.

In 1994 the San Francisco Giants became part of a four-team Western Division in the National League, along with Los Angeles, San Diego, and Colorado. The Central and Eastern Divisions each consisted of five teams. The Atlanta Braves moved to the Eastern Division, making the Giants' journey to the top a little easier. Dusty Baker's crew entered the season with unbridled optimism. They were the team to beat, and were the popular choice to capture the division title. They had lost first baseman Will Clark to free agency but picked up Todd Benzinger to replace him.

San Francisco received a stiff challenge from the Los Angeles Dodgers and the upstart Colorado Rockies during April and May. In fact, the Dodgers spurted past Dusty Baker's boys late in May and ended the month in first place, by 3½ games. Barry Bonds was having a decent season, but not a superstar season. His stats showed a .297 average, with 13 home runs and 32 RBIs in 52 games. No one on the Giant team was in the .300 range, as the team wallowed in 10th place in the league in runs scored. The pitching was decent, with Swift (6–3), Burkett (4–3), and Beck (11 saves), but the strong arms couldn't compensate for the lack of run support.

The Western Division race stayed hot through June, as L.A. maintained a 2½ game lead over San Francisco and a 5½ game lead over Don Baylor's surprising Rockies. The Giants were struggling, and by July 6 their 35–49 record left them 9½ games behind the Dodgers. At the All-Star break they still trailed by 7½. And it was still the run support (or lack of it) that was their undoing. They were 12th in a 14-team league. None of the Giants' batters had made a move. They had no .300 hitters. In fact, Mark Carreon was leading the attack with a .287 average, and only three players had averages above .265. It was a dismal performance.

But Dusty Baker, ever the ultimate motivator, rallied his troops during the three-day break, and they came roaring out of the gate on July 14, pounding Montreal 8–3 behind the slugging of newly signed free agent Darryl Strawberry, who had a single, double, and home run, accounting for five runs batted in. The next night, Barry Bonds sparked a 7–3 Giant rout of the Expos, banging out three base hits, including two home runs. On the 16th, Bonds hit two more homers, driving in three runs, as San Fran edged Felipe Alou's outgunned troops 4–2.

The next night, in Philadelphia, Bonds clubbed another home run, giving him five in three games. He also chipped in with a single, as the Giants won 7–5. Bonds' heroics were particularly notable in view of the fact that he was playing with painful bone chips in his elbow that would require surgery at the end of the season.

The Giant charge continued the remainder of the month, as they ran up a sparkling 11–4 record and closed the gap between them and the front-running Dodgers to a single game. But just when the pennant race was heating up, storm clouds appeared on the horizon. The major league labor agreement, which had been in negotiations since spring, was getting nowhere, and the players union set a strike date of August 12 if an agreement was not reached by that time. If it came to pass, it would be the 8th work stoppage in the last 22 years. After a long session on July 18, both sides were far apart on many subjects, including a salary cap. Richard Ravitch, the owners' top negotiator, appeared dismayed and pessimistic about arriving at an agreement before August 12. Donald Fehr, the executive director of the players union, said a strike would be a last resort, but if it came to that, the players would walk.

With the end of the season staring them in the face 12 days down the road, San Francisco could not maintain their momentum of July, and they dropped six of nine games. Their pitching staff, in particular, took a pounding. They were hammered by Cincinnati 17–4 on the third. Barry Bonds homered in the loss. In their next game they were routed by the Houston Astros, 12–4, behind a 17-hit attack. Houston completed the sweep with 8–7 and 7–4 victories over Dusty Baker's embattled pitching brigade. The Giants bounced back with a sweep of the hapless Cubs, but it was too little, too late.

When the sun rose on August 12, all major league ballparks were empty. The season was over. There would be no stretch-run pennant drive. There would be no post-season playoffs. There would not even be a World Series for the first time in 91 years. When the final out was made on August 11, the Los Angeles Dodgers were the National League Western Division champions, their modest record of 58–56 giving them a 3½ game cushion over San Francisco.

There were many misgivings about the sudden end to the season. Many challenges would go unfulfilled. One of the biggest disappointments was the lost opportunity of Matt Williams, who was challenging Roger Maris' single season home run record. The Giants third baseman had hit 43 home runs in 115 games, a pace that would have given him 61 for the season. Barry Bonds, too, was coming on strong. He had hit 14 home runs over the previous 26 games, giving him 37 for the season. If he had been able to maintain that pace over the final 47 games, he would have ended the season with 62 home runs. But it was not to be. The baseball gods deemed otherwise, and the greedy players and owners prevented the fans from witnessing the exciting pennant races and, perhaps, one or more assaults on baseball's most cherished record. Other players in the home run hunt included Ken Griffey, Jr. (with 40 home runs), Jeff Bagwell (with 39), and Frank Thomas (with 38).

Barry Bonds' strong finish brought his batting average up to .312, with 37 homers and 81 RBIs. He also stole 29 bases.

Negotiations between major league owners and the players union dragged on through the winter and into spring. With a new baseball season approaching, the owners decided to go with replacement minor league players so the major league baseball season would not have to be cancelled. On March 31, just days before the season was to get underway, a U.S. District Court ended the strike by ordering that conditions revert to the rules from 1994 while the owners and players union continued negotiations.

The 1995 major league baseball season got underway three weeks late, and the season was shortened by 18 games. In the National League Western Division the Los Angeles Dodgers were chosen to repeat as division leaders, while the San Francisco Giants were generally picked to finish second or third. In fact, it was worse than that. Dusty Baker's contingent could never get untracked, and they finished last in the four-team division, winning 67 games against 77 losses, and leaving them 11 games behind Tommy Lasorda's Dodgers.

Bad luck plagued the Giants early in the season. Matt Williams, after being selected as the National League Player of the Month for May (on the basis of a .405 average, 12 home runs, and 31 RBIs), broke his foot on a foul tip on June 3; and by the end of June, six of their pitchers, including opening day starter Terry Mulholland, joined him on the DL. The Giants stubbornly hung in the race into July, thanks to some gallant pitching by Mark Portugal (5–2) and Rod Beck (4–2, with 13 saves), and the slugging of Barry Bonds (who was batting .305, with 13 home runs, 45 runs batted in, and 47 runs scored in 61 games). Glenallen Hill, although hitting only .249, contributed 40 RBIs.

On June 20, San Francisco trailed the division-leading Colorado Rockies by only half a game, but when the second half of the season got underway in mid July, Dusty Baker's team gradually slipped back into the pack and, by the end of the month, were a full 9½ games out of first place, with a 39–48 record. When the season came to a merciful close on October 1, the Giants were the cellar dwellers. There were very few bright spots for Dusty Baker. Rod Beck piled up 33 saves, and Mark Leiter finished with a tough 10–12 record and a 3.82 ERA. And there was Barry Bonds.

Bonds tailed off down the stretch but still batted .294, with 33 home runs, 104 RBIs, and 109 runs scored. The measure of a great hitter is his ability to come through in the clutch. And in that regard, Barry Bonds had been the major league's top clutch hitter since 1991. According to statistics compiled by Street and Smith, Bonds and Edgar Martinez were tied for the number one spot, which looked at on-base-percentage (OBP) and slugging percentage (SLG) after the sixth inning in close games. Bonds had led the majors in both OBP and SLG over the previous five years.

The Giant left fielder also stole 31 bases in 1995, making him a 30–30 man for the third time. Bonds was such a powerful offensive threat, however, that his defensive contributions were often overlooked by the fans. In 1995 the strong-armed outfielder had 12 assists, the sixth time in his career he had double-digit assists. His .984 career fielding percentage was five points above the league average, and his 2.10 range factor was 32 points above the league average. He also won five Gold Gloves.

Nineteen-ninety-five had witnessed a historic event in major league baseball. One of its most celebrated records was broken on Wednesday, September 6, when Cal Ripken of the Baltimore Orioles played in his 2131st consecutive game, erasing the mark set by Lou Gehrig in 1939. It had been generally assumed that Gehrig's iron-man feat would last as long as baseball was played, but in 1982 a 21-year-old shortstop in Baltimore began an odyssey that eventually carried him to baseball immortality.

The year also brought sad news to baseball fans around the world. Mickey Mantle, one of the legendary players in the annals of the game, and the game's most powerful switch hitter, passed away at the age of 63. The Mick hit more home runs by the age of 30 than any other player in history, but injuries ended his career prematurely.

The 1996 baseball season was almost a total loss for Dusty Baker and his team. They finished last once again, this time an embarrassing 23 games behind the division-leading San Diego Padres, and a full 15 games behind the third place Colorado Rockies. Long losing streaks did them in: 0–10 run in June, 0–7 streak in July, and another 0–7 streak in August. And to top it off, they went two and fourteen in September. Rookie third baseman Bill Mueller batted .330 in 55 games, filling in for the injured Matt Williams. Glenallen Hill hit .281, with 16 home runs and 63 RBIs. And Barry Bonds, now weighing in at a solid 200 pounds (thanks to a strict weight-training regimen), crushed 42 home runs, drove in 129 runs, and scored 122 runs while batting .308. He also stole 40 bases, making him the major league's second 40–40 man, after Jose Canseco.

As 1997 got underway, major league clubs were still trying to figure out how to get the fans back through the turnstiles. The infamous strike of 1994 caused the fans to desert the ballparks in record numbers. Most people were disgusted with the behavior of both the owners and the players, considering both parties to be excessively greedy. Attendance in 1995 was down an average of 20 percent, and it was still off 14 percent in 1996. A new agreement was finally reached that would extend into the new millennium, but there were a lot of old wounds that would have to be healed before the confidence of the fans could be restored. Would major league baseball survive, or would it shoot itself in the foot again when the new labor contract ran out? Only time would tell.

Giant management, unhappy with the team's last-place finishes over the previous two years, shook up the roster over the winter. They traded popular third baseman Matt Williams to the Cleveland Indians for second baseman Jeff Kent, shortstop Jose Vizcaino, and pitcher Julian Tavarez. Then they obtained first baseman J.T. Snow from the California Angels for two pitchers. Baseball experts were not impressed with San Francisco's maneuverings, and they relegated the Bay Area team to the cellar again. But the shakeup seemed to rejuvenate the team, and when the bell rang, they were off and running.

After dropping their league opener to the Pittsburgh Pirates, 5–2, on April 1, they bounced back to capture game two, 7–5, behind Jeff Kent's five-RBI game. The 6'1" infielder had a two-run homer in the first inning and a two-run double in the fourth. By the end of April, Dusty Baker's bombers were atop the Western Division, tied with the Colorado Rockies, each sporting a 17–7 record. That was rarefied air for the Giants, who could produce only 135 victories in 306 games in 1995–96. Kent set the pace with 26 runs batted in, in 24 games. Glenallen Hill drove in 18 runners. Barry Bonds was off to a slow start, with 13 RBIs on the strength of a .262 batting average and four home runs.

By Memorial Day the Giants had the top spot all to themselves. Their 31–21 record was good enough for a 2½ game lead over the Rockies. One month later they had extended their lead to 4½ games, as the all-around team effort began paying dividends. Jeff Kent slumped in June, but J.T. Snow came on like gangbusters. The big first baseman slammed seven home runs and drove in 21 runs during the month. And Barry Bonds was beginning to show some life. At the halfway mark of the season he had 19 home runs and 43 RBIs, although batting only .275.

Tommy Lasorda's Los Angeles Dodgers grew as hot as the weather in July, and terrorized the league, with 20 victories in 27 games. They wiped out an eight-game San Francisco lead, and caught the Giants by month's end. They had four players with more than 20 home runs, and three players with more than 60 runs batted in. Chan Ho Park and Hideo Nomo led the pitching staff with ten wins each, and Todd Worrell sported 27 saves. The Giants, who led the league by six games at the All-Star break, went eight and thirteen the rest of the month to squander their lead. Bonds was not part of the problem, however, as he raked opposing pitchers for a .340 batting average, with eight home runs and 26 RBIs.

The Dodgers kept the pressure on in August, stretching their lead over the San Franciscans to 2½ games on the strength of a 19–11 mark. Dusty Baker's boys showed a 16–13 slate for the month. The plucky Giants chipped away at the L.A. lead in September, finally catching them on the 11th, on the strength of a 5–3 win over the Philadelphia Phils. Jeff Kent was the big gun, smashing a game-winning two-run homer in the ninth inning. On Wednesday, September 17, the Orange and Black welcomed the enemy into their lair. The Dodgers came to town for a critical two game series. In the opener, Barry Bonds took Chan Ho Park deep with one man on in the first inning, and Kirk Rueter made it stand up, for a 2–1 victory, pulling the Giants to within one game of the Dodgers. The next night, San Francisco stood all alone on top of the National League Western Division, on the strength of a tense, 12-inning victory. The Giants blew a 5–1 lead when L.A. scored two runs in the top of the sixth and two more in the seventh. The Dodgers almost pulled the game out in the tenth inning when they loaded the bases with no outs, but Giant closer Rod Beck bore down and struck out Todd Zeile, then got Eddie Murray to hit into a fast second-to-home-to-first double play. The game stood at 5–5 until catcher Brian Johnson hit a walk-off home run, sending the fans in 3Com Park into a hysterical celebration. Barry Bonds, who had hit a three-run homer earlier in the game, was so excited he hurt his shoulder lifting manager Dusty Baker off the ground. Afterward he said, "Both games had everybody on edge. Regardless of the outcome, we gave baseball what it wanted."

Bob Nightengale, in *USA Today*, noted, "The Giants, with their gang of misfits and castoffs, are like a college fraternity trying to crash baseball's debutante post-season ball…. The Giants have no reason being in this National League West race."

San Francisco moved on to San Diego and took two out of three from the Padres, while Tommy Lasorda's crumbling Dodgers were being swept, three straight, in the mountains of Colorado. Barry Bonds' two-run homer in the sixth inning set the pace for a 7–4 Giant victory in the opener. On Saturday the Padres romped to a 12–2 win, but the next day San Francisco showed its character by scoring three runs in the ninth, giving them a hard fought 8–5 victory. San Diego had tied the game with three runs in the eighth, but Dusty Baker's boys were not to be denied. Barry Bonds hit another home run, a solo job in the fourth. The Giants closed out the Padres with a convincing 11–5 rout on getaway day. Center fielder Darryl Hamilton, another big producer for San Francisco, had a single and a double, and three RBIs. Glenallen Hill hit a solo shot in the second, and J.T. Snow hit number 27 off Andy Ashby, with two men on in the third inning.

The San Francisco Giants held their lead over the last two weeks of the season and captured the Western Division crown by two games over the favored Dodgers. It was Dusty Baker's most satisfying triumph, coming after most experts wrote the Giants off as a bunch of losers. These losers were winners.

The mound corps was led by Shawn Estes, who finished with a 19–6 record. Kirk Rueter went 13–6, and Mark Gardner had 12–9. In the pen, Rod Beck won seven games against four losses, and saved another 37. J.T. Snow batted .281, with 28 home runs and 104 runs batted in. Jeff Kent hit only .250, but slammed 29 home runs and drove in 121 teammates. And Barry Bonds closed strong, batting.291, with 40 home runs, 123 runs scored, and 101 RBIs. He also stole 37 bases, making him a 30–30 man for a record fifth time.

The Giants met the free-spending Florida Marlins in the Division Series, while the Atlanta Braves took on the Houston Astros. The opener of the Florida Series was a tight pitchers' duel that went to the Marlins by a score of 2–1. The Giants held a 1–0 lead after 7½ innings on the strength of a home run to right field by Bill Mueller, but Jim Leyland's team tied it at one-all in the bottom of the inning on a homer by Charles Johnson, and won it in the bottom of the ninth on a run-scoring single by Edgar Renteria off Roberto Hernandez. In game two the Marlins came through in the bottom of the ninth again, and once again Roberto Hernandez was the victim. A single by Moises Alou rescued Gary Sheffield with the game-winner. Barry Bonds had a single and a double in a losing cause. Stan Javier had four hits. Dusty Baker's cohorts went quietly to their graves in the finale, as Florida captured the series in three straight with a 6–2 win at 3Com Park. Julian Tavarez was hit freely by the Floridians; yielding four runs in a sixth-inning uprising that broke open a scoreless game. Jeff Kent was the only Giant to earn his salary, going three for four, with a home run and two RBIs. Barry Bonds was zero for four.

Jim Leyland's fighting fish went on to stun the baseball world by defeating the powerful Cleveland Indians 3–2 in 11 innings in the seventh game of the World Series. A two-out single by Edgar Reneria sent Craig Counsell scurrying across the plate with the championship run.

Nineteen-ninety-eight was another expansion year in the major leagues, with some minor realignments. The Tampa Bay Devil Rays were added to the American League roster, while the Arizona Diamondbacks became the newest members of the National League. At the same time, the Milwaukee Brewers moved from the American League to the National League, leaving the two leagues unbalanced. The National League now had 16 teams, five each in the East and West, and six in the Central, including the Brewers. The American League had just 14 teams, with a four-team Western Division.

It was also the year of the great home run battle between Mark McGwire and Sammy Sosa. The pennant races took a back seat to the dual assault on Roger Maris' home run record. The summer turned into a media frenzy, as newspaper and television reporters stalked the two sluggers unremittingly. When the year finally came to a welcome end for the two combatants, McGwire had set a new record with 70 home runs, and Sosa was close behind with 66. Actually, Sosa was the first to 66, but McGwire came roaring down the stretch, slamming five home runs in his last 11 at-bats, to claim the crown.

In the National League pennant race, the Los Angeles Dodgers were favored to win the Western Division, with a strong mix of hitting (Piazza, Karros, and Eric Davis) and pitching (Nomo, Valdes, Park, and Ramon Martinez).

The Giants didn't read the press clippings, however. They just went out and played baseball. By June 6 they were safely ensconced in first place in their division, after running off an eleven game winning streak. Then disaster struck. Second baseman Jeff Kent, one of the team's sparkplugs, went down with a sprained right knee, sending Dusty Baker's team on a downward spiral. They lost the first four games after Kent went down, and quickly dropped out of the race. By the time he returned in mid–July, the team was in second place, 13 games behind San Diego.

The only good news was that they were still in the running for a wild card slot, trailing the Chicago Cubs and New York Mets by two games. The three teams jockeyed for position throughout September, with first one team, then another taking over the wild card lead. On September 18 it looked like the Giants were out of it, as they trailed the Mets and Cubs by three and four games respectively. But Giant manager Dusty Baker still had one more rabbit to pull out of his hat. His team won seven of its last nine games to finish in a tie with Chicago for the wild card spot. The Giants could have won the wild card spot outright with a victory in the final game of the season, but they came up a run short. The Colorado Rockies scored the winning marker in the bottom of the ninth to frustrate the Giants 9–8. Vinny Castilla's two-run homer off Julian Tavarez, and Neifi Perez's ninth inning homer off Rob Nen, were the key hits.

The day after the regular season ended, the Giants and Cubs met in a one-game playoff in Wrigley Field to determine the National League wild card entry. Things didn't go well for Baker's crew. After 4½ scoreless innings, the Cubs broke through against thirteen game winner Mark Gardner for two runs. Gary Gaetti's round tripper with a man on did the damage. They added two more in the sixth on a pinch hit single by Matt Mieske, and cruised home from there, 5–3. The Giants scored their only runs in the ninth, but they came up two short. The season was over.

In another part of the baseball world, the major league's most amazing streak came to a voluntary end on the last day of the season when Baltimore Oriole third baseman Cal Ripken, Jr., took himself out of the lineup for the first time since 1982, breaking a string of 2,632 consecutive games played. The 38-year-old iron man would go on to accumulate more than 3,000 base hits and 400 home runs in an illustrious career spanning 21 years.

For San Francisco, Barry Bonds had another sensational year, batting .303, with 37 home runs, 120 runs scored, 122 runs batted in, and 28 stolen bases. As usual, he was a one-man wrecking crew, and perhaps the greatest all-around player of his generation. He laid claim to that title by becoming baseball's first 400–400 man, with 411 home runs and 445 stolen bases. Second baseman Jeff Kent finished with a .297 average, 31 homers, and 128 RBIs. Overall, Dusty Baker's bombers had one of the most powerful offenses in the National League, finishing with 845 runs scored, second only to Houston's 874. Unfortunately, the pitching didn't quite match the hitting. The starting pitching was erratic, finishing 12th out of 15 teams. The bullpen was outstanding, however, leading the league in ERA and finishing sixth in total saves.

Barry Bonds had turned 34 on July 24, and Father Time was beginning to catch up with him. He was entering the period in his life where he could no longer take his body for granted. He could no longer go from season to season with only casual conditioning. Now he had to punish his body with a strenuous off-season training regimen in order to be ready for another grueling 162-game schedule. He still had a burning desire to be the greatest player of his time, and to challenge the single-season home run record, and his body was the key to his fulfilling that dream. So he pushed himself five hours a day, five days a week through the winter, lifting weights, doing Nautilus strengthening exercises, practicing martial arts, riding the stationary bike, and running. The program added additional bulk and muscle to his already powerful frame. He now topped the scales at 210 pounds, a far cry from his early days at Pittsburgh, when he was a lanky 165-pounder batting leadoff.

In 1999 the Giants were once again anchored by Barry Bonds and the reliable Jeff Kent, but they still had essentially the same cast of characters that finished 9½ games behind San Diego the previous year. Manager Dusty Baker might have to pull a few rabbits of the hat for the Giants to win the division.

San Francisco jumped out to a 5–0 start when the season opened, sweeping a three game series from Cincinnati in Cinergy Field, and winning two games against the defending division champion San Diego Padres at home, scoring a total of 45 runs and batting .343. Bonds had his magic working early as he piled up nine hits in nineteen at-bats, with two homers and eight RBIs.

Dusty Baker had his charges sitting atop the Western Division on April 17, when the injury jinx reared its ugly head. Barry Bonds, who was rapping the ball at a lusty .366 pace, with four homers and 12 runs batted in in 12 games, went down with a tendon problem in his elbow. Surgery was required, sidelining him for almost eight weeks. It was a long eight weeks for San Francisco, but they managed to stay competitive, thanks to some timely hitting by Rich Aurilia (.307, 9 and 30), Jeff Kent (.290, 7 and 31), and J.T. Snow (.304, 4 and 27). Russ Ortiz, a 4–4 pitcher in '98, was pacing the pitching staff, with a 6–3 record and a sensational 2.54 earned-run-average. Robb Nen had 15 saves out of the bullpen, and John Johnstone was 4–1, with a 1.57 ERA, in a setup role.

Bonds came back from elbow surgery sooner than expected, but after two months of relative inactivity, he had difficulty catching up with the fastball. He started in left field on June 9 against the Anaheim Angels, but drew the collar in four at-bats, as the Giants lost 2–1. He later confessed, "I want to last longer than six innings before getting tired. By the third at-bat, I was a little weary."

Dusty Baker's team was one game out of first when Bonds returned, but a month later they had regained first place, with a 50–38 record, 2½ games better than the Arizona Diamondbacks. They went 17–12 after Bonds' return, although Bonds sat out the last five days with tightness in his groin.

The month of July was unkind to the Giants, as they won only six of sixteen games after the break, dropping into second place, 2½ games behind Arizona. On the last day of the month, Barry Bonds exploded against the Cincinnati Reds, driving in five runs in an 11–1 Giant victory. He blasted two home runs, a three-run job in the first inning and a two-run shot in the third. He had 16 home runs and 49 RBIs to show for his 52 games played. Mark McGwire and Sammy Sosa were locked up in another titanic home run duel, with 40 each. They were both on track to break 60 again.

As the major league season neared its end, several players validated their Hall-of-Fame credentials by passing some notable milestones. Mark McGwire became the 15th man in baseball history to hit more than 500 career home runs. Tony Gwynn entered the prestigious 3000 hit club. Cal Ripken became the first shortstop to hit 400 home runs, and when he corralled his 3000th base hit in 2000, he joined a club (400–3000) that had only six other members—Hank Aaron, Willie Mays, Eddie Murray, Dave Winfield, Stan Musial, and Carl Yastrzemski.

The San Francisco Giants ran out of gas down the stretch. They went as far as their talent could carry them, but it wasn't far enough. They went 36–38 after the All-Star break to finish 14 games behind the division-leading Arizona Diamondbacks. Barry Bonds never got back on average-wise, finishing at .262, but he was still just as dangerous in the clutch, as evidenced by his 34 home runs and 83 runs batted in in just 102 games.

A new millennium meant new hope for major league baseball's also-rans. And that included the San Francisco Giants, who moved into a new ballpark, Pacific Bell Park, to escape the wind and the cold that were constant enemies at Candlestick Park. Never again would a pitcher be blown off the mound like Stu Miller was in the 1961 All-Star game. And never again would a player be able to put his glove up against the outfield wall and have the wind hold it there, as Miller supposedly demonstrated.

San Francisco fans were counting on Barry Bonds and Jeff Kent to lead them to the promised land. The polls picked the Giants to finish third behind the Dodgers and Diamondbacks, but Dusty Baker's only concerns were getting his team ready to play and keeping everyone healthy.

San Francisco's season got underway on April 3 with a loss to the Florida Marlins, 6–4. Giant starter Livan Hernandez was pounded for five runs in six innings, as John Boles' team unleashed a twelve-hit attack. Barry Bonds had a double in four at-bats for the Bay Area club. The Giants took the next two games, then dropped the finale, 5–4, in spite of Bonds' first home run of the season, a two-run shot in the fourth that gave his team a short-lived 4–1 lead.

It was an up-and-down month for San Francisco, and when it ended, the Giants were sitting in last place in the division, with a 10–13 record, five games behind Arizona. The biggest problem Baker had in the early going was the pitching, which was 12th in ERA in the 15 team league. Hernandez was 0–4, Estes was 0–1, and Robb Nen had two blown saves. The team's offense was in the middle of the pack, with only Kent, Bonds, and Ellis Burks performing up to expectations. Bonds, in fact, was playing outstanding baseball. He had clubbed ten home runs in 23 games, and driven in 18 teammates. And his opportunities were limited, as opposing pitchers were giving him very little to hit, choosing instead to walk him, as shown by his 20 bases on balls.

The Giants also had a problem winning in their new ballpark. They lost the first six home games before breaking out against the Montreal Expos. Barry Bonds' eighth inning home run broke a 1–1 tie, giving John Johnstone a victory. The Giants' left fielder hit another home run on Sunday in a 4–3 loss to the Expos, and followed it up with yet another on Monday in a 10–3 rout of the New York Mets.

The Orange and Black finally got back on track after a sluggish start, as Dusty Baker's embattled pitching staff finally settled down, compiling a sparkling 2.94 earned-run-average during the 14 game home stand, which ended with seven victories in the last eight games.

Their winning streak reached seven games before they were brought back to earth by the St. Louis Cardinals. Then the roller coaster season hit the down slope again, as the Giants went 5–12 over the next three weeks, in spite of eight home runs by Barry Bonds. They finished the month strong, winning their last three games. Bonds' home run against the Phils on May 31 gave him ten for the month and 20 for the season.

On June 3 Bonds hit two home runs against the Oakland A's, but Art Howe's troops prevailed, 9–7. Almost unnoticed, the Giant slugger was moving up the all-time home run list. His 21st homer moved him past Dave Winfield and into 20th place on the career list. The next day he hit number 23 against Omar Olivares in the Oakland Coliseum, and the Orange and Black won easily, 18–2. Moving over to Edison International Field, the Giants took the measure of the Anaheim Angels 5–4 in 11 innings, winning it on Bonds' home run. The next night the Angels pulled out a heart-stopping 6–5 victory, with two runs in the bottom of the ninth off Robb Nen. Bonds' solo homer in the third had helped Dusty Baker's cohorts fashion a 3–0 lead, but the bullpen couldn't hold it.

Bonds' four homers in four games catapulted him into the major league lead in home runs, with 25. In the National League, Mark McGwire was second, with 22.

Baseball Weekly noted that, "The Giants are one of the majors' streakiest teams. They've won seven in a row, and also had losing streaks of eight and seven. In their first 17 series, nine were sweeps—The Giants swept five teams and got swept four times."

According to manager Baker, their defense was letting the team down. "A lot of it's defense. When we're in a bad streak, we're usually playing bad defense."

By the time the All-Star break arrived, San Francisco had moved into second place, 3½ games behind the Diamondbacks. The team had gone a respectable 21–14 since Memorial Day, gaining 3½ games in the standings. Jeff Kent was having a career-season, batting a blistering .355, with 23 homers, 70 runs scored, and 85 RBIs. Barry Bonds had 28 homers, 68 runs scored, and 57 RBIs to go along with a .309 average. He had also been walked 56 times.

As the weather heated up, so did the Giants. They caught the Arizona Diamondbacks on the last day of July with a 4–3, 11-inning win over the Milwaukee Brewers, while the Diamondbacks were idle. Ellis Burks' round tripper was the game-winner. Dusty Baker's tenacious crew won 19 games in July, against only 8 losses, in their race for the top. And closer Robb Nen, emerging from the doldrums, boasted 14 saves and a minuscule 0.56 ERA.

The National League pennant race had narrowed down to a two-team affair, matching the pitching of Randy Johnson and Curt Schilling against the slugging of Jeff Kent and Barry Bonds. The Los Angeles Dodgers, one of the pre-season favorites, were quietly fading into the sunset.

Mark McGwire had dropped out of the home run race, with tendonitis in his right knee prematurely ending his season. But new contenders appeared on the horizon to pick up the gauntlet. Gary Sheffield of the Dodgers had 37 home runs, and Sammy Sosa of the Cubs had 36. Four other players, including Bonds, were also in the hunt.

The San Francisco Giants kept the pressure on in August, going 19–10 for the month. Buck Showalter's Diamondbacks, on the other hand, limped along at a 15–12 pace, dropping three back in the race. Arizona's two aces had sub-par months, Johnson going 2–2 and Schilling 3–3. Barry Bonds kept plugging along, hitting seven home runs and driving in 17.

The Giants came roaring down the stretch, winning 16 of 20 games through September 21 to clinch the division crown. The Diamondbacks self destructed, losing 13 of 19 games to drop into third place, a full 12½ games out. Fittingly, Dusty Baker's boys wrapped up the division title at home against Arizona, taking a hard fought 8–7 win in the clincher.

Barry Bonds did not win the home run crown. That honor belonged to Sammy Sosa, who put 50 balls out of National and American League parks. But the Giant slugger did move into 17th place on the all-time

Sammy Sosa has been a media darling since 1998. He never met a microphone he didn't like. (Courtesy James R. Madden, Jr.)

home run list, passing Willie Stargell, Stan Musial, and Lou Gehrig down the stretch.

Once again the playoffs were disastrous for the Bay Area entry. They were eliminated by the New York Mets in four games. Livan Hernandez captured the opener, 5–1, on a five hitter, but after that their tank went dry. The Mets jumped on the Giants' bullpen the next day; scoring three runs in the last two innings for a 5–4 win. Game three was a nail-biter, going 13 innings before the Mets pulled it out 3–2. Bobby Valentine's boys polished off the demoralized west coasters in the finale, 4–0. The Giants went quietly, garnering only one hit off the slants of Bobby J. Jones.

Barry Bonds suffered through another frustrating post-season, batting just .176, with no homers and one RBI in four games.

13. Barry Bonds—
The Home Run King

When Mark McGwire broke Roger Maris' home run record in 1998, setting the mark at a lofty 70 home runs, people felt the new record would last for several decades, as Ruth's and Maris' did. People were wrong. In 1999 McGwire (65) and Sosa (63) once again raised havoc around the National League. But so did eleven other sluggers who hit over 40 home runs apiece. The following year, Chicago's favorite son hit 50 more home runs, and 14 other players hit over 40. McGwire was limited to playing in 89 games because of injuries.

Some of the brawny bombers who were waiting in the wings to challenge Big Mac's record were Jeff Bagwell of the Houston Astros, who averaged 42 homers a year between 1997 and 2000; Ken Griffey, Jr., of the Cincinnati Reds, who averaged 50 home runs a year over the previous five years, including 56 home runs in both 1997 and 1998; Jason Giambi, Oakland's powerful first baseman, who hit 43 homers in 2000; Vladimir Guerrero of the Montreal Expos, who, at 25 years of age, already had two 40-plus home run seasons behind him; and Barry Bonds, who hit 49 homers in 2000, and who already had 494 career home runs to his credit.

Bonds was considered to be the long-shot of the group because his biological clock was ticking away the last years of his major league career. At 37 years old, his best years were thought to be behind him. But Bonds didn't see it that way. He entered the 2001 season like a man on a mission. He had played 15 years in the major leagues without a World Series ring, and he desperately wanted one before he retired. He also wanted a crack at McGwire's record. And he wanted to dispel the rumors that he couldn't hit in the clutch. His career post-season record, totaling five playoff series over five years, consisted of 27 games and 97 at-bats, in which he hit a puny .196, with one home run and six runs batted in. And

Top: Vladimir Guerrero hit 44 home runs in 2000, and, at only 26 years of age, he is a distinct threat to break the single season home run record before he retires. (Courtesy William F. McNeil) *Left:* Ken Griffey, Jr., at 32 years old, has twice hit 56 home runs in a season. (James R. Madden, Jr.)

that didn't count the 1998 wild card playoff game against the Chicago Cubs, in which he went zero for four.

During the off-season, the Giants lost one of their key players to free agency. Ellis Burks, who was one of their most productive offensive weapons, signed with the Cleveland Indians. They also traded away third baseman Bill Mueller. Once again, the Los Angeles Dodgers were the popular choice to win the division, but they had established themselves as underachievers over the past six years, so there was no reason to believe they would suddenly come together as a team in 2001.

Manager Dusty Baker had his team ready to go when the season opened in PacBell Park, and they gave the home fans something to cheer about by defeating the San Diego Padres, 3–2. San Fran scored single runs in the fourth, fifth, and sixth to take the game. Barry Bonds, giving his fans a preview of things to come, launched a 420-foot homer off Woody Williams, with one out in the fifth, to back the strong pitching of Livan Hernandez.

Bonds' favorite weapon in his home run quest would be his specially crafted bat, known as the Rideau Crusher, named after a canal in Ottawa, Canada. The maple bat measured 34 inches long and weighed 32 ounces, almost feather-like in comparison to the war club brandished by Babe Ruth, which weighed in the neighborhood of 42 ounces. Heavy bats were popular in the 1920s and '30s, when players felt that the bigger the bat, the farther the ball would travel. Modern day sluggers follow the philosophy that bat speed is more important than weight, so they generally use light, thin-handled bats that can be whipped through the hitting zone quickly. These bats shatter easily, so players keep dozens of them on hand.

On April 12 the Giants were beaten by the Padres, but Bonds sliced a 417-foot homer to left center field in the first inning, breaking a zero for 21 streak. That homer got the big lefty rolling. He went on to homer in six consecutive games, hitting three against Milwaukee and two against Tommy Lasorda's Dodgers. Unfortunately, the Giants weren't able to take advantage of Bonds' big blasts, winning only three of the six games played.

Barry Bonds passed another milestone in the Giants' game against the Los Angeles Dodgers on April 17. In the eighth inning, with the Giants down 2–1, Bonds tied into a 2–0 pitch from Terry Adams and sent it on a high arc over the right field wall and into McCovey Cove, scoring a runner ahead of him and giving his team a 3–2 victory. It was Bonds' 500th career home run, putting him in select company—alongside men like Ted Williams, Mickey Mantle, and Barry's godfather, Willie Mays. Strangely, none of his teammates came out of the dugout to greet him after his historic trip around the bases, a sign that all was not well in the Giant clubhouse. Jeff Kent, who was a leader on the San Francisco team, once claimed Bonds didn't care about his teammates. Obviously the feeling was mutual.

Dusty Baker's bombers finished the month of April in fourth place in the Western Division, with a 12–12 record, 2½ games behind the front-running Dodgers. Barry Bonds had bounced back from a slow start to account for 11 home runs, good for second place in the National League, two behind Luis Gonzalez of Arizona. Sammy Sosa had seven. Mark

McGwire, with just one home run to his credit, went on the Disabled List and was not expected back until mid–July.

The Giant star continued to climb up the career home run list as the days and months passed. By May 19 he had moved into 13th place, with 514 home runs. He reached that milestone by putting three balls into orbit against the Atlanta Braves in Turner Field. His first homer, in the third inning against southpaw Odalis Perez, was a 416-foot shot into the right field stands. Four innings later he walloped a 440-foot bomb to right, against Jose Cabrera; and in the eighth he capped off his exciting evening by taking Jason Marquis downtown, to dead center field. San Francisco used Bonds' heroics to beat the Braves 6–3. Afterwards, Bonds was quoted by ESPN as saying, "This is crazy. It was just a good day. You don't have days like this every day. I'm happy to have them at all." Chipper Jones of the Braves paid Bonds the highest compliment when he said, "He's the best player in the game, bar none."

Bonds came right back with two home runs the next night. His victims were John Burkett and Mike Remlinger. He connected for a 415-foot blast off Burkett in the top of the first, then slammed a 436-footer to center field off Remlinger in the top of the seventh. But it was not enough to carry the day. The Braves pounded Hernandez and Alan Embree for 11 runs in an 11–6 victory. Bonds also homered the next two nights in Arizona, but the Giants came up empty both times. In all, he hit nine home runs in six consecutive games, but the Giants won only one game.

On the 27th, Barry Bonds hit a 390 foot-chip shot to right field off Colorado southpaw Denny Neagle, as the Giants won 5–4. It was his 11th home run in a ten game span. After the game, as reported by *Baseball Weekly*, he touched on the liveliness of the baseball, something the historians have been questioning for the past eight years. "Balls I used to line off the wall are going out of the park. I can't understand it. I try to figure it out, and I can't figure it out." The statistics bore out what Bonds was saying. In 1961, when Roger Maris hit 61 home runs, teams averaged 145 home runs in 154 games. By 1998, when Mark McGwire broke the record, each team averaged 160 home runs, as noted earlier; and just three years later the average was up to 173.

Bonds experienced a bittersweet moment on May 30. He lit up the Arizona sky with two home runs, both over 400 feet, in a 4–3 loss to the Diamondbacks. The homers were numbers 521 and 522, pushing him past one of his San Francisco idols, Hall-of-Fame first baseman Willie McCovey, as well as the great Red Sox hitting machine Ted Williams.

As the curtain came down on the month of May, Bonds had 28 home runs, including 17 during the month, but his team was mired in last place, five games behind the Diamondbacks, after losing eight of their last eleven games. Jeff Kent had 39 runs batted in, in 56 games, while Bonds had 52. However, the other Giant outfielders had combined for a total of just 59 RBIs. They definitely missed the big bat of Ellis Burks. The pitching staff, as it had been the previous year, was in disarray. Livan Hernandez could do no better than a 3–8 record, with a 6.81 ERA. Kirk Rueter was 5–6, 6.41, and Mark Gardner was 1–4, 5.89. The bullpen had only 15 save opportunities, confirming the ineptitude of the starting staff.

The other division races were being led by Larry Bowa's surprising Philadelphia Phils (who owned an eight game lead over the Atlanta Braves) and the Chicago Cubs in the National League; and the Boston Red Sox, Minnesota Twins, and Seattle Mariners in the American League. The big story in the majors was the amazing performance of Lou Pinella's Seattle team, who had run up a record of 40–12, a winning percentage of .769. They led the second place Oakland Athletics by a whopping 14 games at months end. The Mariners were led by former Japanese legend Ichiro Suzuki, who prefers to be called only by his first name; John Olerud; Bret Boone; and Edgar Martinez; plus a sensational pitching staff headed by Aaron Sele (8–0), Freddy Garcia (6–0), Jamie Moyer (7–1), and Kazuhiro Sasaki (23 saves). Ichiro, who had captured the last seven Japanese League batting titles, was in third place in the American League race, with a .362 average, but he was leading the league in base hits and stolen bases. In the National League home run race, Luis Gonzalez had 21 home runs, seven behind Bonds. Sammy Sosa was off to a slow start with just 15 homers. No one in the American League had more than 18.

The Giants continued to struggle in June, as manager Dusty Baker looked for a way to shift his team into high gear. After sleepwalking through the first ten days of the month with a 5–5 record, the Orange and Black took off on a six game winning streak, thanks primarily to some great pitching. The staff allowed only eight runs over that span. The Giants scored 23, but ten of them came in one game. Barry Bonds went 8 for 19, with four home runs. He hit a home run off Pat Rapp of Anaheim on the 12th to get the winning streak underway. It was a low line drive down the right field foul line in PacBell Park that barely cleared the fence at the 307 foot mark before settling into McCovey Cove. The first-inning solo shot paced the Giants to a 3–2 victory. Bonds homered against the Angels again on the fourteenth, then hit two home runs on the 15th in a 3–1 win over the Oakland Athletics. His first homer, in the first inning, was a slice into the left field stands at PacBell Park, putting San Fran up 1–0. His second homer came in the sixth and gave his team a 3–1 lead. The 375-foot shot to right field was his 36th of the season, putting him twelve games ahead of Mark McGwire's pace. Mark Mulder, the victim of both Bonds home runs, said in an AP article, "You'd think you can make a mistake to him once in awhile, but he hits every one of them."

The home run race began to get interesting in late June, and the media expanded its coverage of Barry Bonds' quest. Under pressure from the news organizations, the Giants agreed to schedule daily news conferences with Barry Bonds, but almost as soon as the media blitz began, the Giant slugger went into a slump. He had one short spurt, between June 19 and June 23, when he hit three more home runs, giving him 39 for the season and 533 for his career, one behind Jimmie Foxx, but that was the extent of his home run production for a period of almost three weeks. It became so frustrating that manager Dusty Baker considered calling off the news conferences. "I wish they'd leave him alone sometimes. Ever since he's gotten this scrutiny, he hasn't been as hot. Sooner or later, I anticipate him or me getting you out of his face."

Barry Bonds' season almost came to an end on June 29 in a game against St. Louis. In the fifth inning of a scoreless contest, Cardinal leadoff batter Albert Pujols sent a drive to deep left that had home run written all over it. But the Giant left fielder went back to the fence and made a leaping catch to rob the Cardinal third baseman of a homer, maintaining the status quo. He banged his wrist in making the catch and sat out the Saturday game, but the injury proved to be minor, and he was back at work on Sunday.

Bonds' slump dragged on for 13 games, during which time the San Francisco team could win only five games. Bonds contributed a measly .214 batting average during that period, with six doubles and no home runs in 42 at-bats. At the All-Star break, Barry Bonds was still hitting .305, with 39 homers and 73 runs batted in. His other half, Jeff Kent, was hitting .297, with 12 homers and 64 RBIs. Rich Aurilia, the Giants' rangy shortstop, picked up some of the slack caused by the loss of Ellis Burks, and the sub-par first half performance of Kent, by ripping the ball at a sizzling .356 pace, with 12 homers and 38 RBIs. The Giants' total offensive statistics put them in the upper half of the league, but their pitching was still disappointing, half a run worse than division leading Arizona.

In the league races, the New York Yankees had nosed in front of the Red Sox by 1½ games, while Minnesota and Seattle retained their positions. Seattle finished the first half with a sensational 60–21 record, including 32–9 on the road. In the Senior Circuit, Bobby Cox's Atlanta Braves had shaved seven games off the Philadelphia lead and now trailed by only one game. The Cubs and Arizona were still on top of the other divisions.

The Baltimore Orioles' "senior citizen," Cal Ripken, Jr., was the big gun in the All-Star game, smashing a third inning home run off Chan Ho Park of the Los Angeles Dodgers to lead the American League to a 4–1 victory over the National League.

When the second half of the season began on Thursday, July 12, Barry Bonds was mentally focused. Facing Paul Abbott of the Seattle Mariners, the muscular southpaw swinger hammered a 429-foot home run to right center field at Safeco Field, giving his team a 1–0 lead. It looked for a while like San Francisco would get off to a winning start for the pennant push, but fate deserted them in the ninth inning when third baseman David Bell hit a one-out home run off Giant closer Robb Nen to tie the score at 3–3. The Mariners went on to win in 11 innings on a two-out single by Tom Lampkin that chased the speedy Mike Cameron across the plate. Bonds' home run was his 40th of the season, putting him one game ahead of Mark McGwire. It was also the 544th of his career, tying him with Jimmie Foxx.

In spite of the home runs, Bonds was still struggling at the plate. It was six more games before he homered again. On July 18 he hit two balls into the California evening sky, leading the Giants to a victory over the Colorado Rockies. His first homer, off Mike Hampton in the fourth inning, came on a 2–1 pitch, and was a 320-foot chippie into the right field seats at PacBell Park. It gave Dusty Baker's team a 1–0 lead. The second, an inning later, was a two-run shot to left field, also off Hampton, putting the Bay Area Bombers in front 4–0. They went on to win, 10–0, as Russ Ortiz extended his record to 11–5 with another strong effort. Bonds' two homers put him in a tie with New York Yankee legend Mickey Mantle for ninth place on the all-time list.

Another week passed, and Barry Bonds had nothing to show for it except two singles in 18 at-bats, for a .111 average. His problems at the plate were aggravated by back spasms, which had bothered him since mid–July and which affected his swing, but he toughed it out, playing every game and not complaining.

The Giants lost four of seven games during Bonds' slump, leaving them languishing in third place, 6½ games off the pace of the Arizona Diamondbacks. In an attempt to get back in the race, the Giants made two significant trades. They picked up slugging first baseman Andres Galarraga from the Texas Rangers, and 28-year-old right handed pitcher Jason Schmidt from the Pittsburgh Pirates. Both moves paid dividends.

Dusty Baker brought his warriors into the lion's den, Arizona's Bank One Ballpark, for a four game series against the division-leading Diamondbacks, beginning on July 26. The Giants began the series seven back. In the opener, Livan Hernandez faced off against Arizona's 14-game winner Curt Schilling. In the top of the fourth inning, with the D'Backs up 1–0, Bonds led off and hit Schilling's first pitch 375 feet into the right center field bleachers to tie the game. The next inning, with Arizona up again, 3–2, with the bases full and one out, Bonds again jumped on the first pitch, and this time he drilled it high and long into the center field seats for a grand slam.

The two homers sent Bonds past Mickey Mantle, with 537 career home runs. His next obstacle on the home run list was the Philadelphia Phils third baseman Mike Schmidt, who finished his career with 548 round trippers. In the single-season race, the Giant slugger had 44 home runs, and was still one game ahead of Mark McGwire's 1998 pace. His closest competitor was Luis Gonzalez of Arizona, who had 41 homers. The 6'2", 180-pound D'Backs slugger was having a career season of his own. He was hitting .350, with 102 RBIs in 105 games. Gonzalez had spent nine years in the major leagues before going to Arizona, and he never had more than 23 home runs or 79 RBIs in a season. He experienced a rebirth in the desert country, hitting 26 homers in 1999 and 31 homers in 2000. His RBI totals for those two years were 111 and 114 respectively, and he had a combined batting average of .323, 55 points above his previous career average.

Mike Schmidt hit 548 home runs during an 18 year major league career. (Author's collection)

In game two of the crucial series, Dusty Baker's team ripped Bob Brenly's boys again. This time the score was 9–5. Arizona's Brian Anderson took a 2–1 lead into the fourth inning, but when the lefty tried to sneak a 1–1 pitch past Barry Bonds, the Giant slugger tomahawked it 436 feet into the right field grandstand, tying the game. The Giants took it from there. After Kent was retired, Andres Galarraga hit a solo shot, giving San Fran a 3–2 lead. They added a big six spot in the fifth and coasted home. The loss dropped Arizona out of the top spot for the first time since May 24. They were replaced by Tommy Lasorda's Los Angeles Dodgers. Dusty Baker was elated at the team's resurgence, according to an AP source. "Up and down the lineup, guys are starting to swing the bat pretty good now. I don't know why. It just happens."

The Saturday game was another laugher for the Bay Area crew. Giant ace Russ Ortiz was opposed by journeyman right hander Albie Lopez, who was acquired from Tampa Bay on July 25. The 29-year-old Lopez, who was 5–12 at Tampa Bay, was manhandled by Baker's fired-up crew, particularly by center fielder Marvin Benard, shortstop Rich Aurilia, and right fielder Armando Rios. Benard ripped five base hits in six at-bats, Aurilia was three for five (with two home runs and five runs batted in), and Rios was three for five, with a double and a home run. Barry Bonds' triple and single went almost unnoticed. Ortiz retired after six innings, with a comfortable 10–4 lead, picking up his 12th victory of the season.

The getaway game on Sunday was a good old-fashioned pitchers' duel between Shawn Estes and Randy Johnson, two of the National League's premier southpaws. The fireballing Johnson was on his game, sending 12 batters back to the bench dragging their bats behind them. But Estes was almost as good. As the game entered the eighth inning, the D'Backs were protecting a slim 2–1 lead, fashioned by a two-run homer by former Giant Matt Williams in the second inning. In the top of the eighth, Rich Aurilia took Randy Johnson deep for his 21st home run of the year, tying the game at 2–2. Brenly dipped into his bullpen in the ninth, calling on lightning-fast Byung-Hyun Kim to hold the Bay Area crew in check. The side-wheeling right hander had appeared in 50 games for Arizona, fanning 89 batters in just 66 innings, but this time his speed wasn't good enough. Marvin Benard stepped up with one on and two out, and put a fast ball over the fence to give his team a big 4–2 lead. The D'Backs nicked Robb Nen for a run in the bottom of the ninth, but the Giant closer kept the lid on, and the Giants won again, 4–3. The L.A. lead was now 1½ games over Arizona, with San Francisco just four games out.

The big questions now were, could the Arizona Diamondbacks regroup, or would they drift back into the pack as they did last year? And could the Dodgers hold on to the top spot with the multitude of injuries that had decimated their lineup? Their top three pitchers, Kevin Brown, Andy Ashby, and Darren Dreifort, were all out with season-ending injuries, and many of the position players had been on the DL at one time or another during the season. Grudzielanek and Sheffield were playing hurt, and third baseman Adrian Beltre had never recovered from an off-season appendectomy and subsequent infection.

Manager Dusty Baker felt good about his team's position as the hot August sun turned the infield clay to cement. He had a set lineup, with outstanding firepower in Galarraga, Kent, Aurilia, and Bonds, and he had a revitalized pitching staff headed by Ortiz (12–6), Rueter (10–7), Estes (8–5), Hernandez (9–11, but 6–2 after a slow start), and Robb Nen (30 saves, 2.96 ERA). He was ready to take on the world.

On August 1 Barry Bonds hit a two-out, first-inning home run to give his team a 1–0 lead over the Pittsburgh Pirates. The 400-foot shot, number 46 on the year, landed on the walkway on top of the right field fence at PacBell Park. Jason Schmidt, in his San Francisco debut, endeared himself to the Giant faithful by tossing seven innings of one-hit ball, and the Orange and Black won 3–1. The next night, Kirk Rueter threw a three-hitter at the Bucs, and Dusty Baker's boys won again, 3–0, as Barry Bonds took a night off. Jeff Kent knocked in two runs with a double, and Marvin Benard homered. The Giants were now only one game out of first place, and a ½ game behind the Arizona Diamondbacks.

Philadelphia moved into PacBell on August 3 and were quickly vanquished, 4–2, when Andres Galarraga hit a two-out, two-run, walk-off homer in the bottom of the ninth off Phillie reliever Turk Wendell. It was the Giants' ninth consecutive victory following their acquisition of Galarraga. Barry Bonds played but was not a factor, going zero for two. It was a tough loss for the Phils, who now trailed Atlanta by two games. The next night Bonds slammed a two-run homer into McCovey Cove off Nelson Figueroa, but Terry Francona's crew roughed up the Orange and Black, 12–2, ending their nine-game streak. Bonds' blast, a 405-footer, brought the Giants back to 5–2, but it was all downhill after that. The Phils scored five in the seventh and two in the eighth to stay within two games of the Atlanta Braves in the Eastern Division.

The Sunday finale turned out to be the Giants' 62nd victory of the season. After spotting the Phils two runs in the top of the first, Baker's bombers roared back to score three in the third and three in the fourth. Rich Aurilia's 23rd homer of the year, a three-run shot off Robert Person in the third inning, was all the Giants needed. They added two more runs in the bottom of the eighth on Aurilia's double, making the final score 8–4.

After Philadelphia left town, Barry Bonds and the San Francisco Giants went on a mini-tear. The Giants won seven of nine games, and Bonds rapped out nine hits in 30 at-bats, six of them for the distance, accounting for 15 runs batted in. On August 7 the Giants beat the Cincinnati Reds in Cinergy Field, 9–3, in 11 innings, with Bonds delivering what turned out to be the game-winning blow, a 430-foot bomb to straight-away center field. San Fran added five more runs before the bleeding could be stopped.

Two days later they beat the Reds again, 6–4, and once again Barry Bonds produced the eventual game-winner. His 350-foot fly ball over the right field fence in the third inning put his team on top, 3–2, and they never looked back. They added single runs in the fourth and fifth innings, in support of Russ Ortiz, who won his 13th game.

The game on the 11th was another milestone for the San Francisco left fielder. After sitting out the opener against the Chicago Cubs in Wrigley Field, a game won by the Cubs 9–3, Barry Bonds was back in action in game two. And this time the Giants won, by a 9–4 margin. They blew the game open in the second inning, pushing over six big runs against Joe Borowski, who was making his first major league start after 57 relief appearances. Three runs were already in, and the Giants had two men on base and two out, when Bonds stepped to the plate to face the right hander. He tied into a 2–2 pitch from Borowski and hit a line drive to deep center, the ball carrying over the ivy-covered wall before bouncing back onto the field. The Giant slugger had to wait for the umpire's call before circling the bases. It was Bonds' 50th home run of the year, putting him within 20 home runs of Mark McGwire's record, with 45 games remaining. The home run put him in select company, along with Willie Mays and Johnny Mize, as the only New York-San Francisco Giants player to hit 50 home runs in a season. It also made Bonds the oldest player ever to hit 50. After the game, the kid from San Carlos showed measurable relief at his accomplishment. "I hope that will finally get my godfather off my back. He said I should have hit 50 years ago." Livan Hernandez was the beneficiary of the San Francisco attack, winning his fifth consecutive start and evening his record at 11–11.

Three days later, in the cozy confines of PacBell Park, Dusty Baker's crew met the Florida Marlins, while Arizona hosted the lowly Pittsburgh Pirates. Only a single game separated the two teams after 119 games. The Dodgers had slipped into third place, three games behind, after losing six of ten. The stretch run promised to be exciting from both a division championship standpoint and the home run chase. In the opener of the series, the Bay Area Bombers came out swinging. They drove Marlin starter

Jesus Sanchez to cover in less than three innings, scoring three runs in the first, two in the second, and three more in the third. Sanchez pitched carefully to Bonds, walking him twice in the first two innings, but Barry's teammates made the skinny right-hander pay for it. Andres Galarraga knocked in two runs with a double, Eric Davis put one over the wall, and Jeff Kent singled in two more. In all, the Giants pounded Sanchez for eight runs on ten hits and three walks. Bonds, after just missing a homer in the third, came to bat in the sixth with the bases loaded against journeyman right-hander Ricky Bones. This time he didn't miss. He crushed an 0–2 pitch, driving it 410 feet over the right field wall and into McCovey Cove. It was number 51. Newly acquired Jason Schmidt won his eighth game of the season.

On Thursday, August 16, San Francisco completed a three game sweep of Florida with a 5–3 victory. The game was a pitchers' duel between 24-year-old A.J. Burnett of the Marlins and Shawn Estes of the Giants. Tony Perez' team nicked Estes for a run in the top of the fourth, but the Giants got it right back in the bottom half of the inning when Barry Bonds popped a 310-foot home run over the short right field wall. The ball hit the sidewalk and bounced into the water. The score stayed 1–1 until the seventh, when Alex Gonzalez blooped a bases-loaded single to right field for two runs and a 3–1 lead. But, again, the Giants roared back. In the bottom of the eighth inning, Pedro Feliz doubled and came home on a single by Marvin Benard, narrowing the Florida lead to 3–2. Rich Aurilia singled, and Bonds, facing L.A. native Vic Darensbourg, hit a monstrous shot to right center field. The ball carried well over the fence before settling into McCovey Cove. The Giant slugger stood and admired his homer for a few seconds, while dozens of kayaks, canoes, and row boats raced to the splash-down area. The PacBell crowd practically brought the light towers down with their screams and whistles, a riotous ovation that lasted for several minutes, until their hero stepped from the dugout and tipped his cap.

Barry Bonds' two home runs gave him yet another record. His 53rd homer sent him past Willie Mays to become the greatest home run hitter in Giant history. It also put him within 17 home runs of McGwire's record. The San Francisco left fielder even seemed to be in awe of himself, as he reported to AP: "I'm accomplishing things I never thought I could do. I was surprised by 50 homers, because I had never done it. I just hope I can carry it on all the way through." When he was reminded that his team had taken 17 of 20 games since July 25, and that he had hit 11 home runs and driven in 28 runs in those games, he replied, "This is a time when you have to excel. The finish line is getting closer and closer."

And Bonds was getting closer and closer to the single season home run record. His 53 home runs through 121 games put him six home runs ahead of Mark McGwire. His nearest competitor in the race, Luis Gonzalez, had 45 home runs and was slowly falling out of contention. Sammy Sosa had 43.

The Giants' five-game win streak finally ended with a 2–1 loss to the Atlanta Braves. Greg Maddux made Dusty Baker's boys his 16th victim of the year, limiting them to six hits and no walks. San Fran starter Livan Hernandez deserved a better fate. He hurled a complete game two-hitter, but was victimized by an error, a Chipper Jones triple, and Brian Jordan's sacrifice fly that gave Bobby Cox's crew the winning runs in the eighth inning. Jeff Kent had given the Giants a 1–0 lead with a home run in the seventh.

That loss seemed to put the Bay Area boys in a downward spiral. They finished the month 5–9, giving them an overall record of 16–12 for August and leaving them a full four games behind the Arizona Diamondbacks. They also trailed the Chicago Cubs by a game and a half in the wild card race. Barry Bonds hit four home runs in the last 14 games of the month, one in a pinch hit role, to give him 57 for the season. Sammy Sosa had 52 homers, while Luis Gonzalez had 51. Sosa's record was particularly impressive. Since 1998 he had hit 231 home runs through August 31, and had two fifty-homer seasons and two sixty-homer seasons, and was on his way to a third sixty-homer season.

The division pennant races were all still up for grabs in the National League. Atlanta led Philadelphia by one game, and the Houston Astros had moved in front of Chicago by four games. In the Junior Circuit, Joe Torre's Yankees opened a seven game lead over the rapidly fading Red Sox, and the Cleveland Indians had taken over the top spot in the Central Division by 5½ games over the Twins. In the individual competitions, Ichiro had moved into first place in the AL batting race, with an average of .351, while Jim Thome led in home runs with 43, and Roger Cedeno was setting the pace in stolen bases with 51. In the National League, Moises Alou was showing the way with a .350 average, and Jimmy Rollins had 40 steals. The most incredible story on the pitchers mound was New York's Roger Clemens, who, at the ripe old age of 38, was almost unbeatable, running off 18 victories against a single loss.

As the month of September began, the media scrutiny kicked into high gear to chronicle the great home run chase. But for some reason the newspaper and television coverage was not nearly as intense as it had been for the McGwire-Sosa chase. Some people thought it was because when Big Mac and Sammy were on the trail of Roger Maris' record, they were chasing a record that had stood the test of time for 37 years, a record that had been broken only once in 74 years. Things were different this time. The record was only three years old, and most baseball people felt the home run had been cheapened considerably since 1993, and even more so since 1998. Major league home runs, which had been relatively stable from 1961 through 1993, suddenly jumped by 17 percent per team between 1993 and 1998, and another 12 percent from '98 to 2001. Also, the new major league baseball stadiums, constructed over the previous twelve years, were bandboxes compared to the spacious ballparks that challenged Babe Ruth and Roger Maris, particularly in the power alleys and center field. And there is evidence that baseballs manufactured since 1994 were livelier. All these factors, coupled with the fact that Barry Bonds was not a fan favorite, resulted in a less-than-enthusiastic atmosphere surrounding his historic quest.

Bonds' adversarial relationship with the media was legendary, and the September scrutiny intensified it. He didn't like the press, and he let them know it in *USA Today*: "I understand their jobs, but I really don't much care for them.... I come to the ballpark to do my job.... I just don't like to be bothered at work."

His relationship with his teammates and with the fans was not much better. The players resented his arrogance and aloofness. They didn't like the special treatment he received, like four lockers and a recliner. They didn't like the fact that he didn't fraternize with them, play cards or backgammon with them, or stretch with them. Bonds kept pretty much to himself, and when the game was over he drove off alone on his Harley-Davidson, or left in his personal limousine. Fans booed and heckled him wherever he went, unlike the friendly reception accorded to McGwire and Sosa when they were chasing the record. He was occasionally bombarded with food and paper products on the field, and was greeted with negative comments.

Barry Bonds sat out the September 1 game, but the Giants beat the Colorado Rockies 2–1. The game was tied at 1–1 in the last of the ninth, when the Big Cat, Andres Galarraga, hit a dramatic two-out, game-winning home run. Robb Nen was the winner in relief. Two days later the Giant slugger put a Jason Jennings sinker-that-didn't-sink into orbit, sending it 435 feet over the wall in right center field; but Jennings settled down and won the game 4–1. On September 4 the Arizona Diamondbacks arrived in PacBell for a big three game series. It would be the last head-to-head series between the two adversaries, and with the Giants trailing the D'Backs by 2½ games in the National League West, it was crucial that they take at least two of the games. In the opener, Jason

Schmidt ran his record to 5–1 since his trade to the Giants on July 30, out pitching Bobby Witt and Greg Swindell to win 5–2. Dusty Baker's gladiators pushed over three runs in the seventh, breaking a 2–2 tie. The teams traded runs on infield outs before Rich Aurilia, San Fran's most recent slugger, hit his 30th home run of the year in the fifth, giving his team a temporary 2–1 lead. Arizona tied the game again in the sixth, and that's where it stood when the Giants batted in the seventh. Aurilia stepped to the plate with one man out to face Miguel Batista, who had come on in relief to start the inning. With Eric Davis on base after singling, and Bonds on deck, the Arizona righty challenged Aurilia, and the Giant shortstop made him regret the decision, hitting his second home run of the game. As he was taking a curtain call to quiet the noisy, sold-out stadium, Barry Bonds launched a Batista fastball 420 feet over the right center field wall.

It was a good start for Dusty Baker's boys. They had closed the gap between them and the D'Backs to 1½ games, and closed to within ½ game of the Cubs for the wild card spot. For Bonds, it was number 59, putting him closer to his destiny. It was also the fastest anyone had hit 59 homers. Mark McGwire had accomplished the feat in 140 games in 1998, and Sammy Sosa had duplicated it in 1999.

Game two in the big series pitted 19-game winner Curt Schilling against the Giants' 14-game winner Russ Ortiz. It was no contest. The big Diamondback righty, who had won five of his six previous decisions, captured his 20th victory of the season with a strong outing. He pitched eight innings in a 7–2 victory, holding the Giants to five hits while fanning twelve. Ortiz, San Francisco's top pitcher, was saddled with his ninth loss. He was knocked out of the box in the fifth inning after yielding three runs on seven base hits. The Arizona attack was led by Craig Counsell, who went four for five, with four runs scored; Reggie Sanders, who was three for five; and Schilling, who went three for four, with two runs scored. Bonds was zero for two, with a walk and a strikeout.

The finale of the series was a huge game for San Francisco, who needed a victory to keep from falling 3½ games behind. Dusty Baker handed the ball to rookie Ryan Jensen, who was making his seventh start of the year. Bob Brenly sent Albie Lopez to the mound in search of his fourth victory. The game turned into a donnybrook that saw 42 players make an appearance, 23 of them wearing Arizona uniforms. The Diamondbacks called on six pitchers in an attempt to stem the tide of Giant runs, while Dusty Baker used seven pitchers in trying to stop the D'Backs. Arizona got off the mark quickly, pushing over two runs in the top of the first on Reggie Sanders' three-bagger and Steve Finley's single. The

Giants, undaunted, came storming back in the bottom half with a four-run barrage. A single by Aurilia, a walk to Bonds, singles by Galarraga and Vander Wal, another walk to Santiago, and a single by Martinez did the damage. In the second inning, with two men out, Barry Bonds made history one more time by hitting a 2–2 pitch 420 feet to right center field. It was home run number 60, making him just the fifth man in major league history to reach that elevated plateau. Babe Ruth, Roger Maris, Mark McGwire, and Sammy Sosa preceded him. The noise from the 41,155 Giant fanatics was deafening. They forced the big slugger to come out of the dugout for a final salute before the game could continue.

After Finley cut the margin to 5–3 with an RBI triple in the third, things quieted down for a few innings. Then, in the bottom of the sixth, the Bay Area Bombers struck again. Three more Giant runners crossed the plate on a two-run single by Aurilia and a double by Galarraga. That essentially ended Arizona's hopes for victory, as Aurilia hit one out in the eighth, and the San Fran bullpen held the D'Backs to two runs in the ninth, clinching a hard fought 9–5 victory.

Barry Bonds savored his achievement in the clubhouse after the game, as reported by AP: "That homer was nice. My heart was racing as I rounded the bases." But as much as he relished the adulation of the Pac-Bell faithful, he tried to keep his comments to the men of the press focused on the pennant race. He told the reporters that with a tight race between the Giants and the Diamondbacks, he didn't expect to see too many more good pitches. He expected opposing pitchers to start pitching around him, so it would be up to the men batting behind him, especially Kent and Galarraga, to take up the slack.

The Giants hit the road after the Arizona series for a short, three-game visit to Coors Field, a slugger's paradise. It was estimated that there were 69 percent more homers hit in Coors Field than in the average National League stadium. But two games passed without a Bonds home run. Dusty Baker's cohorts dropped the opener 3–2 in 12 innings. Barry Bonds reached base six times in six trips to the plate, three times on walks, once on a double, and twice on singles. He had one RBI, but with Kent out of the lineup and Galarraga going one for six, his efforts were wasted. The next day the Giants got back on the winning track by taking a 7–3 decision from Buddy Bell's cellar dwellers. Kirk Rueter won his 14th game of the year, with help from three relievers. Jeff Kent and J.T. Snow accounted for five runs batted in between them. Kent had a single, a double, and a home run, while Snow had a two-run double. Bonds was held to a single in five attempts.

On Sunday Barry Bonds exploded, and the Giants needed all his efforts to win 9–4 in 11 innings. The powerful left fielder led the San Fran hit parade with three home runs, one of them a titanic blast off Scott Elarton in the first inning. That homer, following a home run by Rich Aurilia, came on a 1–1 pitch and was a 488-foot drive that carried over the right center field wall, striking a beer sign. It was the third longest home run in Coors Field history, and it put his team up 2–0. They added another run before the inning ended, upping the margin to 3–0. Colorado scored one in the fourth. Then, in the top of the fifth, Bonds did more damage with a leadoff home run, again off Elarton. This time the ball traveled a mere 361 feet, barely clearing the right field wall. The Rockies pushed over one run in the fifth, then tied the game at 4–4 with two more in the sixth. That's where the score stood after ten innings. In the top of the 11th, J.T. Snow, who had battled injuries and a season-long slump, came to the plate with one out and slammed a two-run home run, his eighth of the year, giving the Giants a 6–4 lead. A walk to Eric Davis and a single by Rich Aurilia set the stage for more Bonds heroics. Number 25, facing southpaw Todd Belitz, tied into a 0–1 pitch and drove it on a high arc to right field, the ball coming to earth 394 feet from home plate.

Barry Bonds was still in a daze in the clubhouse. According to an AP article, Bonds said, "I've been in disbelief over a lot of things I've done this year. Everything is unreal. That was fun today." Bonds' pyrotechnics set new standards in several areas. His three home runs gave him 63 for the year, sending him past Roger Maris, and putting him hot on the trail of Sosa and McGwire. It also established a record for the most home runs ever hit by a left handed batter. Number 63 came in the team's 144th game, giving him an eight game bulge over Mark McGwire. The three homers also gave him 32 home runs on the road, tying the mark set by Babe Ruth and matched by McGwire. Sammy Sosa was sitting on 54 home runs after 142 games, and Luis Gonzalez had 51.

Just as the big home run race was about to enter its final three weeks, tragedy struck America's heartland. At precisely 8:45 AM, EDT, a Boeing 767 jet airliner, American Airlines Flight 11, en route from Boston's Logan Airport to Los Angeles, was hijacked by Arab terrorists and diverted to New York City, where it was intentionally flown into the North Tower of the World Trade Center. As thousands of people witnessed the horror on television, a second airliner, American Airlines Flight 175 from Boston, also bound for Los Angeles, crashed into the South Tower at 9:03, sending huge fireballs of jet fuel spewing skyward. The devastation was unimaginable, with steel, glass, and debris blanketing the ground for blocks around the Trade Center. Finally, in one last ghastly scene, both 110-story towers began to shudder, then collapsed inward and fell to earth, with the loss of more than 3000 lives.

At the same time this was taking place in New York, two other airliners had been hijacked and were on their way to targets in Washington, D.C., one to the White House and the other to the Pentagon. United Airlines Flight 93 is believed to have been on its way to the White House when several passengers, who had learned of the Trade Center disaster from a cell phone conversation, took matters into their own hands. They attacked the highjackers, causing the plane to go out of control and crash into a field in Pennsylvania. The heroic passengers, none of whom survived, foiled the hijackers' plan and saved the White House from destruction. The last hijacked plane, United Flight 77 from Washington, nosedived into the Pentagon, killing several hundred people.

These were acts of terror never before experienced in the United States, and they brought the horrors of war home to all Americans in nightmarish terms. The mastermind behind the terrorist acts was a Saudi Arabian multi-millionaire radical named Osama Bin Laden. Bin Laden had also been linked to other acts of terrorism against American targets, such as the bombings of American embassies in Africa, and the suicide bombing of the Navy ship U.S.S. *Cole* at anchor in Yemen.

Over the next few months, Bin Laden's terrorist organization, and other terrorist organizations, would be fiercely attacked by U.S. military forces in Afghanistan. President George W. Bush, promising the American people that our government would not rest until terrorism was eradicated around the world, said, "Make no mistake. The United States will hunt down and pursue those responsible for these cowardly actions." He warned this might take years to complete.

In the wake of the September 11 attacks, the major league baseball season was interrupted to let the nation mourn its dead and to grieve for the families who were directly affected by the devastation.

The pennant race and the chase for the home run crown were resumed after a week, but the enthusiasm that had permeated the thrill of the chase just a few days earlier was no longer evident in the responses of the fans. Baseball was put in proper perspective. It was, after all, just a child's game.

When the schedule resumed on September 18, the San Francisco Giants returned home to do battle with the Central Division–leading Astros. It was a tough start to the stretch run for Dusty Baker's crew, as they went down to defeat 3–2 when Houston pushed over two runs in the top of the ninth against the Giants' closer, Robb Nen. The next two games didn't get any better, as Larry Dierker's crew dismantled the confused Bay Area club 10–4 in game two, then squeaked out another close victory, this time by a score of 5–4, in the finale, a sweep that opened Houston's lead over St. Louis to 4½ games, and dropped the Giants two games behind Arizona. In the Sunday getaway game, Barry Bonds hit a two-run homer over the 410-foot mark in center field off Wade Miller in the fifth inning to give his team a 4–1 lead, but the bullpen blew it. And Robb Nen failed for the second time in three days, yielding the winning run in the tenth inning.

The Giant clubhouse was like a morgue after the game, and Barry Bonds was in no mood to talk to the media. The pennant race was slowly slipping away, and the terrorist attack of the previous week still preyed on his mind: "It's going to be a long time before we stop thinking about all of this." In Bonds' mind, home run number 64 was unimportant.

Dusty Baker tried to rally his troops after their poor showing against Houston. He reminded them that they still had 15 games to play, including the next six on the road—in San Diego and Los Angeles—and they needed to focus their energies on their objective, one game at a time. The team responded to their manager's plea. Jason Schmidt heard his manager loud and clear, and he strode to the mound in Qualcomm Stadium and proceeded to shut down the Padre offense on seven scattered hits, winning 2–0 on RBI singles by Calvin Murray and Barry Bonds. Bonds' drive, a 330-foot line drive down the right field line, hit the scoreboard above the right field fence. It would have been a home run prior to 1996, when the scoreboard was erected.

Bruce Bochy's team bounced back on Saturday and edged San Francisco 4–3 in ten innings. It was another heartbreaking loss for the Orange and Black, their third one-run loss in five games, and their second in extra innings. Once again the Giant bullpen collapsed. After Shawn Estes had left his team with a 2–0 lead after six innings, the Padres bounced back against the pen-men. Fultz, Worrell, and Boehringer all failed to stem the tide. Sunday's game was different. Baker's bombers unleashed a 17-hit attack, making it easy for Russ Ortiz, who took his 15th decision of the year, 11–2. Five different Giant players knocked in two runs, including Bonds. San Fran scored three runs in the top of the first and never let up. Bonds upped the margin to four runs in the second with his 66th, a 411-foot blast off the second wall in center field. Two innings later he followed Rich Aurilia's 35th by slicing a high fly ball to left field. The 365-footer dropped just over the wall, giving the Giants a comfortable 7–1 lead.

Bonds, who left the game with a stiff back in the seventh inning, did not endear himself to the fans when he let go a tirade in the clubhouse after the game. After hitting home runs number 65 and 66, and helping the Giants win an important game, he should have been happy, but he wasn't. Instead, he lashed out at his real or imagined critics. Some of his more self-serving comments included: "Mark McGwire never had to go through the things I've had to go through.... Everyone has taken their shots at me all year—*Sports Illustrated*, Jeff Kent. You name it.... Everyone has been on my case. But I'm still here." Bonds did have kind things to say about his friend Tony Gwynn, who gave him words of encouragement when he was slumping, according to AP. "He just told me to do the things I do normally ... that I was pressing and going after pitches out of the strike zone ... that I was trying too hard to lift the ball.... He just made some good, valid points, and I took advantage of them."

Barry Bonds' two home runs tied him with Sammy Sosa and brought him to within four home runs of Mark McGwire, with 12 games to play. At his present pace, he would finish the year with 71 home runs and a new single season home run record. Sosa, the only other slugger in the race, now that Luis Gonzalez had bogged down at 53 home runs, was on track to hit 63.

Prior to the game against the Dodgers in Los Angeles, Bonds held his daily press conference to answer some of the same inane questions he had been answering daily for two months. Do you think you will break McGwire's record? Do you think the Dodger pitchers will give you anything to hit? Do you think you will catch Hank Aaron? Outside the clubhouse, the usual Hollywood extravaganza was unfolding. Lights, cameras, and video recorders were everywhere. Celebrities like Robin Williams and Tom Hanks were on hand to witness the historic chase. Businessmen and con men were both vying for Bonds' time, trying to convince him to promote their product or invest in their scheme. The only quiet time Bonds had was when the game was in progress. Then they couldn't get to him. Then he was happy.

James Baldwin, obtained from the Chicago White Sox on July 26 to help the Dodgers in their pennant push, started for Los Angeles. The big right-hander, who was only 2–4 since being acquired by the Dodgers, pitched one of his better games, but it wasn't good enough. Rich Aurilia and Jeff Kent hit doubles in the third inning for the first run of the game, and that was all the scoring through the first six. Then, in the seventh, the hammer dropped. Bonds stepped to the plate to face Baldwin, with the bases empty and two men out. After taking a slider and a fast ball, Bonds got another fast ball and lined it into the lower box seats in the right field corner—number 67. L.A. took one back in the bottom of the inning on Adrian Beltre's 13th homer of the year, but that's as close as they came. Livan Hernandez pitched three-hit ball for seven innings, and Robb Nen shut them down in the ninth for his 41st save.

Barry Bonds was able to relax a little before game two. He had a chance to get together with Gary Sheffield, the Dodgers' most explosive hitter and a distant relative of his. According to Bob Nightengale in *Baseball Weekly*, Bonds rose early in the morning and took his white stretch limousine to Sheffield's 10,000 square foot Bel Air mansion, arriving at 1:30 PM. After a tour of the $2.8 million house, Sheffield's wife DeLeon prepared lunch, consisting of shish kebabs, turkey wings, and rice. Later the two baseball legends traveled to Dodger Stadium together to prepare for game two. Off the field, they were close friends—on the field, they were adversaries.

Game two was all L.A. It was a tight pitchers' duel between Kirk Rueter and Chan Ho Park for five innings, with the Giants clinging to a slim 1–0 lead. Then in the sixth inning Rueter's world collapsed. Jim Tracy's sleeping giants awoke and pounded the Giant starter and his replacement, Brian Boehringer, for seven runs, including Shawn Green's 48th home run of the season. Park shut Bonds down three times and walked him twice. The final score was 9–5. The loss kept San Francisco from gaining ground on Arizona, who dropped a 9–4 contest to Milwaukee. Dusty Baker's crew was still 1½ games off the top spot.

On September 26 both teams won, with San Fran nipping the Dodgers 6–4, thanks to a three-run uprising in the ninth. L.A. held a 4–3 lead after eight, but closer Jeff Shaw blew his ninth save of the season when John Vander Wal blooped a two-out, two-run single to center field. Bonds didn't homer, but he did play a big part in the outcome. He reached base four times, on three walks and a single, and scored the go-ahead run after receiving his 162nd walk of the season in the ninth. The former Arizona State University All-Star was not only on track to break McGwire's home run record, but he was also on track to break Babe Ruth's single season bases-on-balls record of 170.

The season was nearing its end as the Giants went home to meet the Padres in a three game series. Thursday, September 27th, was an off-day for the Giants, but it was a sad and traumatic day for Barry Bonds. His friend and former bodyguard, Franklin Bradley, who was in the hospital for abdominal surgery, died from complications at age 37. Bonds raced to the hospital but didn't arrive in time to say goodbye to his buddy. He sat by the bed and cried uncontrollably.

The next day, facing Jason Middlebrook in the second inning, Bonds slammed a 3–0 cripple 438 feet over the right center field wall. As he crossed home plate, he threw both arms skyward—that was for you,

Franklin. He returned to the dugout and sat down at the end of the bench, weeping quietly for his friend. The home run made the score 4–0, and Dusty Baker's bombers went on from there to pin down a 10–5 victory, keeping them within two games of first place. After the game, Bonds said, "It felt good to do something for him. He will be with me forever. I can move on now." The dejected Bonds dressed quickly, donned his black leather jacket, avoided reporters, and slipped out the door. He jumped on his silver and black Harley-Davidson and headed down the Junipero Serra Freeway to his home in Los Altos Hills.

Barry Bonds' home run was number 68, leaving him two behind the magic number. His two walks gave him the all-time National League single season bases-on-balls record, with 164, breaking the old mark of 162 set by Mark McGwire in 1998. He needed seven more to break the major league mark.

Eight games remained in the tension-filled season for the San Francisco slugger, but he seemed relaxed most of the time. He often arrived at the stadium four or five hours before game time, spending some time with the chiropractor, taking a nap, doing stretching exercises, spending time in the batting cage, and visiting with friends. He also attended the daily press conference. As game time approached, he would begin the mental preparation, trying to focus on the game ahead.

On Saturday he faced rookie Brett Jodie, who was appearing in just his fifth major league game. The game was tied at 1–1 after five innings, and Jodie left the game after holding Bonds zero for one, with one walk. In the sixth, leading off, Barry Bonds caught hold of a Chuck McElroy serve and hit a tremendous shot to right field. The ball cleared the wall with plenty to spare and splashed down in McCovey Cove, some 437 feet from home plate. San Francisco scored another run on singles by Kent and Galarraga, and held on behind Russ Ortiz and Robb Nen to win 3–1.

On Sunday, Giant fans—and media hordes, were out in force to see Bonds break or tie the record. ESPN was there to broadcast the game with dozens of crew members, headed by commentator Charlie Steiner. Commissioner Bud Selig was there, as well as Willie Mays, Barry's mother and father, his wife Elizabeth, and his children, Aisha, Nikolai, and Shikara. Outside the stadium, in McCovey Cove, pandemonium reigned, as dozens of small boats, inner tubes, and surf boards jockeyed for position. Even swimmers and canine retrievers were prepared to do battle for the historic ball. Unfortunately, the home folks were disappointed. San Diego held Barry Bonds in check, and prevented Dusty Baker's team from gaining ground on the Diamondbacks by edging the Giants 5–4, while the D'Backs were dropping a 2–1 decision to the Los Angeles Dodgers.

Brian Tollberg and three relievers held the Giants to eight hits, while Padres' bats raked Livan Hernandez for four runs and nine hits in less than four innings. Bonds was zero for one, with two walks. He was also hit by a pitch.

San Francisco moved on to Houston to tangle with the Astros, who were leading the Central Division by the slim margin of one game, and who were determined to hold their position. Enron Field was packed to the rafters with 43,548 screaming fans, all rooting for Larry Dierker's team to take no prisoners. Even those fans who were hoping to see Barry Bonds break the home run record didn't want him to do it in a game-winning situation.

Dusty Baker received outstanding pitching from Kirk Rueter and the bullpen crew, and the Giants won the opener 4–1. Ramon Martinez went deep for the Bay Area team, and Murray, Kent, and Vander Wal all had RBIs. The loss dropped Houston into a first place tie with St. Louis, who whipped Milwaukee 5–1. Bonds went one for two, with two walks, and scored a run.

In game two, San Fran won again, this time by a score of 11–8. The game was a real donnybrook, with Houston jumping out to a 2–0 lead in the first, then watching the Giants take the lead with two runs in the fourth and two more in the fifth before coming back with one of their own in the sixth. That was it as far as Houston was concerned, however. Dusty Baker's determined bombers put the game away by pushing over three runs in the seventh, then adding a brace of runs in both the eighth and ninth innings. Kent and Galarraga had three hits each, Benito Santiago hit a homer, and Kent drove in three runs, giving him 100 for the season. Once again, Barry Bonds was in the middle of the action, with a single in two at-bats, plus three bases-on-balls, good for three runs scored. But no home runs. He was still stuck on 69. He did break one record, however; his three walks giving him 173 for the season, breaking Babe Ruth's major league record of 170 bases-on-balls, set in 1923. When the evening ended, the Giants still trailed Arizona by two games, and the Astros remained tied with the Cardinals.

Thursday, October 4, was a red letter day in major league baseball. Barry Bonds moved into a tie with Mark McGwire as the all-time single-season home run leader, with 70 circuit blows. All the dignitaries, celebrities, and media personnel were on hand to witness the historic event. Bonds' son, Nikolai, was the Giants' batboy. The game, although critical to the pennant hopes of both teams, took a back seat to the momentous event that unfolded in Enron Field. Another full house of 43,734 fans were there to cheer on their beloved Astros. The game stayed close for four innings, with the Giants clinging to a 2–0 lead; but in the fifth, San Francisco's bats came to life, breaking the game open with a four run outburst. They coasted from there, winning 10–2 behind another fine effort from Russ Ortiz. Barry Bonds drew a two-out walk in the first inning, eventually coming around to score ahead of Jeff Kent's 22nd homer of the year. He grounded out to second in the third, walked again in the fifth, and was intentionally passed in the sixth. By the time the ninth inning rolled around, the crowd was tired and restless and, with the game out of reach, most of them were cheering for Bonds to hit one out. Barry quickly obliged. Leading off against 22-year-old, Wilfredo Rodriguez, he scorched a 1–1 fastball, sending a towering drive to right center field that settled into the upper deck of the grandstand, 454 feet from home plate. Enron Field exploded with excitement, with clapping, screaming, whistling, and foot stomping greeting the co–home run king. Bonds dropped his bat and watched his record breaking clout sail into the Texas night. Then he trotted around the bases, pointing to the heavens as he crossed the plate. He was greeted by his teammates and by his son Nikolai. Minutes later he had to make two curtain calls to quiet the crowd. After the game, in the clubhouse, Bonds was at peace with himself. He had caught one of his idols. "I'm glad the chase is over. It's an honor to share the record with him. He put the home run record where it is." The game statistician noted that Bonds saw 64 pitches during the game, and only 14 were strikes. But Bonds hit one of those strikes out of the park.

The loss dropped Houston one game behind the St. Louis Cardinals in the Central Division. But Larry Dierker's team played the Cardinals in the season-ending series and took two of the three games to win the division.

The Western Division pennant race headed into the last weekend of the season, with San Francisco hosting the Los Angeles Dodgers, while the Arizona Diamondbacks visited the hapless Milwaukee Brewers. One day after a joyous party in Houston, celebrating Barry Bonds remarkable achievement, a dark cloud descended over PacBell Park. In a wild exhibition of long ball hitting, Jim Tracy's Big Blue Machine eked out an 11–10 victory over Dusty Baker's exhausted troops, eliminating the Giants from both the division race and the wild card race. Neither starter stayed around long. In fact, Shawn Estes hit the showers after just two-thirds of an inning, as the Dodgers raked him for five runs on five hits. Pitcher Chan Ho Park's bases-loaded single off Mark Gardner brought in the last two runs. In the bottom of the first, history was made. Bonds came to the plate with two men out and the bases empty. He waved his Rideau Crusher several times, choked up on the bat as he had done every at-bat since he was four years old, and stepped in to face Park. The Korean flame-thrower was determined to challenge the Giant slugger with his best stuff. But this time his best wasn't good enough. Bonds tattooed a 1–0 pitch, sending it 442 feet into the dry California air. It splashed down in the friendly waters of McCovey Cove for a new single season home run record. His mark of 71 homers broke the old mark established by Mark McGwire in 1998. And Bonds wasn't through. In the third inning he took Park downtown again, sending a fast ball over the center field fence at the 404 foot mark. That shot narrowed the Dodger lead to 8–5 and, after a Shawn Green home run in the top of the fourth, Dusty Baker's hardened warriors cut the lead still further in the bottom half with a three run uprising. Gary Sheffield put one out in the top of the sixth, but the Orange and Black finally got even in the same inning when Rich Aurilia homered with a man on, his 37th of the year. Jim Tracy's boys pushed over the eventual winning tally in the seventh, on a single, an error, and an infield out. A dejected Barry Bonds sat in the Giants clubhouse long after the game ended, trying to make some sense out of the crazy season. He had just set a new home run record, but he couldn't enjoy it because his team had been eliminated from post-season play.

San Francisco and Los Angeles had two more games to play before they could go home, lick their wounds, and dwell on what might have been. In the Saturday game the Dodgers won 6–2 behind Jim Baldwin. Barry Bonds sat it out. In the last game of the season, won by the Giants 2–1, knuckleballer Dennis Springer of the Dodgers faced Kirk Rueter. Barry Bonds gave the fans what they came to see, in the bottom of the first. With two men out and the bases empty, Springer threw the Giant strong boy a

Bonds broke Mark McGwire's single season home run record when he hit number 71 on October 5. (© S.F. Giants)

72 mile-per-hour knuckler, and Bonds skied it down the right field line. He watched as it disappeared over the right field fence, 380 feet from home plate. It was Bonds' 73rd and last home run of the season.

When the season ended, the division winners were Atlanta, Houston, and Arizona, in the National League, and New York, Cleveland, and Seattle, in the American League. The Wild Card entries were St. Louis and Oakland. The Arizona Diamondbacks shocked the baseball world by downing Joe Torre's supposedly invincible Bronx Bombers, four games to three, in the World Series. They scored the tying and winning runs in the bottom of the ninth inning of game seven off legendary Yankee closer, Mariano Rivera.

The San Francisco Giants couldn't grab the brass ring in 2001, but Barry Bonds hauled in a handful. He was baseball's new single season home run king, smashing 73 circuit blows in just 476 official at-bats. His average of 6.5 at-bats per home run bettered Mark McGwire's mark of 7.3, set in 1998. Bonds also broke Babe Ruth's single season bases-on-balls record by walking 177 times. And his unbelievable .863 slugging percentage surpassed Ruth's .847, again knocking the Babe off the top rung. Giants manager, Dusty Baker, put it in perspective when he said, "It seems Babe isn't gonna have many records, is he? It's the greatest year I've ever seen from a single player."

Barry Bonds launches home run number 73, a 380 foot shot, off Dodger knuckleballer Dennis Springer on October 7. (© S.F. Giants)

To cap off his fairy tale season, Bonds was selected as the National League's Most Valuable Player, making him the only four-time winner in major league history. He was subsequently rewarded with a new five year, $90 million contract by Giants President and General Partner Peter Magowan, guaranteeing he would finish his career in San Francisco.

As great as Barry Bonds was in 2001, he may have been even better in 2002. After a frantic season-long battle with the Arizona Diamondbacks and Los Angeles Dodgers, Dusty Baker's club came roaring down the stretch, winning 29 of their last 39 games, to finish in second place, just 2½ games behind Arizona.

Bonds was sensational from beginning to end, even though National League pitchers were wary of him after his record-breaking season, and seldom gave him a good pitch to hit. His 198 bases-on-balls broke his own major league record, and his .582 on-base percentage toppled Ted Williams' mark of .551 set in 1941 when Williams tattooed the ball at a .406 clip. And in spite of his limited opportunities, the future Hall-of-Famer still hammered 46 home runs in 403 official at-bats. He then put the frosting on his cake by capturing his first batting crown with an average of .370.

Barry Bonds continued to be a formidable presence in post season play, helping San Francisco dispose of the Atlanta Braves in the Division Series, three games to two, then crush the St. Louis Cardinals in the National League Championship Series, four games to one. The big slugger seemed to be in the middle of every Giant rally, reaching base 22 times in ten games, eight times on base hits and 14 times on walks. He batted a respectable .287, with ten runs scored, four home runs, and 10 RBI's. In the final game against the Cardinals, Barry went 0 for 2, but drove in the tying run with a sacrifice fly in the eighth inning. David Bell carried the pennant-winning run across the plate in the bottom of the ninth, on a two-out single by Kenny Lofton.

Dusty Baker's warriors met Mike Scioscia's Anaheim Angels in the World Series, the first time two Wild Card entries had ever met in the Fall Classic. The second place Angels, winners of 99 games during the regular season, stormed through the American League playoffs, stunning the proud New York Yankees in the Division Series, three games to one, then polishing off the upstart Minnesota Twins in the ALCS, four games to one, taking the finale, 13–5.

The 2002 World Series may have been the signature event that validates Barry Bonds' legacy. The Giant slugger had a reputation for being a choker in 27 previous post season appearances, based on his .197 batting average, one home run, and six RBI's. But that stigma disappeared

The burden of a hero. Barry Bonds engulfed by autograph seekers during spring training, 2002. (Courtesy James R. Madden, Jr.)

in his first World Series at-bat, when he electrified the big crowd in Edison Field by putting a Jarrod Washburn heater into orbit, 418 feet over the right field wall. It was the first run of the Series, and it sparked the Giants to a 4-3 victory.

The World Series was an exciting affair, with the Angels finally wearing down the Giants in seven games, but Bonds was sensational, batting .471, with four home runs and six runs-batted-in. And he set World Series records for on-base-percentage (.700), slugging average (1.294), and bases on balls (13), for a seven game Series.

Barry Bonds had the two greatest back-to-back seasons ever put together by a major league baseball player, in 2001 and 2002. In addition to winning a batting championship, he broke three of baseball's "unbreakable" single season records; home runs (73), bases-on-balls (198), and on-base percentage (.582). He is also in line to win an unprecedented fifth Most Valuable Player trophy. These accolades, plus his spectacular post season performance, put him at or near the top of the list of the greatest players in major league history.

In the short span of two years, Barry Lamar Bonds has gone from being an outstanding major league player to being a legend in his own time.

14. The Champions—
Side by Side

The preceding chapters have reviewed the lives and careers of Babe Ruth, Roger Maris, Mark McGwire, Sammy Sosa, and Barry Bonds, the five single-season home run champions, with special emphasis placed on each of their record breaking seasons.

The five historic seasons covered a period of 75 years, encompassing a world war, a painful depression, several recessions, a number of small military "land actions" in such places as Korea, Vietnam, Iraq, Panama,

Barry Bonds had the greatest offensive season in baseball history, with an .863 slugging percentage and a .515 on-base percentage, in addition to setting new records in home runs (73) and bases on balls (173). (© S.F. Giants)

and Grenada, and a heinous terrorist attack on the New York World Trade Center.

This chapter will study the five combatants, side by side, comparing the various cultural and social conditions that existed during their careers, as well as the factors in baseball, that may have affected each player's home run totals.

Ruth, Maris, McGwire, Sosa, and Bonds— Their Backgrounds

Each player's background had a profound effect on his subsequent ability to handle the on- and off-field pressures associated with his pursuit of the home run record. Babe Ruth and Sammy Sosa had similar backgrounds, and those backgrounds may have given them an advantage in their battle for the crown. Psychologists say poverty toughens a person and makes him a survivor. If that's the case, then Ruth and Sosa were survivors.

George Herman "Babe" Ruth was born into a poor family on the south side of Baltimore, Maryland. He ran in the streets almost from the time he could walk, while his parents tried to carve out a living in a bar. He spent ten of his first 19 years in a home for wayward boys, learning how to fend for himself. Ruth was bigger and stronger than other boys his age, and he used his bulk to exercise control over them. He also learned how to manipulate the people he couldn't intimidate, such as the Xaverian Brothers that ran the Home, the Yankee fans, and the New York newspapermen who followed the team and wrote about his exploits.

Ruth learned to handle pressure as a seven-year-old. Surviving on the streets of Baltimore, day and night, taught him how to cope with adversity and how to overcome unpleasant situations. Adhering to the strict discipline of "the Home" taught him how to operate within the rules of a system. When he became an adult, he used his survival instincts to become the greatest player in baseball history. He delighted in playing a kid's game for big money. And when he closed in on his own home run record, he was able to do so in a casual and relaxed atmosphere. He controlled his environment.

Sammy Sosa was born into abject poverty in the Dominican Republic. He worked as a shoeshine boy, after school, from the time he was 7 years old. He became street smart at an early age, learning how to charm people with an engaging smile and a keen sense of humor. He struggled to take home two dollars a day to help his mother put food on the table.

Young Sosa learned how to handle pressure in his early teens. His struggle to become a professional baseball player, to help support his family, began when he was just 14. It was a heavy burden to carry. However, it made him into a strong man who enjoys playing baseball yet can separate it from the important things in life. In the overall scheme of things, family is important, and being a good person is important. Baseball is just a game.

Roger Maris was born into a blue collar family in North Dakota. He grew up to be an outstanding high school athlete. He played sports aggressively, both on the football field and the baseball diamond. On the gridiron, he was a standout on both offense and defense. On the diamond, he could do it all—hit, hit with power, run, field, and throw.

Throughout his amateur and professional career, Maris performed brilliantly on the field of play. But his lack of people skills caused him serious problems off the field when he became the subject of a mini media blitz during his pursuit of Babe Ruth's home run record. His early life had not prepared him for the pressures of celebrity, and the public scrutiny almost destroyed him.

Mark McGwire is the son of a dentist, brought up in an affluent middle class neighborhood in California. He led a sheltered life, protected from the pressures of the outside world by his mother and father. His day to day life was one of family, study, and athletics. He and his four brothers were all superior athletes who starred in several sports during their high school and college years.

McGwire traveled through the first 21 years of his life in blissful ignorance of the realities of the world. He never wanted for anything. He had a loving family, a comfortable home, all the luxuries associated with upper middle class living, a distinguished athletic career, and the advantage of a college education. But, like Maris, he had no experience handling the pressures that were part of his pursuit of the home run record.

Barry Bonds is the son of major league slugger Bobby Bonds, and the godson of all-world outfielder Willie Mays. He was raised in an upper middle class neighborhood in San Carlos, California. Like McGwire, he never wanted for anything. And he was never exposed to the harsh realities of the outside world. His childhood activities included having the run of the San Francisco Giant clubhouse, and cavorting with the major league players before games in Candlestick Park.

His entire life revolved around baseball. He spent three years at Arizona State University refining his baseball skills, then signed a professional contract with the Pittsburgh Pirates. With professional baseball, however, came media attention that focused not only on his baseball skills but also on his private life. And Barry Bonds' privileged childhood left him ill equipped to deal with it.

Babe Ruth and Sammy Sosa had a significant advantage over Roger Maris, Mark McGwire, and Barry Bonds, based on their backgrounds. They were survivors of a distressed childhood who grew up well prepared to handle the off-field pressures associated with their season-long chase of history.

Their Personalities

The personalities of the five home run champions, like their backgrounds, had a significant effect on their ability to handle the off-field pressures associated with their quest.

Babe Ruth was a big, undisciplined kid who never grew up. He played a kid's game, and he played it with enthusiasm. Off the field, he was an extrovert who lived life to the fullest. He had a good sense of humor and he used it effectively, both for his own well-being and for putting other people at ease. The pressures of early childhood on the streets, combined with the challenges of his teenage years in the "Home," prepared Ruth for any eventuality. Baseball was never a struggle for him. The pursuit of the home run record was not something to be feared. It was just a game. He enjoyed the moment, and whatever happened, happened.

His happy-go-lucky attitude endeared him to both fans and newspapermen. They always supported him in his conflicts with management, and they cheered his every move on the baseball diamond. When he was chasing a new record, they were there, urging him on to new conquests.

Sammy Sosa is an extrovert, an entertainer who enjoys the spotlight and who plays to his audience. The chase for the crown, and the associated media blitz, were sheer pleasure for the former shoeshine boy. Sosa was born into poverty with a smile on his face. He enjoyed life as a child, even when the struggle was oppressive. His religion taught him to accept whatever happened with grace and humility. His mother taught him to be a good person. His genes allowed him to face each day with a smile.

His career with the Chicago Cubs has been one long love affair, particularly with the fans in the right field stands. Sosa has endeared himself to the "Bleacher Bums" over a period of seven years, and he never forgets to salute them each time he goes out to his position. They were his secret weapon in his pursuit of the home run record. They kept his adrenalin pumping day after day with their enthusiastic support. And he, in return, kept their adrenalin pumping with his good natured friendship and his titanic blasts.

Roger Maris was an introvert who cherished and protected his privacy. His dour personality put him at a decided disadvantage when he became a celebrity and had to face the press. The Yankee right fielder never learned the art of controlling an interview to his own advantage. He answered every question honestly and to the point, without considering the ramifications of seeing his quotes in print. In addition, he lacked the sense of humor needed to charm his interviewers with clever retorts and one-liners.

The North Dakota native was a blue collar player from a blue collar background. He expected to do an honest days work for a days pay. He couldn't handle the public relations aspect of his job.

Mark McGwire was shy and quiet as a youth, but he had a restrained sense of humor which stood him in good stead over the years. He also had a private side, fostered by his father that did not permit anyone to see his inner feelings. He learned how to get along with people as his baseball career developed, but he was never subjected to strong pressures of any kind until the home run race began.

The big redhead was unprepared for the intense scrutiny of the press during the 1998 season. His claustrophobia increased daily as spring turned into summer, and the size of the media circus grew from a couple of dozen reporters to more than two hundred frantic writers and cameramen. He was beginning to wear down when Sammy Sosa came along to support him.

On the field, Mark McGwire was better prepared to meet the challenges of the home run race than his four cohorts. He was the ultimate professional hitter, who mentally prepared himself before each at-bat, putting himself in a trance-like state and blocking out everything else around him. His ability to visualize the pitch being thrown may be unequaled in baseball history.

Barry Bonds has an arrogant and abrasive personality. He is the product of an affluent middle class family whose father was away much of the time playing professional baseball. He grew up with a chip on his shoulder, an introvert who was driven to prove he was better than other people. His knack for alienating people began in high school and carried through college and into the professional baseball ranks. He had few friends on the Pittsburgh Pirates, and is not well-liked in the San Francisco clubhouse, even today. He and Jeff Kent, in particular, are like oil and water. His relationship with the press is well known. One writer called him rude, condescending, and short. Another said he was baseball's biggest jerk.

On the field, Bonds is in his element. He enjoys playing the game, particularly hitting a baseball, and he is successful in achieving his goals because he can concentrate completely on the task at hand and block out the off-field distractions, from the media as well as from other real or imagined affronts.

Ruth and Sosa had outgoing personalities that disarmed people. They knew how to deal with people and how to enjoy the media blitz that accompanied the home run chase. On the field, however, McGwire and Bonds had a distinct advantage.

Social Climate

When Babe Ruth was entering the peak years of his professional baseball career, the country was just coming out of "The War to End All Wars." Soldiers returning home from the war with the sights and sounds of human slaughter fresh in their memory had a fatalistic attitude toward life in general. The motto of the "Lost Generation" that populated the United States in the 1920s was "Eat, drink and be merry, for tomorrow we die."

It was also the Golden Age of Sports, when athletes of every type were idolized by the entire country. Heavyweight boxing champion Jack Dempsey and home run king Babe Ruth were at the forefront.

Babe Ruth could do no wrong. Every home run was a celebration. Every misdemeanor was forgiven. Babe was not isolated from the hedonistic night life in the big cities around the American League. He was right in the middle of it, often partying until dawn, then making his way back to the hotel. The big, jovial, moon-faced kid was loved by all.

The young slugger broke the home run record four different times— in 1919, 1920, 1921, and 1927. Every time, except the first time, he was chasing his own record, so he was never under any pressure to set a new standard. The New York fans were so blasé they didn't even consider it noteworthy when he hit 60 home runs in 1927. They thought he would be setting home run records for years to come.

In Roger Maris' case, it was entirely different. He had the most difficult chore of all—trying to dethrone a god. Ruth was beloved the world over. Baseball fans in general rooted against Maris because they didn't want anyone to unseat the mighty Babe. The Yankee management, fans, and players were pulling for Mantle, because he was a homegrown player. Maris was considered to be a hired gun, not a genuine New York Yankee. The New York newspapermen were openly hostile toward the new challenger for the same reason. Their questions were often pointed and embarrassing. Even the Baseball Commissioner plotted against him, declaring that Babe Ruth's record had to be broken in 154 games or it would be identified with an asterisk. It's no wonder Maris' hair began to fall out in clumps before the season ended.

Mark McGwire and Sammy Sosa had an easier task than Maris, although not as easy as Ruth. The quality of baseball declined after 1961; the new-age players were selfish, crude, and greedy, and the strike of 1994 alienated many of the fans. Baseball was in desperate need of a hero; so when McGwire and Sosa came along, they were welcomed with open arms by both the fans and the media alike. Whereas Maris was confronted by 10 to 20 hostile newspapermen during the last three months of the season, McGwire and Sosa had to face hundreds of reporters, writers, and cameramen daily; but their sessions were generally friendly and light hearted, particularly when Sammy Sosa participated.

Mark McGwire was fortunate that Sosa was a co-challenger, because the happy-go-lucky Dominican taught his American friend that the media attention was something to be enjoyed.

Barry Bonds performed in the same arena and in the same generation as McGwire and Sosa, but unfortunately he was chasing a record that was only three years old, and many fans had become disenchanted with home runs. Most people felt that home runs had become cheap, and the home run record was not as prestigious as it had been in the days of Ruth and Maris. For example, when Sammy Sosa hit 64 home runs in 2001, it was the third time he had exceeded the 60 mark, giving him more 60+ home run seasons than the total of all major league players prior to 1998.

To make matters worse for Bonds, it was the age of "people want to know," and the tabloid mentality of the press sent reporters scurrying off on witch hunts, hoping to uncover some kind of scandalous behavior on the part of the reigning hero. Bonds' short temper and persecution complex came into direct conflict with the objectives of the media, turning San Francisco town into a battleground.

Roger Maris and Barry Bonds were at a tremendous disadvantage compared to the other three challengers. They were the only ones who faced a hostile environment, although in Bonds' case, much of it was self-inflicted.

Physical Size and Conditioning of the Home Run Champions

All five challengers were big men, all six feet tall or taller, and all weighing 200 pounds or more. Babe Ruth was a big man in his day, standing 6'2" tall and weighing a muscular 215 pounds. Once he became an established star, however, he let his finely muscled physique deteriorate. His love of food, drink, and city night life added pounds of fat to his body and affected his play on the field. Periodically, the Bambino would punish himself over the winter to get himself physically fit for the new season. In 1927 he was in top physical condition, having spent the winter in the gym, lifting weights, doing aerobics, and running. Back home, in the country, he chopped wood, cleared brush, and jogged. He came into the season weighing a trim 220 pounds.

Roger Maris was a solidly built six foot, 200-pound slugger who was always in condition to play. He was a dedicated player who worked out daily during the season, and who maintained his weight and physical fitness over the winter.

Sammy Sosa was another rugged six foot, 200-pound slugger. Like Maris, he was dedicated to the game, and he worked out religiously during the season, lifting weights, running and doing various aerobic exercises. He, like many major leaguers, also took a number of legal dietary supplements.

Mark McGwire became a physical fitness fanatic after the 1991 season, when his career almost self-destructed. His brother J.J., a personal trainer, put Mark on a physical fitness program designed to maximize his strength and stamina. The regimen centered around, but was not limited to, weight training. He added 20 pounds of muscle over the winter of '91–92, arriving in spring training at a muscular 235 pounds on a big 6'5" frame. He added another 15 pounds over the next six years, bringing his weight up to a full 250 pounds. He also took dietary supplements, including androstenedione, but, as discussed earlier, the andro did not appear to contribute to his home run surge. He was hitting titanic blasts long before he started taking andro.

Barry Bonds was tall and slender when he first broke into major league baseball; but over the years, he built himself up from a 165-pound speedster into a muscular 210-pound slugger. The Giant outfielder always kept himself in top physical condition, and, as he got older, he became more and more dedicated to a rigid off-season conditioning program.

In baseball, as in boxing, bigger is better. A good big man will always defeat a good small man, all other things being equal. In baseball, a good big man will normally hit more home runs than a good small man. Mark McGwire is a good big man. Barry Bonds is a good small man, and his career home run average reflects his smaller size. But he was able to wrest the single-season home run title away from McGwire because he stayed in a zone for 162 games. His home run swing was consistent from beginning to end. It was compact, exceptionally quick, and had an uppercut arc that sent balls sailing toward the distant outfield fences.

The appendix contains a chart showing the physical size of the major league all-star teams from the 19th century to the present, as well as the average number of home runs hit by the all-stars. A rough estimate indicates that every 3.3 pounds of muscle a player adds will result in one home run a year. The physical size and average number of home runs hit by the five single-season home run champions are shown below.

Name	Height	Weight	Home Runs
Babe Ruth	6'2"	220 lbs.	50
Roger Maris	6'	195 lbs.	30
Mark McGwire	6'5"	235 lbs.	52
Sammy Sosa	6'	200 lbs.	38
Barry Bonds	6'2"	190 lbs.	39

Using the factor of 3.3 pounds per home run, and using Mark McGwire as the base point, if McGwire rapped out an average of 52 home runs a year, Babe Ruth could be expected to hit 49 home runs (based on his average weight), Barry Bonds 42, Sammy Sosa 44, and Roger Maris 43. Babe Ruth's projected total is almost dead-on to his actual career home run total. Barry Bonds and Sammy Sosa may yet reach their projected number based on their performance over the past several years. But Roger Maris hit 13 home runs less than predicted, which is not surprising. Maris was not a home run hitter in the true sense of the word. He had a smooth, fluid swing that sent line drives to all fields, but not necessarily over the fence. His career home run average, excluding 1961, was a modest 26 home runs per year. He just had one phenomenal year.

The total number of home runs hit in the major leagues increased from 73 home runs per team per year during the decade from 1920 to 1930, to 153 home runs per team per 154-game year during the period from 1990 to 2000 (see appendix). And from 1999 through 2001 the average was an astronomical 175. If the estimate of the home run increase on the all-star teams is accurate, and can be extended to each major league team roster, then approximately 30 percent of the total increase in home runs over the last seven decades can be attributed to the increased size of the players, as well as the improvement in their physical fitness.

Mark McGwire had a significant advantage in size. All the champions were physically fit during their record year.

Ballpark Dimensions

The playing field dimensions of baseball stadiums have changed dramatically over the past 70 to 90 years. Until recently, most parks favored left handed batters, as shown in the tables in the appendix. During Babe Ruth's time, the average distance to right field in American League parks was 329 feet, compared to 386 feet in right center, and 446 feet in straight away center. Left field was a healthier 339 foot shot from home plate.

In 1961, when Roger Maris was taking dead aim at Ruth's record, right field was 325 feet from home, the power alley in right center was 380 feet, and center field was 422 feet. Left field was 336 feet.

When McGwire, Sosa and Bonds made their runs, the average park was symmetrical at 330 feet down the left and right field foul lines, 374 feet to the alleys, and 406 feet to center.

The numbers confirm that the parks have become progressively smaller since Babe Ruth took aim at the fences, particularly in the power alleys and center field. The power alleys are about 15 feet closer to the batter than they were in Ruth's day, and the center field fence is a whopping 39 feet closer. A review of Mark McGwire's home runs shows that six of his home runs to center field traveled less than the average 446 foot center field distance of Ruth's day, and two of his home runs to the power alley were less than the 386-foot distance of Ruth's day. However, even if eight home runs were deducted from McGwire's totals, he still would have hit 62 home runs within the 162 game format, or 59 home runs in a 154 game format. In Barry Bonds' case, 15 of his 16 home runs to center field traveled less than 446 feet, and five of his 19 home runs to right center field traveled less than 386 feet. Additionally, two of his home runs to right field would have stayed in the park in Ruth's time. Therefore, if Barry Bonds had played in the same parks that Ruth did, it is estimated he would have lost 22 home runs, giving him 51 home runs over a 162 game schedule, or 48 home runs over a 154 game schedule.

Each of the parks associated with the home run champions has a home run factor (HRF) associated with it. The HRF is the number of home runs hit in a particular park compared to the average number of home runs hit in all the league parks. The Yankee Stadium HRF is 1.03, meaning that 1.03 home runs are hit in the Stadium for every home run hit in the average league park. The HRF in Wrigley Field is 1.16, the HRF in Busch Stadium is 1.05, and the HRF in PacBell Park is 0.94.

Only Sammy Sosa came close to approximating his home park's HRF. Sammy hit 35 of his 66 home runs at home, for a HRF of 1.13. Mark McGwire hit 38 of his 70 home runs at home, indicating the big slugger had more adrenalin pumping when playing before the home folks.

Curiously, both Babe Ruth and Roger Maris hit more home runs on the road than at home. Their detractors have always claimed they set their records by hitting into the friendly right field stands at Yankee Stadium, a 296-foot chip shot from home plate. The facts prove otherwise. Babe Ruth actually hit 50 percent of his career home runs on the road. Maris hit 54 percent of his Yankee round trippers away from the Stadium.

There is one additional factor that affects the home run history of the various major league baseball parks. Teams are now located all across the country, from the Pacific Ocean to the Atlantic, and from the Canadian border to Mexico. At the present time, one city seems to have a decided home run advantage caused by the unique atmospheric conditions surrounding its park. Home runs fly out of Coors Field in Denver at a 69 percent higher rate than in the average National League Park. Fulton County Stadium in Atlanta, the Braves' home park from 1966 through 1996, had a HRF of 1.43, but that advantage seems to have disappeared in their new park; Turner Field has recorded a HRF of just 0.93 since 1997.

Mark McGwire and Sammy Sosa had a distinct field advantage (both home and away) over Babe Ruth, Roger Maris, and Barry Bonds, from a home run factor standpoint. But McGwire, Sosa, and Bonds had an enormous advantage over Babe Ruth when it came to the size of the parks they played in. If the ballparks had been the same size for all the competitors, Babe Ruth's single season home run record would still be intact, all other factors being equal.

Equipment—Baseballs and Pitching Mounds

Baseballs have always had a decided effect on the number of home runs hit in the major leagues. When the lively ball was introduced in 1920, the home run became the single most important offensive weapon. In 1930, when the seams of the ball were recessed, home runs jumped up more than 30 percent over 1928. Since 1994, the baseballs have been manufactured in Costa Rica. Coincidentally or not, home runs have increased by 30 percent since that time.

Another modification to the rules that benefited the batter was lowering the pitcher's mound from a maximum of 15" to 10" in 1969. This change was designed to give parity to the batter, after a decade of pitching dominance in the 1960s.

Mark McGwire, Sammy Sosa, and Barry Bonds have all benefited from the livelier balls and the lower pitching mounds.

Integration

In 1945 the Brooklyn Dodgers signed Jackie Robinson to play baseball for them, thus ending more than 57 years of segregated major league baseball. Some of the great Negro League players who entered the major leagues at that time, in addition to Robinson, included Willie Mays, Ernie Banks, Monte Irvin, Roy Campanella, and Larry Doby, all Hall-of-Famers.

In Babe Ruth's time, the great black baseball players were not allowed to compete in the major leagues, so they had to play in their own segregated league. As a result, the Bambino did not have to face the likes of Satchel Paige, "Smokey Joe" Williams, "Cannonball" Dick Redding, "Bullet Joe" Rogan, Willie Foster, or dozens of other legendary black pitchers. If he had to bat against the great Negro league pitchers of his day, it is doubtful he could have hit 60 home runs in one season.

Babe Ruth had a big advantage over the other challengers in not having to bat against the top black pitchers of the '20s and '30s.

Expansion—and a Dilution of Talent

Several major league teams, like the Boston Braves, Brooklyn Dodgers, and New York Giants, moved their franchises to other cities during the 1950s. In 1961, Los Angeles and Washington were added to the American League. The following year, New York and Houston were added to the National League.

Over the past 37 years major league baseball has increased from 16 teams to 30 teams. The population of the United States in 1920 was 106 million. However, blacks were not allowed to play organized baseball, so the number of people eligible to play baseball was just 95 million. In 1961, the total population was 175 million, and in 1998 it was 270 million.

It can be assumed from these population numbers that the quality of baseball increased substantially from 1920 to 1961 because the population almost doubled, and integration permitted blacks to play in the major leagues, while the number of teams remained constant. In fact, the period from 1950 to 1965 is frequently referred to as "The Golden Age of Baseball."

Since 1961, several factors have influenced the quality of America's National Pastime. First, the population has increased by just 57 percent over that period, while the number of major league teams has increased by a whopping 88 percent. But the true story is even grimmer. Other professional sports have drained away some of the talent that would have previously been channeled into professional baseball.

In 1950 there were 11 professional basketball franchises and 13 professional football franchises. By 1998, these sports had grown to 29 and 30 teams respectively, an increase of 146 percent. Basketball and football are particularly attractive to college athletes because the players can go directly from school into a high paying professional career; whereas in baseball they usually have to spend four or five years in the minor leagues before they reach the majors, where the big money is—if they make it at all.

In addition to the above mentioned sports, baseball has also lost players to tennis, golf, hockey, and a host of minor sports. And now, with college education being more accessible to athletes, some of the finite talent pool is choosing to begin a business career rather than buck the odds to play professional baseball.

Baseball, within its own borders, has seen other areas where talent has been dangerously diluted. It is most noticeable on the mound, where pitchers are so protected it is actually causing more physical harm than good. Going back to the Babe Ruth era, major league teams had a four-man pitching rotation, and the starters were expected to finish what they started. During the 1920s, major league teams averaged 80 complete games a year over a 154 game schedule. During the '40s and '50s, teams averaged 40 to 60 complete games a year. In 1996 the 28 major league teams averaged 10 complete games over a 162 game schedule. Four years later, the average was down to 4.5 complete games per team per year. The entire pitching staff of the Colorado Rockies tossed only one complete game in 1995, a measure of ineptness matched by the Tampa Bay Devil Rays in 2000.

Today, major league teams have five-man pitching rotations, and any pitcher who can throw six innings is considered to be a quality pitcher. Starting pitchers are under a "pitch count," and are removed from the game after reaching a specified limit, usually about 100 pitches. The philosophy is that it is desirable to bring a "fresh arm" into the game after the sixth inning, even if it means replacing a Greg Maddux with a Russ Springer. Imagine if Walter Johnson, Lefty Grove, or even Sandy Koufax had been under a 100-pitch count. With that scenario, Nolan Ryan never would have made it past the fifth inning. Pitchers today average about two innings per start less than pitchers of 20 to 30 years ago. And yet the injuries to pitching arms continue to mount. On July 27, 1997, for instance, 68 major league pitchers were on the disabled list, an average of more than two per team. Almost a year later, on June 28, 1998, there were a total of 79 pitchers from 30 teams on the DL. Perhaps today's pitchers need to work more, not less.

Major league pitching quality has deteriorated to the point where it is about on par with the high minor league pitching of the 1950s.

Mark McGwire, Sammy Sosa, and Barry Bonds have a definite advantage facing today's diluted pitching talent. All things considered, taking into account expansion, the drain of other professional sports, and the dilution of pitching talent due to pitch counts and middle relievers, perhaps half the pitchers in the major leagues today are of minor league caliber.

Travel—Night Baseball

Travel and night games affect the performances of the major league players. In the days before expansion, travel was relatively simple. An overnight train ride, or a two hour flight, was all that was required to reach the most distant city in the major leagues, St. Louis. There were only eight teams in each league, so the 154-game schedule was broken down into 22 games with each opposing team, 11 at home and 11 away.

Travel was much easier for Babe Ruth, somewhat more difficult for Roger Maris, and much more difficult for McGwire, Sosa, and Bonds.

Babe Ruth had another advantage over his four opponents in that he played all his games in the daylight. It was usually more comfortable, and easier on the muscles, playing under a warm sun. And the balls carried farther. Night games, with cold, damp weather, create minor health problems and reduce the number of home runs hit in a game.

Sammy Sosa, for example, has hit 32 percent more home runs in the sunlight than he has hit in the evening (the major league average is eight percent). He had played in more than 1200 major league games through 1998, about half of them during the day. In 2259 daytime at-bats, Sosa averaged 37 home runs for every 550 at-bats. Under the moon, he averaged just 28 home runs in 2401 at-bats.

Babe Ruth had the benefit of having a comfortable travel schedule, and of playing all his games in the warm sunlight. Maris, McGwire, Sosa, and Bonds were at a disadvantage in both cases.

Individual Performances

Babe Ruth, Roger Maris, Mark McGwire, Sammy Sosa, and Barry Bonds all dominated their league during their record breaking season. But no one ever dominated a league like Babe Ruth dominated the American League from 1919 to 1934. In 1919, the last year of the dead ball, the Sultan of Swat hit 29 home runs to break the record for the dead ball era. In the process, he out-homered four of the other seven teams. The next year, the first year of the lively ball, he did even better. He smashed 54 home runs, while the runner-up, George Sisler, had just 19. And Babe out-homered every other team in the American League. In 1921 and 1926 he out-homered five of the seven teams, and in his 60 home run season he once again out-homered every other team. In fact, the other teams averaged only 40 home runs apiece.

Over a six year period, from 1919 to 1924, Babe Ruth accounted for 10.8 percent of all home runs hit in the American League. From 1926 to 1931 he accounted for 9.5 percent of all home runs hit in the league.

From 1920 through 1933, American League teams averaged 67 home runs a year. Babe Ruth, by himself, averaged 46 home runs a year in just 489 at bats.

In his record year of 1927, the Bambino hit an unbelievable 13.7 percent of all the American League home runs hit that year. To put that in perspective, in 1961 Roger Maris hit five percent of all American League home runs (based on an eight team league). To match Ruth's performance of hitting 13.7 percent of the league home runs, Maris would have had to hit 167 home runs in 1961. Mark McGwire, Sammy Sosa, and Barry Bonds were in the same boat. McGwire hit 5.5 percent of all the National League home runs (based on an eight team league), while Sosa hit 5.1 percent and Bonds hit 4.7 percent. To match Ruth's percentage, McGwire would have had to hit 174 homers, Sosa 177, and Bonds 211.

Maris, McGwire, Sosa, and Bonds cannot match Babe Ruth's complete domination of a league, statistics-wise. The Babe revolutionized the game.

Summary

McGwire, Sosa, Bonds, Maris, and Ruth each enjoyed certain advantages over the other four players during their race for the crown. The players, and the areas they enjoyed an advantage in, are shown below.

Babe Ruth	Roger Maris	Mark McGwire	Sammy Sosa	Barry Bonds
Background			Background	
Personality			Personality	
Social climate		Social climate	Social climate	
Chasing himself				
		Concentration		Concentration
Friendly Press		Friendly Press	Friendly Press	
Segregation				
Physical fitness	Physical fitness	Physical fitness	Physical fitness	Physical fitness
		Dietary supplements	Dietary supplements	Dietary supplements
Physical size		Physical size		
Travel	Travel			
Day games				
	Expansion	Expansion	Expansion	Expansion
		Smaller parks	Smaller parks	Smaller parks
		Atmospheric conditions	Atmospheric conditions	Atmospheric conditions
		Dilution of Pitching	Dilution of Pitching	Dilution of Pitching
		Lively Balls	Lively Balls	Lively balls
		Sosa	McGwire	

Certain facts seem obvious.

• Babe Ruth set the single-season home run record—not once, but four times. In 1927, when he hit 60 home runs, he out-homered every other team in the league and accounted for 13.7 percent of the league's entire home run production.

The "Sultan of Swat" had a number of advantages in his quest for the home run crown, the most important of which was that he wasn't chasing any record or any record holder. He already held the record. Anything he did over and above that was a bonus.

• Sammy Sosa was the first man in baseball history to hit 66 home runs in a single season.

• Mark McGwire broke Roger Maris' single-season home run record of 61. He subsequently broke Sammy Sosa's record of 66, then established a new record when he hit his 70th home run on September 26, 1998.

McGwire and Sosa together had advantages in several areas, most notably having a friendly press, enthusiastic fans, smaller parks, livelier baseballs, diluted pitching talent, and each other to feed off.

• Barry Bonds broke Mark McGwire's record when he hit his 71st and 72nd home runs on October 5, 2001. He hit number 73 on October 7. He enjoyed the advantages of smaller parks, livelier baseballs, and diluted pitching talent.

• Roger Maris, on the other hand, had the worst of all worlds. He was chasing an icon, Babe Ruth, and no one—fans, teammates, or press—wanted him to break the record. His taciturn personality alienated the newspapermen. As noted above, he had almost none of the advantages enjoyed by Ruth, McGwire, Sosa or Bonds. He was too late to reap the benefits of segregation and of playing his games in the daylight. And he was too early to capitalize on expansion, poor pitching, smaller parks, and livelier baseballs. The fact that he was able to break Babe Ruth's home run record under almost unbearable conditions speaks volumes about the heart and courage of this most private baseball player.

It is impossible to compare players from one era with players from another era. Ruth's dominance in the American League occurred during a time when the game was in transition from a Punch and Judy game to a slugging game. He most likely would not have had the same advantage had he played in the 1990s. Modern day players are bigger and stronger, and most of them are swinging from the heels, going for the long ball. The Babe would still be a great home run hitter, without question, and might still be the major league home run champion. But he would definitely not hit 13.7 percent of the league's home runs. Competition would be stiffer.

All five home run champions were deserving of their achievements and accolades. It is not possible to single out one of the five as the greatest single-season home run champion of all time. They all overcame tremendous obstacles to accomplish a truly amazing feat. Each was a champion in his own time.

PART TWO : THE STATISTICS

1. Playing Statistics

George Herman "Babe" Ruth

Born Baltimore, MD, Feb. 6, 1895; *died* New York, NY, Aug. 16, 1948.
Height 6'2"; *weight* 215 pounds; *Bats* left; *throws* left

Year	Team	League	Pos	G	AB	R	H	D	T	HR	RBI	BA
1914	Boston	AL	P	5	10	1	2	1	0	0	2	.200
1915	Boston	AL	P	42	92	16	29	10	1	4	21	.315
1916	Boston	AL	P	67	136	18	37	5	3	3	15	.272
1917	Boston	AL	P	52	123	14	40	6	3	2	12	.325
1918	Boston	AL	P-OF-1	95	317	50	95	26	11	11	66	.300
1919	Boston	AL	P-OF	130	432	103	139	34	12	29	114	.322
1920	New York	AL	OF-1-P	142	458	158	172	36	9	54	137	.376
1921	New York	AL	OF-1-P	152	540	177	204	44	16	59	171	.378
1922	New York	AL	OF-1B	110	406	94	128	24	8	35	99	.315
1923	New York	AL	OF-1B	152	522	151	205	45	13	41	131	.393
1924	New York	AL	OF	153	529	143	200	39	7	46	121	.378
1925	New York	AL	OF	98	359	61	104	12	2	25	66	.290
1926	New York	AL	OF-1B	152	495	139	184	30	5	47	146	.372
1927	New York	AL	OF	151	540	158	192	29	8	60	164	.356
1928	New York	AL	OF	154	536	163	173	29	8	54	142	.323
1929	New York	AL	OF	135	499	121	172	26	6	46	154	.345
1930	New York	AL	OF-P	145	518	150	186	28	9	49	153	.359
1931	New York	AL	OF-1B	145	534	149	199	31	3	46	163	.373
1932	New York	AL	OF-1B	133	457	120	156	13	5	41	137	.341
1933	New York	AL	OF-P	137	459	97	138	21	3	34	103	.301
1934	New York	AL	OF	125	365	78	105	17	4	22	84	.288
1935	Boston	NL	OF	28	72	13	13	0	0	6	12	.181
Totals	22 years			2503	8399	2174	2873	506	136	714	2213	.342

Pitching—career totals

Years	Team	G	IP	W	L	Pct.	SO	BB	ERA
1914–19	Boston Red Sox	158	1190	89	46	.659	483	425	2.20
1920–33	New York Yankees	5	31	5	0	1.000	5	16	5.52

Roger Eugene Maris

Born Hibbing, MN, Sept. 10, 1934; *died* Houston, TX, Dec. 14, 1985
Height 6'; *weight* 205 pounds; *Bats* left; *throws* right

Year	Team	League	Pos	G	AB	R	H	D	T	HR	RBI	BA
1957	Cleve.	AL	OF	116	358	61	84	9	5	14	51	.235
1958	Cleve-KC	AL	OF	150	583	87	140	19	4	28	80	.240
1959	K.City	AL	OF	122	433	69	118	21	7	16	72	.273
1960	New York	AL	OF	136	499	98	141	18	7	39	112	.283
1961	New York	AL	OF	161	590	132	159	16	4	61	141	.269
1962	New York	AL	OF	157	590	92	151	34	1	33	100	.256
1963	New York	AL	OF	90	312	53	84	14	1	23	53	.269
1964	New York	AL	OF	141	513	86	144	12	2	26	71	.281
1965	New York	AL	OF	46	155	22	37	7	0	8	27	.239
1966	New York	AL	OF	119	348	37	81	9	2	13	43	.233
1967	St. Louis	NL	OF	125	410	64	107	18	7	9	55	.261
1968	St. Louis	NL	OF	100	310	25	79	18	2	5	45	.255
Totals	12 years			1463	5101	826	1325	195	42	275	850	.260

Note: The individual playing statistics for Ruth and Maris are from *The Historical Register*, compiled by Bob Hoie and Carlos Bauer.

Mark David McGwire

Born Pomona, CA, Oct. 1, 1963
Height 6'5"; *weight* 250 pounds; *Bats* right; *throws* right

Year	Team	League	Pos	G	AB	R	H	D	T	HR	RBI	BA
1986	Oakland	AL	3B	18	53	10	10	1	0	3	9	.189
1987	Oakland	AL	1-3-OF	151	557	97	161	28	4	49	118	.289
1988	Oakland	AL	1B-OF	155	550	87	143	22	1	32	99	.260
1989	Oakland	AL	1B	143	490	74	113	17	0	33	95	.231
1990	Oakland	AL	1B	156	523	87	123	16	0	39	108	.235
1991	Oakland	AL	1B	154	483	62	97	22	0	22	75	.201
1992	Oakland	AL	1B	139	467	87	125	22	0	42	104	.268
1993	Oakland	AL	1B	27	84	16	28	6	0	9	24	.333
1994	Oakland	AL	1B	47	135	26	34	3	0	9	25	.252
1995	Oakland	AL	1B	104	317	75	87	13	0	39	90	.274
1996	Oakland	AL	1B	130	423	104	132	21	0	52	113	.312
1997	Oak-St. L.	AL-NL	1B	156	540	86	148	27	0	58	123	.274
1998	St. Louis	NL	1B	155	509	130	152	21	0	70	147	.299
1999	St. Louis	NL	1B	153	521	118	145	21	1	65	147	.278
2000	St. Louis	NL	1B	89	236	60	72	8	0	32	73	.305
2001	St. Louis	NL	1B	97	299	48	56	4	0	29	64	.187
Totals	16 years			1874	6187	1167	1626	252	6	583	1414	.263

Samuel Peralta Sosa

Born San Pedro de Macoris, Dominican Republic, Nov. 12, 1968
Height 6'; *weight* 195 pounds; *Bats* right; *throws* right

Year	Team	League	Pos	G	AB	R	H	D	T	HR	RBI	BA
1989	Tex-Chic	AL	OF	58	183	27	47	8	0	4	13	.257
1990	Chicago	AL	OF	153	532	72	124	26	10	15	70	.233
1991	Chicago	AL	OF	116	316	39	64	10	1	10	33	.203
1992	Chicago	NL	OF	67	262	41	68	7	2	8	25	.260
1993	Chicago	NL	OF	159	598	92	156	25	5	33	93	.261
1994	Chicago	NL	OF	105	426	59	128	17	6	25	70	.300
1995	Chicago	NL	OF	144	564	89	151	17	3	36	119	.268
1996	Chicago	NL	OF	124	498	84	136	21	2	40	100	.273
1997	Chicago	NL	OF	162	642	90	161	31	4	36	119	.251
1998	Chicago	NL	OF	159	643	134	198	20	0	66	158	.307
1999	Chicago	NL	OF	162	625	114	180	21	2	63	141	.288
2000	Chicago	NL	OF	156	604	106	193	38	1	50	138	.320
2001	Chicago	NL	OF	160	577	146	189	34	5	64	160	.328
2002	Chicago	NL	OF	150	556	122	160	19	2	49	108	.288
Totals	14 years			1875	7026	1215	1955	297	43	499	1347	.278

Barry Lamar Bonds

Born: Riverside, CA, July 24, 1964
Height: 6' 2"; *weight:* 210 pounds; *Bats* left; *throws* left

Year	Team	League	Pos	GG	AB	R	H	D	T	HR	RBI	BA
1986	Pitts.	NL	OF	113	413	72	92	26	3	16	48	.223
1987	Pitts.	NL	OF	150	551	99	144	34	9	25	59	.261
1988	Pitts.	NL	OF	144	538	97	152	30	5	24	58	.283
1989	Pitts.	NL	OF	159	580	96	144	34	6	19	58	.248
1990	Pitts.	NL	OF	151	519	104	156	32	3	33	114	.301
1991	Pitts.	NL	OF	153	510	95	149	28	5	25	116	.292
1992	Pitts.	NL	OF	140	473	109	147	36	5	34	103	.311
1993	San Fr	NL	OF	159	539	129	181	38	4	46	123	.336
1994	San Fr	NL	OF	112	391	89	122	18	1	37	81	.312
1995	San Fr	NL	OF	144	506	109	149	30	7	33	194	.294
1996	San Fr	NL	OF	158	517	122	159	27	3	42	129	.308
1997	San Fr	NL	OF	159	532	123	155	26	5	40	101	.291
1998	San Fr	NL	OF	156	552	120	167	44	7	37	122	.303
1999	San Fr	NL	OF	102	355	91	93	20	2	34	83	.262
2000	San Fr	NL	OF	143	480	129	147	28	4	49	106	.306
2001	San Fr	NL	OF	153	476	129	156	32	2	73	137	.328
2002	San Fr.	NL	OF	143	403	117	149	31	2	46	110	.370
Totals	17 years			2439	8335	1830	2462	514	73	613	1652	.295

2. Side by Side Comparisons

	Ruth	Maris	McGwire	Sosa	Bonds
DOB	2/6/1895	9/10/34	10/1/63	11/12/68	7/24/64
Place	Baltimore, MD	Hibbing, MN	Pomona, CA	San Pedro de Macoris, D.R.	Riverside, CA
Residence	Deceased	Deceased	Long Beach, CA	Santo Domingo, D.R.	Los Altos, CA
Religion	Catholic	Catholic	Catholic	Catholic	
Height	6'2"	6'	6'5"	6'	6'2"
Weight	215	200	250	195	210
Throws	Left	Right	Right	Right	Left
Bats	Left	Left	Right	Right	Left
Position	1B-P-OF	OF	1B	OF	OF
Primary Team	Yankees	Yankees	Athletics	Cubs	Giants
HR Record Team	Yankees	Yankees	Cardinals	Cubs	Giants
HR Record, Year	1927	1961	1998	1998	2001
Age, HR Record Year	32	27	34	29	37
Team, League Standing	1 World Champ	1 World Champ	3 —	2 Playoff	2 —
Games, Season	154	163	162	163	162
Games Played	151	161	155	158	153

	Ruth	Maris	McGwire	Sosa	Bonds
ABs	540	590	509	639	476
Hits	192	159	152	196	156
Runs	158	132	130	132	129
HRs	60	61	70	66	73
HR's per 550 ABs	61	57	76	57	84
RBI	164	142	147	158	137
Strikeouts	89	67	155	170	93
BBs	138	94	162	73	177
OBP	.487	.376	.470	.376	.515
SA	.772	.620	.752	.648	.863
BA	.356	.269	.299	.307	.328
Awards: MVP	No	Yes	No	Yes	Yes
Player of the Year	—	—	Yes	Yes	Yes

3. Home Run Statistics

	Ruth	Maris	McGwire	Sosa	Bonds
Year	1927	1961	1998	1998	2001
HRs	60	61	70	66	73
HRs by Month					
March	0	0	1	0	0
April	4	1	10	6	11
May	12	11	16	7	17
June	9	15	10	20	11
July	9	13	8	9	6
August	9	11	10	13	12
September	17	9	15	11	12
October	0	1	0	0	4
HRs by July 4	26	30	37	33	39
HRs by Labor Day	50	53	60	58	57
Date, 50th HR	Sept. 11	Aug. 22	Aug. 20	Aug. 23	Aug. 11
Game	138	125	125	130	117
Date, #60	Sept. 30	Sept. 26	Sept. 5	Sept. 12	Sept. 6
Game	154	159	141	149	141
Date, #61	—	Oct. 1	Sept. 7	Sept. 13	Sept. 9
Game	—	163	143	150	144
Date, #62	—	—	Sept. 8	Sept. 13	Sept. 20
Game	—	—	144	150	147
Date, #66	—	—	Sept. 25	Sept. 25	Sept 28
Game	—	—	161	160	154
Date, #67	—	—	Sept. 26	—	Sept. 29
Game	—	—	162	—	155
Date, #70	—	—	Sept. 27	—	Oct. 4
Game	—	—	163	—	159

	Ruth	Maris	McGwire	Sosa	Bonds
Date, #71					Oct. 5
Game	—	—	—	—	160
Date, #73		—	—	—	Oct. 7
Game					162
HRs—Home	28	30	38	35	37
HRs—Away	32	31	32	31	36
HRs off RH Pitcher	42	52	55	54	56
HRs off LH Pitcher	18	9	15	12	17
HR, % of League	13.7	4.0	2.7	2.6	2.5
HR, % If 8 Team Lge	13.7	5.0	5.5	5.1	4.7
HRs by Team					
Chicago W.S.	6	13	2	3	—
Washington	8	9	—	—	—
Cleveland	9	8	2	0	—
Phila. A's	9	—	—	—	—
Detroit Tigers	8	8	0	2	—
Boston Red Sox	11	7	—	—	—
St. L. Browns	9	—	—	—	—
Kansas City A's	—	5	—	—	—
L.A. CA Angels	—	4	—	—	2
Minnesota Twins	—	4	1	1	—
Balt. Orioles	—	3	—	—	—
K. C. Royals	—	—	1	0	—
Ariz. D'backs	—	—	4	5	9
Atlanta	—	—	2	3	7
Chic. Cubs	—	—	7	—	2
Cincinnati	—	—	1	4	4
Colo. Rockies	—	—	2	3	10
Fla. Marlins	—	—	7	4	4
Houston Astros	—	—	5	4	2
L.A. Dodgers	—	—	4	1	6
Milw. Brewers	—	—	4	12	4
Montreal Expos	—	—	6	3	1
N.Y. Mets	—	—	4	2	2
Phil. Phillies	—	—	5	8	2
Pitts. Pirates	—	—	3	2	2
St. L. Cards	—	—	—	3	3
San Diego	—	—	5	3	1
San Francisco	—	—	5	3	11
Seattle Mariners	—	—	—	—	1
Texas Rangers	—	—	—	—	0
Totals	60	61	70	66	73
HR Distance					
300-349'	—	—	3	3	3
350-399'	—	—	20	23	23
400-449'	—	—	26	34	44

	Ruth	Maris	McGwire	Sosa	Bonds
HR Distance					
450–499'	—	—	16	5	3
500+'	—	—	5	1	0
Average, ft.	—	—	423	407	404
Longest, ft.	500+	450 est.	550	500	488
Total, ft.	—	—	29,610	26,730	29,493
HR, Direction					
Left Field	—	0	37	13	3
LCF	—	9	17	15	4
CF	—		13	18	16
RCF	—		3	11	19
Right Field	—		0	9	31
HRs, Day	60		21	33	26
HRs, Night	—		49	33	47
HRs, Grass	60	61	60	57	71
HRs, Artificial	—	—	10	9	2
2-HR games	9	7	8	10	8
3-HR games	1	0	2	1	2

4. Homer by Homer Comparisons

HR No.	Ruth	Maris	McGwire	Sosa	Bonds
1	04-15	04-26	03-31	04-04	4-02
2	04-23	05-03	04-02	04-11	4-12
3	04-24	05-06	04-03	04-15	4-13
4	04-29	05-17	04-04	04-23	4-14
5	05-01	05-19	04-14	04-24	4-15
6	05-01	05-20	04-14	04-27	4-17
7	05-10	05-21	04-14	05-03	4-18
8	05-11	05-23	04-17	05-16	4-20
9	05-17	05-28	04-21	05-22	4-24
10	05-22	05-30	04-25	05-25	4-26
11	05-23	05-30	04-30	05-25	4-29
12	05-28	05-31	05-01	05-27	5-02
13	05-29	06-02	05-08	05-27	5-03
14	05-30	06-03	05-12	06-01	5-04
15	05-31	06-04	05-14	06-01	5-11
16	05-31	06-06	05-16	06-03	5-17
17	06-05	06-07	05-18	06-05	5-18
18	06-07	06-07	05-19	06-06	5-19
19	06-11	06-11	05-19	06-07	5-19
20	06-11	06-11	05-19	06-08	5-19
21	06-12	06-13	05-22	06-13	5-20
22	06-16	06-14	05-23	06-15	5-20
23	06-22	06-17	05-23	06-15	5-21
24	06-22	06-18	05-24	06-15	5-22
25	06-25	06-19	05-25	06-17	5-24
26	07-03	06-20	05-29	06-19	5-27
27	07-08	06-22	05-30	06-19	5-30
28	07-09	07-01	06-05	06-20	5-30
29	07-09	07-02	06-08	06-20	6-01
30	07-12	07-02	06-10	06-21	6-04
31	07-24	07-04	06-12	06-24	6-05
32	07-26	07-05	06-17	06-25	6-07

HR No.	Ruth	Maris	McGwire	Sosa	Bonds
33	07-26	07-09	06-18	06-30	6-12
34	07-28	07-13	06-24	07-09	6-14
35	08-05	07-15	06-25	07-10	6-15
36	08-10	07-21	06-27	07-17	6-15
37	08-16	07-25	06-30	07-22	6-19
38	08-17	07-25	07-11	07-26	6-20
39	08-20	07-25	07-12	07-27	6-23
40	08-22	07-25	07-12	07-27	7-12
41	08-27	08-04	07-17	07-28	7-18
42	08-28	08-11	07-17	07-31	7-18
43	08-31	08-12	07-20	08-05	7-26
44	09-02	08-13	07-26	08-08	7-26
45	09-06	08-13	07-28	08-10	7-27
46	09-06	08-15	08-08	08-10	8-01
47	09-06	08-16	08-11	08-16	8-04
48	09-07	08-16	08-19	08-19	8-07
49	09-07	08-20	08-19	08-21	8-09
50	09-11	08-22	08-20	08-23	8-11
51	09-13	08-26	08-20	08-23	8-14
52	09-13	09-02	08-22	08-26	8-16
53	09-16	09-02	08-23	08-28	8-16
54	09-18	09-06	08-26	08-30	8-18
55	09-21	09-07	08-30	08-31	8-23
56	09-22	09-09	09-01	09-02	8-27
57	09-27	09-16	09-01	09-04	8-31
58	09-29	09-17	09-02	09-05	9-03
59	09-29	09-20	09-02	09-11	9-04
60	09-30	09-26	09-05	09-12	9-06
61		10-01	09-07	09-13	9-09
62			09-08	09-13	9-09
63			09-15	09-16	9-09
64			09-18	09-23	9-20
65			09-20	09-23	9-23
66			09-25	09-25	9-23
67			09-26		9-24
68			09-26		9-28
69			09-27		9-29
70			09-27		10-04
71					10-05
72					10-05
73					10-07

5. Babe Ruth
in 1927

Date	HR No.	Pitcher	Team	Location
04-15	1	H. Ehmke	Phil. A's	New York
04-23	2	R. Walberg	Phil. A's	Philadelphia
04-24	3	S. Thurston	Washington	Washington
04-29	4	S. Harriss	Boston	Boston
05-01	5	J. Quinn	Phil. A's	New York
05-01	6	R. Walberg	Phil. A's	New York
05-10	7	M. Gaston	St. Louis	St. Louis
05-11	8	E. Nevers	St. Louis	St. Louis
05-17	9	R. Collins	Detroit	Detroit
05-22	10	B. Karr	Cleveland	Cleveland
05-23	11	S. Thurston	Washington	Washington
05-28	12	S. Thurston	Washington	New York
05-29	13	D. MacFayden	Boston	New York
05-30	14	R. Walberg	Phil. A's	Philadelphia
05-31	15	J. Quinn	Phil. A's	Philadelphia
05-31	16	H. Ehmke	Phil. A's	Philadelphia
06-05	17	E. Whitehill	Detroit	New York
06-07	18	T. Thomas	Chicago	New York
06-11	19	G. Buckeye	Cleveland	New York
06-11	20	G. Buckeye	Cleveland	New York
06-12	21	G. Uhle	Cleveland	New York
06-16	22	T. Zachary	St. Louis	New York
06-22	23	H. Wiltse	Boston	Boston
06-22	24	H. Wiltse	Boston	Boston
06-30	25	S. Harriss	Boston	Boston
07-03	26	H. Lisenbee	Washington	Washington
07-08	27	D. Hankins	Detroit	Detroit
07-09	28	K. Holloway	Detroit	Detroit
07-09	29	K. Holloway	Detroit	Detroit
07-12	30	J. Shaute	Cleveland	Cleveland
07-24	31	T. Thomas	Chicago	Chicago

Date	HR No.	Pitcher	Team	Location
07-26	32	M. Gaston	St. Louis	New York
07-26	33	M. Gaston	St. Louis	New York
07-28	34	L. Stewart	St. Louis	New York
08-05	35	G. Smith	Detroit	New York
08-10	36	T. Zachary	Washington	Washington
08-16	37	T. Thomas	Chicago	Chicago
08-17	38	S. Connally	Chicago	Chicago
08-20	39	J. Miller	Cleveland	Cleveland
08-22	40	J. Shaute	Cleveland	Cleveland
08-27	41	E. Nevers	St. Louis	St. Louis
08-28	42	E. Wingard	St. Louis	St. Louis
08-31	43	T. Welzer	Boston	New York
09-02	44	R. Walberg	Phil. A's	Philadelphia
09-06	45	T. Welzer	Boston	Boston
09-06	46	T. Welzer	Boston	Boston
09-06	47	J. Russell	Boston	Boston
09-07	48	D. MacFayden	Boston	Boston
09-07	49	S. Harriss	Boston	Boston
09-11	50	M. Gaston	St. Louis	New York
09-13	51	W. Hudlin	Cleveland	New York
09-13	52	J. Shaute	Cleveland	New York
09-16	53	T. Blankenship	Chicago	New York
09-18	54	T. Lyons	Chicago	New York
09-21	55	S. Gibson	Detroit	New York
09-22	56	K. Holloway	Detroit	New York
09-27	57	L. Grove	Phil. A's	New York
09-29	58	H. Lisenbee	Washington	New York
09-29	59	P. Hopkins	Washington	New York
09-30	60	T. Zachary	Washington	New York

6. Roger Maris in 1961

Date	HR No.	Pitcher	Team	Location
04-26	1	P. Foytack	Detroit	Detroit
05-03	2	P. Ramos	Minnesota	Minnesota
05-06	3	E. Grba	Los Angeles	Los Angeles
05-17	4	P. Burnside	Washington	New York
05-19	5	J. Perry	Cleveland	Cleveland
05-20	6	G. Bell	Cleveland	Cleveland
05-21	7	C. Estrada	Baltimore	New York
05-24	8	G. Conley	Boston	New York
05-28	9	C. McLish	Chicago	New York
05-30	10	G. Conley	Boston	Boston
05-30	11	M. Fornieles	Boston	Boston
05-31	12	B. Muffett	Boston	Boston
06-02	13	C. McLish	Chicago	Chicago
06-03	14	B. Shaw	Chicago	Chicago
06-04	15	R. Kemmerer	Chicago	Chicago
06-06	16	E. Palmquist	Minnesota	New York
06-07	17	P. Ramos	Minnesota	New York
06-09	18	R. Herbert	Kansas City	New York
06-11	19	E. Grba	Los Angeles	New York
06-11	20	J. James	Los Angeles	New York
06-13	21	J. Perry	Cleveland	Cleveland
06-14	22	G. Bell	Cleveland	Cleveland
06-17	23	D. Mossi	Detroit	Detroit
06-18	24	J. Casale	Detroit	Detroit
06-19	25	J. Archer	Kansas City	Kansas City
06-20	26	J. Nuxhall	Kansas City	Kansas City
06-22	27	N. Bass	Kansas City	Kansas City
07-01	28	D. Sisler	Washington	New York
07-02	29	P. Burnside	Washington	New York
07-02	30	J. Klippstein	Washington	New York
07-04	31	F. Lary	Detroit	New York

Date	HR No.	Pitcher	Team	Location
07-05	32	F. Funk	Cleveland	New York
07-09	33	B. Monbouquette	Boston	New York
07-13	34	E. Wynn	Chicago	Chicago
07-15	35	R. Herbert	Chicago	Chicago
07-21	36	B. Monbouquette	Boston	Boston
07-25	37	F. Baumann	Chicago	New York
07-25	38	D. Larsen	Chicago	New York
07-25	39	R. Kemmerer	Chicago	New York
07-25	40	W. Hacker	Chicago	New York
08-04	41	C. Pascual	Minnesota	New York
08-11	42	P. Burnside	Washington	Washington
08-12	43	D. Donovan	Washington	Washington
08-13	44	B. Daniels	Washington	Washington
08-13	45	M. Kutyna	Washington	Washington
08-15	46	J. Pizarro	Chicago	New York
08-16	47	B. Pierce	Chicago	New York
08-16	48	B. Pierce	Chicago	New York
08-20	49	J. Perry	Cleveland	Cleveland
08-22	50	K. McBride	Los Angeles	Los Angeles
08-26	51	J. Walker	Kansas City	Kansas City
09-02	52	F. Lary	Detroit	New York
09-02	53	H. Aguirre	Detroit	New York
09-06	54	T. Cheney	Washington	New York
09-07	55	D. Stigman	Cleveland	New York
09-09	56	M. Grant	Cleveland	New York
09-16	57	F. Lary	Detroit	Detroit
09-17	58	T. Fox	Detroit	Detroit
09-20	59	M. Pappas	Baltimore	Baltimore
09-26	60	J. Fischer	Baltimore	New York
10-01	61	T. Stallard	Boston	New York

7. Mark McGwire
in 1998

Date	HR No.	Pitcher	Location	Distance	Direction
03-31	1	R. Martinez	L.A. @ St. Louis	364	LF
04-02	2	F. Lankford	L.A. @ St. Louis	368	LF
04-03	3	M. Langston	S.D. @ St. Louis	367	LF
04-04	4	D. Wengert	S.D. @ St. Louis	430	CF
04-14	5	J. Suppan	Ariz. @ St. Louis	424	LF
04-14	6	J. Suppan	Ariz. @ St. Louis	347	LF
04-14	7	B. Manuel	Ariz. @ St. Louis	462	CF
04-17	8	M. Whiteside	Phil. @ St. Louis	410	LF
04-21	9	T. Moore	Montreal	440	LCF
04-25	10	J. Spradlin	Philadelphia	410	CF
04-30	11	M. Pisciotta	Chicago	380	LCF
05-01	12	R. Beck	Chicago	362	LCF
05-08	13	R. Reed	New York	358	LF
05-12	14	P. Wagner	Milw. @ St. Louis	527	LCF
05-14	15	K. Millwood	Atlanta @ St. Louis	381	RCF
05-16	16	L. Hernandez	Florida @ St. Louis	550	CF
05-18	17	J. Sanchez	Florida @ St. Louis	478	LF
05-19	18	T. Green	Philadelphia	440	CF
05-19	19	T. Green	Philadelphia	471	LCF
05-19	20	W. Gomes	Philadelphia	451	LF
05-22	21	M. Gardner	San Fran. @ St. Louis	425	LF
05-23	22	R. Rodriguez	San Fran. @ St. Louis	366	LF
05-23	23	J. Johnstone	San Fran. @ St. Louis	477	LCF
05-24	24	R. Nenn	San Fran. @ St. Louis	394	LF
05-25	25	J. Thomson	Colo. @ St. Louis	432	LF
05-29	26	D. Miceli	San Diego	388	LCF
05-30	27	A. Ashby	San Diego	423	LCF
06-05	28	O. Hershiser	San Francisco	410	CF
06-08	29	J. Bere	Chic. White Sox	358	LF
06-10	30	J. Parque	Chic. White Sox	410	CF

Date	HR No.	Pitcher	Location	Distance	Direction
06-12	31	A. Benes	Arizona	451	LF
06-17	32	J. Lima	Houston	349	LF
06-18	33	S. Reynolds	Houston	450	LF
06-24	34	J. Wright	Cleveland	433	LF
06-25	35	D. Burba	Cleveland	461	LF
06-27	36	M. Trombley	Minnesota	431	LCF
06-30	37	G. Rusch	K. C. @ St. Louis	471	LF
07-11	38	B. Wagner	Houston @ St. Louis	463	LF
07-12	39	S. Bergman	Houston @ St. Louis	403	LCF
07-12	40	S. Elarton	Houston @ St. Louis	403	LF
07-17	41	B. Bohanon	L.A. @ St. Louis	511	LF
07-17	42	A. Osuna	L.A. @ St. Louis	425	LF
07-20	43	B. Boehringer	San Diego	454	LCF
07-26	44	J. Thomson	Colorado	452	LF
07-28	45	M. Myers	Milw. @ St. Louis	414	RCF
08-08	46	M. Clark	Chic. @ St. Louis	377	LF
08-11	47	B. Jones	Mets @ St. Louis	467	LCF
08-19	48	M. Karchner	Chicago Cubs	430	LF
08-19	49	T. Mulholland	Chicago Cubs	406	CF
08-20	50	W. Blair	New York	369	LF
08-20	51	R. Reed	New York	385	LF
08-22	52	F. Cordova	Pittsburgh	477	RCF
08-23	53	R. Rincon	Pittsburgh	392	LCF
08-26	54	J. Speier	Florida @ St. Louis	509	CF
08-30	55	D. Martinez	Atlanta @ St. Louis	501	CF
09-01	56	L. Hernandez	Florida	450	CF
09-01	57	D. Pall	Florida	472	CF
09-02	58	B. Edmondson	Florida	497	LF
09-02	59	R. Stanifer	Florida	458	LF
09-05	60	D. Reyes	Cinci. @ St. Louis	381	LF
09-07	61	M. Morgan	Cubs @ St. Louis	430	LF
09-08	62	S. Trachsel	Cubs @ St. Louis	341	LF
09-15	63	J. Christiansen	Pitt. @ St. Louis	385	LCF
09-18	64	R. Roque	Milwaukee	414	LCF
09-20	65	S. Karl	Milwaukee	422	LF
09-25	66	S. Bennett	Mont. @ St. Louis	375	LF
09-26	67	D. Hermanson	Mont. @ St. Louis	403	LF
09-26	68	K. Bullinger	Mont. @ St. Louis	435	CF
09-27	69	M. Thurman	Mont. @ St. Louis	377	LF
09-27	70	C. Pavano	Mont. @ St. Louis	370	LF

8. Sammy Sosa
in 1998

Date	HR No.	Pitcher	Location	Distance	Direction
04-04	1	M. Valdes	Mont. @ Cubs	371	RF
04-11	2	A. Telford	Montreal	350	RCF
04-15	3	D. Cook	New York	430	LF
04-23	4	D. Miceli	S.D. @ Cubs	420	CF
04-24	5	I. Valdes	Los Angeles	430	CF
04-27	6	J. Hamilton	San Diego	434	CF
05-03	7	C. Politte	St. L. @ Cubs	370	LCF
05-16	8	S. Sullivan	Cincinnati	420	CF
05-22	9	G. Maddux	Atlanta	440	CF
05-25	10	K. Millwood	Atlanta	410	RCF
05-25	11	M. Cather	Atlanta	420	CF
05-27	12	D. Winston	Phil. @ Cubs	460	LF
05-27	13	W. Gomes	Phil. @ Cubs	400	RF
06-01	14	R. Dempster	Florida @ Cubs	430	LCF
06-01	15	O. Henriquez	Florida @ Cubs	410	LCF
06-03	16	L. Hernandez	Florida @ Cubs	370	LCF
06-05	17	J. Parque	Chic. W.S. @ Cubs	370	RCF
06-06	18	C. Castillo	Chic. W.S. @ Cubs	410	CF
06-07	19	J. Baldwin	Chic. W.S. @ Cubs	380	CF
06-08	20	L. Hawkins	Minnesota	340	RF
06-13	21	M. Portugal	Philadelphia	410	RF
06-15	22	C. Eldred	Milw. @ Cubs	420	RCF
06-15	23	C. Eldred	Milw. @ Cubs	410	LF
06-15	24	C. Elderd	Milw. @ Cubs	415	LCF
06-17	25	B. Patrick	Milw. @ Cubs	430	LF
06-19	26	C. Loewer	Phil. @ Cubs	380	LCF
06-19	27	C. Loewer	Phil. @ Cubs	378	LF
06-20	28	M. Beech	Phil. @ Cubs	366	LCF
06-20	29	T. Borland	Phil. @ Cubs	500	LF
06-21	30	T. Green	Phil. @ Cubs	380	RF
06-24	31	S. Greisinger	Detroit	390	CF

Date	HR No.	Pitcher	Location	Distance	Direction
06-25	32	B. Moehler	Detroit	400	CF
06-30	33	A. Embree	Ariz. @ Cubs	364	LF
07-09	34	J. Juden	Milwaukee	432	RCF
07-10	35	S. Karl	Milwaukee	450	CF
07-17	36	K. Ojala	Florida	440	CF
07-22	37	M. Batista	Mont. @ Cubs	365	RCF
07-26	38	R. Reed	Mets @ Cubs	420	CF
07-27	39	W. Blair	Arizona	349	RF
07-27	40	A. Embree	Arizona	430	RCF
07-28	41	B. Wolcott	Arizona	395	LCF
07-31	42	J. Wright	Colo. @ Cubs	378	RCF
08-05	43	A. Benes	Ariz. @ Cubs	377	LCF
08-08	44	R. Croushore	St. Louis	400	CF
08-10	45	R. Ortiz	San Francisco	366	CF
08-10	46	C. Brock	San Francisco	420	LCF
08-16	47	S. Bergman	Houston	360	RCF
08-19	48	K. Bottenfield	St. L. @ Cubs	368	LF
08-21	49	O. Hershiser	San Fran. @ Cubs	430	CF
08-23	50	J. Lima	Houston @ Cubs	440	LCF
08-23	51	J. Lima	Houston @ Cubs	380	LCF
08-26	52	B. Tomko	Cincinnati	439	LCF
08-28	53	J. Thomson	Colorado	414	RCF
08-30	54	D. Kile	Colorado	482	LCF
08-31	55	B. Tomko	Cinci. @ Cubs	364	LF
09-02	56	J. Bere	Cinci. @ Cubs	370	RF
09-04	57	J. Schmidt	Pittsburgh	387	CF
09-05	58	S. Lawrence	Pittsburgh	411	RCF
09-11	59	B. Pulsipher	Milw. @ Cubs	464	RF
09-12	60	V. de Los Santos	Milw. @ Cubs	430	LF
09-13	61	B. Patrick	Milw. @ Cubs	480	LF
09-13	62	E. Plunk	Milw. @ Cubs	480	LF
09-16	63	B. Boehringer	San Diego	434	LF
09-23	64	R. Roque	Milwaukee	344	RF
09-23	65	R. Henderson	Milwaukee	410	CF
09-25	66	J. Lima	Houston	462	LF

9. Barry Bonds in 2001

Date	HR No.	Pitcher	Location	Distance	Direction
4-02	1	W. Williams	San Diego @ Giants	420	CF
4-12	2	A. Eaton	San Diego	417	LCF
4-13	3	J. Wright	Milwaukee	440	RF
4-14	4	J. Haynes	Milwaukee	410	RF
4-15	5	D. Weathers	Milwaukee	390	LCF
4-17	6	T. Adams	Los Angeles @ Giants	417	RF
4-18	7	C. H. Park	Los Angeles @ Giants	420	RF
4-20	8	J. Haynes	Milwaukee @ Giants	410	CF
4-24	9	J. Brower	Cincinnati @ Giants	380	RCF
4-26	10	S. Sullivan	Cincinnati @ Giants	430	CF
4-29	11	M. Aybar	Chicago @ Giants	370	RF
5-02	12	T. Ritchie	Pittsburgh	420	LCF
5-03	13	J. Anderson	Pittsburgh	400	RCF
5-04	14	B. Chen	Philadelphia	360	RF
5-11	15	S. Trachsel	N. Y. Mets @ Giants	410	RCF
5-17	16	C. Smith	Florida	420	RCF
5-18	17	M. Remlinger	Atlanta	391	RF
5-19	18	O. Perez	Atlanta	416	RF
5-19	19	J. Cabrera	Atlanta	442	RF
5-19	20	J. Marquis	Atlanta	410	CF
5-20	21	J. Burkett	Atlanta	415	RCF
5-20	22	M. Remlinger	Atlanta	436	CF
5-21	23	C. Schilling	Arizona	430	CF
5-22	24	R. Springer	Arizona	410	LCF
5-24	25	J. Thompson	Colorado @ Giants	400	RF
5-27	26	D. Neagle	Colorado @ Giants	390	RF
5-30	27	R. Ellis	Arizona @ Giants	420	RF
5-30	28	R. Ellis	Arizona @ Giants	410	CF
6-01	29	S. Chacon	Colorado	420	RF
6-04	30	B. Jones	San Diego @ Giants	410	CF

Date	HR No.	Pitcher	Location	Distance	Direction
6-05	31	W. Serrano	San Diego @ Giants	410	CF
6-07	32	B. Lawrence	San Diego @ Giants	450	CF
6-12	33	P. Rapp	Anaheim @ Giants	320	RF
6-14	34	L. Pote	Anaheim @ Giants	430	RCF
6-15	35	M. Mulder	Oakland @ Giants	380	LF
6-15	36	M. Mulder	Oakland @ Giants	375	RF
6-19	37	A. Eaton	San Diego	375	RCF
6-20	38	R. Myers	San Diego	347	RF
6-23	39	D. Kile	St. Louis	380	RCF
7-12	40	P. Abbot	Seattle	429	RCF
7-18	41	M. Hampton	Colorado @ Giants	320	RF
7-18	42	M. Hampton	Colorado @ Giants	360	LF
7-26	43	C. Schilling	Arizona	375	RCF
7-26	44	C. Schilling	Arizona	370	CF
7-27	45	B. Anderson	Arizona	436	RF
8-01	46	J. Beimel	Pittsburgh @ Giants	400	RCF
8-04	47	N. Figueroa	Philadelphia @ Giants	405	RF
8-07	48	D. Graves	Cincinnati	430	CF
8-09	49	S. Winchester	Cincinnati	350	RF
8-11	50	J. Borowski	Chicago Cubs	396	CF
8-14	51	R. Bones	Florida @ Giants	410	RF
8-16	52	A. Burnett	Florida @ Giants	310	RF
8-16	53	V. Darensbourg	Florida @ Giants	430	RCF
8-18	54	J. Marquis	Atlanta @ Giants	415	RF
8-23	55	G. Lloyd	Montreal	380	RF
8-27	56	K. Appier	N. Y. Mets	375	RCF
8-31	57	J. Thompson	Colorado @ Giants	400	RF
9-03	58	J. Jennings	Colorado @ Giants	435	RCF
9-04	59	M. Batista	Arizona @ Giants	420	RCF
9-06	60	A. Lopez	Arizona @ Giants	420	RCF
9-09	61	S. Elarton	Colorado	488	RCF
9-09	62	S. Elarton	Colorado	361	RF
9-09	63	T. Belitz	Colorado	394	RF
9-20	64	W. Miller	Houston @ Giants	410	CF
9-23	65	J. Middlebrook	San Diego	411	CF
9-23	66	J. Middlebrook	San Diego	365	LF
9-24	67	J. Baldwin	Los Angeles	360	RF
9-28	68	J. Middlebrook	San Diego @ Giants	438	RCF
9-29	69	C. McElroy	San Diego @ Giants	437	RF
10-04	70	W. Rodriguez	Houston	454	RCF
10-05	71	C. H. Park	Los Angeles @ Giants	442	RF
10-05	72	C. H. Park	Los Angeles @ Giants	404	CF
10-07	73	D. Springer	Los Angeles @ Giants	380	RF

10. Major League Park Field Dimensions

American League—1927

	Distance, Feet				
Location	LF	LCF	CF	RCF	RF
Yankee Stadium	281	395	490	429	295
Shibe Park	312	405	468	393	307
Comiskey Park I	365	375	455	375	365
Fenway Park	321	379	488	405	359
Tiger Stadium	345	365	467	370	370
Griffith Stadium	358	391	421	378	328
Sportsmans Park III	355	379	430	354	320
League Park II, Cleveland	376	415	420	400	290
Average	339	388	446	386	329

American League—1961

	Distance, Feet				
Location	LF	LCF	CF	RCF	RF
Yankee Stadium	301	402	461	407	296
Fenway Park	315	379	420	380	302
Tiger Stadium	340	365	440	370	325
Memorial Stadium, Baltimore	309	380	410	380	309
Comiskey Park I	352	375	415	375	352
Cleveland Stadium	320	380	410	380	320
Metropolitan Stadium, Minneapolis	329	402	412	402	329

	Distance, Feet				
Location	**LF**	**LCF**	**CF**	**RCF**	**RF**
Griffith Stadium	388	372	421	373	320
Wrigley Field, Los Angeles	340	345	412	345	339
Municipal Stadium, Kansas City	370	390	421	387	353
Average	336	379	422	380	325

National League—1998–2001

	Distance, Feet				
Location	**LF**	**LCF**	**CF**	**RCF**	**RF**
Joe Robbie Stadium	335	380	410	380	345
Shea Stadium	338	371	410	371	338
Veterans Stadium	330	371	408	371	330
Olympic Stadium	325	375	404	375	335
Turner Field	335	380	401	390	330
Three Rivers Stadium	335	375	400	375	335
PNC Park	325	389	399	375	330
Busch Stadium	330	375	402	375	330
Wrigley Field	355	360	400	368	353
County Stadium, Milwaukee	315	392	402	392	315
Riverfront Stadium	330	375	404	375	330
Astrodome	330	375	400	375	330
Dodger Stadium	330	375	400	375	330
Qualcomm Stadium	327	370	405	370	327
3Com Park	335	365	400	365	335
Pacific Bell Park	335	370	404	370	307
Bank One Ballpark	330	369	407	371	334
Coors Field	347	390	424	375	350
Average	332	373	406	375	330

Major League Stadiums— Home Run Factors (HRF)

Location	**HRF**
Yankee Stadium	1.03
Busch Stadium	1.05
Wrigley Field	1.16
Kingdome Seattle	1.41
Safeco Field	0.78
Fenway Park	0.88

Location	HRF
Jacobs Field	0.99
The Ballpark at Arlington	1.12
PacBell Stadium	0.94
Dodger Stadium	0.91
Coors Field	1.69
Turner Field	0.93
Enron Field	1.15
Shea Stadium	0.85

HRF: The number of home runs hit in that park compared to the average number of HRs hit in the league.

11. Home Run Factors

Major League Home Runs

Factors Affecting Major League Home Runs—From 1920 to 1998

Average major league team home runs per year:
> 1920   39 home runs per team per year
> 1998   140 home runs per team per year
>   An increase of 121 home runs

Factors

	% home run increase (decrease)/ team/year	No. of HR increase (decrease)/ team/year
Player size, physical fitness, weight training, personal trainers, dietary supplements	9	11
New livelier basenball, 1994	18	21
Homer friendly parks, dimensions	3	4
Atmospheric conditions, Colorado, Atlanta	3	4
Babe Ruth syndrome	49	59
Ralph Kiner syndrome	27	33
Integration	8	10
Designated hitter	5	6
Night Baseball	(-8%)	(-10)
Expansion, travel, free agency	(-14%)	(-17)
Total	100%	121

Babe Ruth Syndrome

Babe Ruth's home run heroics affected the batting philosophy of a generation of home run hitters, but the full effect of his influence on home run production wasn't felt until the next generation of hitters arrived on the scene in the 1930s. Ruth's contemporaries, except in a few cases, could not, or did not want to, change their batting strokes.

Ralph Kiner Syndrome

This was similar to the Babe Ruth syndrome. Kiner's effect on home run output was noticeable during the 1950s and '60s. His famous comment, "Home run hitters drive Cadillacs. Singles hitters drive Chevys," influenced a whole generation of young hitters.

Integration

The Negro League players were, in general, more productive home run hitters than the average major league player. The effect of the movement of these players into the major leagues was noticeable during the 1950s and '60s.

Major League Home Run Production

Average Home Runs per Year per Team
Based on a 154-Game Schedule

Years	Home Runs/Team/Year	Comments
1921–30	73	16 major league teams
1931–40	84	16 major league teams
1941–50	84	16 major league teams
1951–60	133	16 major league teams; Integration
1961–70	136	18 to 24 major league teams
1971–80	115	24 to 26 major league teams; Changed baseball manufacturer from Spalding to Rawlings in 1976
1981–90	125	26 major league teams; Baseballs manufactured in Haiti
1991–98	147	26 to 30 major league teams
1991	124	26 teams
1992	111	26 teams
1993	137	28 teams
1994	154	28 teams—Baseballs manufactured in Costa Rica

Years	Home Runs/Team/Year	Comments
1995	156	28 teams
1996	168	28 teams
1997	165	28 teams
1998	160	30 teams

Number of Home Runs Hit per Team per Year

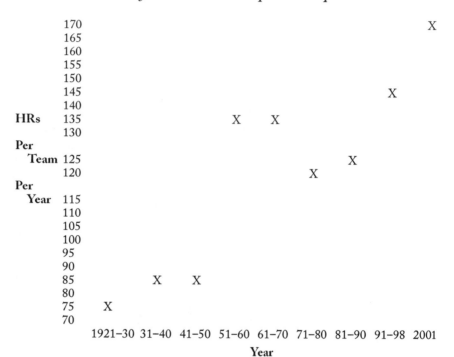

The Effect of Player Size on Home Runs

Period	Major League All-Star Team Average Size of 18 Players		Avg HRs/Man Adjusted for Lively Ball	Players Weighing 200 Pounds or More
19th Century	5'10"	175 pounds	15	Brouthers, Connor, Thompson
1901–25	5'10"	181 pounds	15	Bresnahan, Wagner, J. Jackson
1926–50 Williams,	6'	188 pounds	20	Gehrig, Ruth, Greenberg, Terry

Period	Major League All-Star Team Average Size of 18 Players		Avg HRs/Man Adjusted for Lively Ball	Comments Players Weighing 200 Pounds or More
1951–75	6'	194 pounds	25	Campanella, Bench, Hodges, J. Robinson, McCovey, Killebrew
1976–99	6'1"	195 pounds	19	Fisk, Murray, Ripken, Winfield, Puckett
1990–99	6'2"	208 pounds	26	I. Rodriguez, Thomas, M.Vaughn, McGwire, Baerga, Ripken M. Williams, Caminiti, Griffey, J. Gonzalez, Belle, Bichette, Buhner, J. Carter

All other things being equal, the bigger the batter, the more home runs he will hit. From 1926 to 1999 the average number of home runs increased by six, and the average weight of the players increased by 20 pounds.

Added muscle = more home runs

Example: Mark McGwire at 250 pounds weighs 50 pounds more than Sammy Sosa, which would give him a formidable 15 home run edge.

Through 1998, McGwire has averaged 49 home runs for every 550 at-bats during his career. Sosa has averaged 32 home runs for every 550 at-bats during his career.

Effect of Player Size on Home Runs

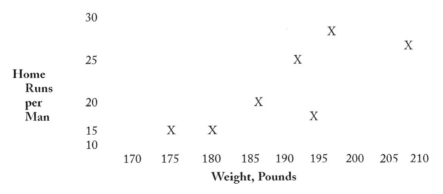

12. Top Home Run Seasons, per At-Bat

Player	Team	Year	AB	HR	HR per 550 AB
Barry Bonds	San Francisco Giants	2001	476	73	84
Mark McGwire	St. Louis Cardinals	1998	509	70	76
Mark McGwire	Oakland Athletics	1995	317	39	68
Mark McGwire	Oakland Athletics	1996	423	52	68
Babe Ruth	New York Yankees	1920	458	54	65
Barry Bonds	San Francisco Giants	2002	403	46	63
Babe Ruth	New York Yankees	1927	540	60	61
Babe Ruth	New York Yankees	1921	540	59	60
Mark McGwire	Oakland–St. Louis	1997	540	58	59
Mickey Mantle	New York Yankees	1961	514	54	58
Hank Greenberg	Detroit Tigers	1938	556	58	57
Roger Maris	New York Yankees	1961	590	61	57
Sammy Sosa	Chicago Cubs	1998	639	66	57
Hank Aaron	Atlanta Braves	1973	392	40	56

Note: Seasons with less than 10.00 at bats per home run

13. Top Home Run Careers, per At-Bat

Player	AB	HR	HR/550 AB	Weight, lbs.
Mark McGwire	6,187	583	52	250
Babe Ruth	7,289	665	50 (1920–1935)	220
Barry Bonds	8,335	613	40	210
Ralph Kiner	5,205	369	39	195
Harmon Killebrew	8,147	573	39	210
Sammy Sosa	6,470	450	38	205
Ken Griffey, Jr.	6,716	460	38	205
Ted Williams	7,706	521	37	205
Albert Belle, Jr.	5,853	381	36	200
Mickey Mantle	8,102	536	36	201
Dave Kingman	6,677	442	36	215
Jimmie Foxx	8,134	534	36	195
Mike Schmidt	8,352	548	36	195
Hank Greenberg	5,193	331	35	210
Hank Aaron	12,364	755	34	190
Willie Mays	10,881	660	33	187
Eddie Mathews	8,537	512	33	195
Reggie Jackson	9,864	563	31	195
Duke Snider	7,161	407	31	200
Roger Maris	5,101	273	30	195

Bibliography

Bamberger, Michael. "Sammy: You're the Man." *Sports Illustrated*, September 28, 1998, 44–50.

Baseball Weekly. Arlington, Va: Gannett, 1998–2001.

Beard, Charles A., and Mary R. Beard. *The Rise of American Civilization*. New York: Macmillan, 1937.

Benson, Michael. *Ballparks of North America*. Jefferson, N.C.: McFarland, 1989.

Brown, Gene, Arleen Keylin and Daniel Lundy, eds. *Sports of the Times*. New York: Arno, 1982.

Carter, Craig, ed. *Daguerreotypes*. 8th ed. St. Louis: Sporting News, 1990.

Caruso, Gary. *The Braves Encyclopedia*. Philadelphia: Temple University Press, 1995.

Castle, George. *Sammy Sosa: Clearing the Vines*. Champaign, Ill.: Sports Publishing, 1998.

Cohen, Richard M., and David S. Neft. *The World Series*. New York: Collier, 1986.

Creamer, Robert W. *Babe: The Legend Comes to Life*. New York: Fireside, 1992.

Davenport, John Warner. *Baseball's Pennant Races*. Madison, Wis.. First Impressions, 1981.

Friend, Tom. "Crush Hour." *ESPN*, September 1998, 122–126.

Gallagher, Mark. *The Yankee Encyclopedia*. Champaign, Ill.: Sagamore, 1996.

"The Great Home Run Race," *Sports Illustrated*. Time Inc. 1998.

Hoffman, Robert M., ed. *News of the Nation*. Englewood Cliffs, N.J.: Prentice-Hall, 1975.

Honig, Donald. *A Donald Honig Reader*. New York: Fireside, 1988.

Houk, Ralph, and Robert W. Creamer. *Season of Glory*. New York: G.P. Putnam's Sons, 1988.

Johnson, Lloyd, and Miles Wolff, eds. *Encyclopedia of Minor League Baseball*. Durham, N.C.: Baseball America, 1993.

Kaplan, David A., and Brad Stone. "Going...Going...." *Newsweek*, September 14, 1998, 54–56.

Kermisch, Al. "The Babe Ruth Beginning." *Baseball Research Journal*, 4 (1975):45–51.

Koenig, Bill. "The Babe." *Baseball Weekly*, no. 21 (1998): 28–31.

Krich, John. *El Béisbol.* New York: Prentice Hall, 1989.

Lowry, Philip. J. *Green Cathedrals.* Reading, Mass.: Addison-Wesley, 1992.

The Mac Attack: The Road to 62 and Beyond. Tulsa, Okla.: Paragon Communications Group, 1998.

McConnell, Bob, and David Vincent, eds. *SABR Presents the Home Run Encyclopedia.* New York: Macmillan, 1996.

McGwire, Mark, with Tom Verducci. "Where Do I Go from Here?" *Sports Illustrated,* September 21, 1998, 52–55.

McKinney, Susan M., ed. *Home Run: The Year the Records Fell.* Champaign, Ill.: Sports Publishing, 1998.

McNeil, William F. *The Dodgers Encyclopedia.* Champaign, Ill.: Sports Publishing, 1997.

_____. *The King of Swat.* Jefferson, N.C.: McFarland, 1997.

Menke, Frank G. *The New Encyclopedia of Sports.* New York: A.S. Barnes and Company, 1947.

Morse, Joseph Laffan, ed. *The Universal Standard Encyclopedia.* New York: Unicorn, 1954.

Muskat, Carrie. "Sammy Sosa." *Cubs Quarterly,* 16, no. 1 (1997): 34–41.

Nemec, David. *Great Baseball Feats, Facts, & Firsts.* New York: New American Library, 1987.

Oh, Sadaharu, and David Falkner. *Sadaharu Oh.* New York: Vintage Books, 1985.

Okrent, Daniel, and Steve Wulf. *Baseball Anecdotes.* New York: Harper & Row, 1990.

Oleksak, Michael M., and Mary Adams Oleksak. *Béisbol.* Indianapolis: Masters Press, 1986.

Peary, Danny, ed. *Cult Baseball Players.* New York: Fireside, 1990.

Pirone, Dorothy Ruth. *My Dad, the Babe.* Boston: Quinlan Press, 1988.

Rains, Rob. *Mark McGwire, Home Run Hero.* New York: St. Martin's, 1998.

Reichler, Joseph L., ed. *The Baseball Encyclopedia.* New York: Macmillan, 1979.

_____, and Jack Clary. *Baseball's Great Moments.* New York: Gallahad Books, 1990.

Reidenbaugh, Lowell. *Baseball's Hall of Fame, Cooperstown.* New York: Arlington House, 1988.

Reilly, Rick. "The Good Father." *Sports Illustrated,* September 7, 1998, 32–45.

Rice, Grantland. *The Tumult and the Shouting.* New York: A.S. Barnes, 1954.

Ritter, Lawrence, and Mark Rucker. *The Babe: A Life in Pictures.* New York: Ticknor & Fields, 1988.

Rodriguez Suncar, Osvaldo, ed. *La Pelota Nuestra.* Santo Domingo, Dominican Republic: Productores Asociados, n.d.

Ruiz, Yuyo. *The Bambino Visits Cuba.* San Juan, P.R.: La Esquina del Left Field, n.d.

Rushin, Steve. "Sam the Ham." *Sports Illustrated,* September 14, 1998, 34–35.

Schott, Tom, and Nick Peters. *The Giants Encyclopedia.* Champaign, Ill.: Sports Publishing, Inc., 1999.

Shatzkin, Mike, ed. *The Ballplayers.* New York: Arbor House, 1990.

Smelser, Marshall. *The Life that Ruth Built*. Lincoln.: University of Nebraska Press, 1975.

Smith, Gary. "Heaven and Hell." *Sports Illustrated*, December 21, 1998, 54–72.

_____. "The Mother of All Pearls." *Sports Illustrated*, September 14, 1998, 56–59.

_____. "The Race Is On." *Sports Illustrated*, September 14, 1998, 48–51.

Smith, Ron, ed. *Celebrating 70*. St. Louis: Sporting News, 1998.

Sports Illustrated, October 7, 1998.

Street & Smith's Baseball, Charlotte, N.C.: 1988–2002.

Thorn, John, et al., eds. *Total Baseball*. 5th ed. New York: Viking, 1997.

Torres, Angel. *The Baseball Bible*. Glendale, Calif.: GWP, 1983.

Veducci, Tom. "Larger Than Life." *Sports Illustrated*, October 7, 1998, 24–31.

_____. "The Greatest Season Ever." *Sports Illustrated*, October 5, 1998, 38–52.

_____. "Goin' Yard." *Sports Illustrated*, October 7, 1998, 36–41.

_____. "Stroke of Genius." *Sports Illustrated*, December 21, 1998, 44–63.

_____. "Making His Mark." *Sports Illustrated*, September 14, 1998, 30–33.

Wendel, Tim. "Roger Maris." *Baseball Weekly*, 8, No. 22, August 19–25, 1998.

Index